AppleWorks:™
Tips and
Techniques

AppleWorks:™
Tips and Techniques

ROBERT ERICSON

Berkeley • Paris • Düsseldorf • London

Cover design: Kurt Fink
Book design: Joseph Roter

Library of Congress Card Number: 85-62543
ISBN 0-89588-303-1
Printed by Haddon Craftsmen
Manufactured in the United States of America
10 9 8 7 6 5 4 3 2 1

To Ann, Grandpa, and good teachers

Acknowledgments

This book benefitted most from timely encouragement, some of which predated AppleWorks. I am particularly indebted to Hunter Dupree and Tom Galloway. Carole Alden and Rick Talcott encouraged me to work with SYBEX.

Many people provided helpful comments. Each of the following provided at least one important insight that would almost certainly have escaped me: Bruce Benedict, Richard Blanco, David Burger, Giorgio Cupertino, Lawrence Eaton, Tom Ewing, John Farley, Robert Fortuno, Bruce Guenard, Debra Hara, Frank Howell, Philip Kaplan, Jim Long, Sherry Lowry, Steven Morrisby, Ann Moskol, Robert Netro, Bill Newell, Bruce Ristow, Al Salerno, Susan Smith, Bruce Sprague, David Teskey, Rick Talcott, Paul Taylor, and Roger Vancil.

At SYBEX, Barbara Gordon managed the project with competence, style, and understanding. Valerie Robbins edited the book with insight and offered many helpful suggestions. Dan Tobler reviewed the book with a critical technical eye, and Olivia Shinomoto word processed the editing with skill and care. Other SYBEX people who contributed to the production of this book include Brenda Walker and Donna Scanlon, typesetting, and Eileen Walsh and Jon Strickland, proofreading.

Finally, I was greatly encouraged by the concurrent development of substantive applications that can be used with AppleWorks. I would particularly like to note the work of Penny Alexander in management, Deane Arganbright in mathematics, Anthony Filipovitch in planning, and Jeffrey Jacques in statistics.

Table of Contents

Introduction

his book began at a national planning conference in Minneapolis, in the spring of 1984, during a discussion with Anthony Filipovitch, a professor who was developing much-needed spreadsheet templates for analytical methods used in town planning and management. We both knew that the Apple IIe was widely used in school and library management, so why not in town planning? Common applications in that field also required database management and word processing, so why not AppleWorks? Over the next year, Tony completed an eminently practical set of methods templates in VisiCalc notation, and I developed a number of integrated applications for AppleWorks, including several based on his work.

AppleWorks quickly proved to be a very effective tool. I began a notebook to document everything I learned while transferring classic VisiCalc templates and developing integrated applications from scratch. The notebook grew larger as I learned more about AppleWorks, and I was surprised in several ways.

First, I found AppleWorks remarkably fun to learn. The programs in AppleWorks gently encourage thought: they have useful options waiting to be combined in new ways. This is an inherent benefit of integrated software, and the AppleWorks designer, Rupert Lissner—remarkable architect that he is—has made the most of it. There is a theory in environmental design that says we find a special contentment in building things from an assortment of parts. That theory has always impressed me, but even more so in recent months. AppleWorks is very much an integrated assortment of parts, and it is, above all else, fun to learn and easy to teach.

Second, I found that AppleWorks has a number of undocumented options that make it easy to develop advanced applications. Experienced users can use these options to find interesting ways around apparent limitations. For example, there are ways to print multicolumn Word Processor text, manage more than 30 Data Base categories, and add additional functions to the Spreadsheet. These are among the many options documented in this book.

Third, I discovered that AppleWorks has undocumented problems that require some caution. For example, before you develop a Data Base application, read about specific problems with record-selection rules. And before you use wide worksheets, read about formula capacities in rows. Once understood, the undocumented problems can be effectively isolated.

Fourth, I learned that AppleWorks has an unusually large capacity. With additional memory in an Apple IIe or Apple IIc, AppleWorks can manage more than 5,000 database records in random-access memory (RAM). And it remains remarkably fast and dependable at that level. The traditional "small-yet-serious" image of the Apple II has been greatly enhanced by AppleWorks.

As the AppleWorks notebook grew, it helped others learn about applications development. Someone suggested converting the notebook to technical notes that could be easily shipped by airmail. The resulting package was primarily intended for people working in environmental design and information science. Experienced users found the documentation and tips contained in the notes helpful, and many of them kindly sent me their own insights along with information about interesting projects they were working on.

The technical notes attracted a far broader audience than I expected. I learned that many people master AppleWorks quickly, begin developing interesting applications, and find that they need additional AppleWorks information. When SYBEX wrote to me, the notes were being used in more than 20 countries, and we both knew that it was time for an advanced AppleWorks reference book.

USING THE BOOK

This book is designed primarily as a reference for intermediate and advanced users. I use these terms humbly, and only in a relative sense, because we all have more to learn. If you are new to AppleWorks, you can also use this book to learn the basics more efficiently. Begin by studying the AppleWorks manuals. Try things out on your Apple. Write questions and comments as you go along, and then refer to this book for specific additional information. In my experience it was that additional information that reinforced points in the AppleWorks manuals and made everything fit together.

In the pages that follow, I have outlined some keys to understanding and using the book.

Many people are beginning, intermediate, and advanced users in different ways at the same time.

These terms must always be used cautiously. Some people know a great deal about the Word Processor, but they rarely use the other AppleWorks programs. Some people have mastered Spreadsheet accounting applications, but they know little about about other applications for the same program. Most of us learn according to our individual needs and interests, which means that we tend to learn somewhat unevenly. Almost everyone will find at least one thing in the book that they already know. Likewise, almost everyone will find something that they will probably never need to know.

The AppleWorks information applies to the Apple IIc, the IIe, and the enhanced IIe, all of which use exactly the same program.

Apple now calls these three personal computers the Apple II series. At least three utilities are currently available to modify AppleWorks for the earlier Apple II and II+ models. If you are using such a utility, keep close at hand a list of the keys that correspond to the standard AppleWorks commands, and ignore all references in this book to memory expansion and allocation.

The Apple III uses a version of AppleWorks known as III E-Z Pieces. It can exchange files with the Apple II version of AppleWorks. If you are using III E-Z Pieces, read the cautions about undocumented problems first, test them on your version, and note the ones that apply. Ignore all references in this book to memory expansion and allocation.

All the tips in this book apply to AppleWorks version 1.2 USA unless otherwise noted.

References to "earlier versions" mean versions 1.0 and 1.1. Both have many undocumented problems that were corrected in version 1.2.

I have included the most significant undocumented problems in earlier versions of AppleWorks. Note them when they are mentioned in the book, even if you have the latest version. When you develop a good template that others can use, it may not work well on earlier versions of AppleWorks. A surprising number of people continue to use the earlier versions: they forget to send in the registration card and never upgrade.

The information in this book combines technical insights with management concepts.

Some people develop superb applications and then misplace their files. Others manage their files well but need to learn more about developing applications. This book addresses both sets of problems. Sometimes the information is simple and almost obvious; sometimes it is subtle and more difficult. In every case the intent is to document additional capabilities. In AppleWorks and in general, simple insights are often the most valuable.

Tips and techniques are utility information. The tips consist of useful pieces of information or simply reminders of some feature in AppleWorks. Techniques are procedures requiring special knowledge, often the result of using several tips in combination. Techniques appear within tip headings, although they are not always specifically noted.

Along with tips and techniques, the book includes cautions about undocumented problems and possible unwanted effects of specific procedures. Each caution includes a suggested way around the problem. You may want to read the cautions first, just to make certain that undocumented problems have not affected work already completed.

This book uses a modular design.

The component tips, techniques, and cautions are grouped in ways that most readers will want to study them. If you want to find utility information related to financial applications for the Spreadsheet, you can check the Table of Contents and find the information in one place. If you want to find all the information related to the command for saving files, you can look in the Index under "Files, saving" or "Saving files" for page references throughout the book. By using the Table of Contents and Index to complement one another, you can quickly find almost anything.

This book focuses primarily on working within AppleWorks, although it includes instructions for transferring data to and from AppleWorks.

You will normally work within AppleWorks, and there is much information to cover at this level. When you need to go beyond AppleWorks, look for specialized software that offers Apple-Works design conventions and built-in data transfer capabilities. AppleWorks can also create and use ASCII and DIF files, both of which have been well documented in other sources. For specific references, read the annotated bibliography in Appendix D.

The research for this book followed this path: over a period of fifteen months, I developed and tested many large applications in environmental design and management, almost always as part of other work. This kind of real-world testing worked surprisingly well. It created a critical mass of information to which others added their findings.

There are other logical and potentially productive paths for studying AppleWorks. For example, I have included suggestions and references in Appendix A for those readers who want to explore AppleWorks byte by byte.

Learn to appreciate the subtle craftsmanship of AppleWorks.

AppleWorks gets things done efficiently. It has become a quiet workhorse in many professional fields, accomplishing more than almost anyone had expected. But surprisingly few people know that AppleWorks can perform the important common functions—replacing text, arranging records, calculating interest—faster than far more expensive integrated software running on far more expensive systems.

The templates used in this book can be purchased on a disk.

The cost is $12 postpaid from Robert Ericson, P.O. Box 16064, Rumford, RI 02916. The templates use both sides of the disk, and many are extended versions of examples used in this book. Template files can save time in applications development, particularly when the templates include complex formulas or large amounts of needed data.

Finally, and most importantly, comments and suggestions are welcome and appreciated.

Please send them to the address given above. I will send collected information on undocumented problems to Apple. Authors of tips and cautions published in later editions of this book will be gratefully acknowledged.

DESIGN OF THE BOOK

This book is, above all, a reference book for serious users. The main chapters follow the order of AppleWorks files on the

Desktop: Word Processor, Data Base, and Spreadsheet. The chapter on printer configuration comes last, although you may want to read it first if you have problems getting your printer to work correctly. Note that the AppleWorks Reference Manual follows a similar order, except that its Data Base chapters come before the Word Processor chapters. Knowing this, you will find it easy to use this book and the AppleWorks Reference Manual together.

The tips, techniques, and cautions follow a logical order within each chapter. Most of the AppleWorks commands, functions, and options have been included in the book, but some receive more detailed treatment than others. There are several good reasons for any imbalance in the quantity of information provided on different topics.

First, the need for cautions varies from program to program within AppleWorks. For example, the Data Base record-selection rules have serious undocumented problems, whereas parts of other programs work flawlessly. This is certainly not an unusual situation. Almost every software package has undocumented problems that are unevenly distributed. These problems also tend to be discovered after the user manuals have been written.

Second, the level of documentation in the AppleWorks Reference Manual varies considerably from program to program, and within each program. For example, the exponentiation function in the Spreadsheet receives surprisingly little attention in the Apple-Works Reference Manual, whereas other functions, such as @CHOOSE, are explained in detail.

Third, some options have far more potential than others for advanced AppleWorks applications. Remember that the materials from Apple, which include excellent disk-based tutorials, were written primarily for beginning users. At that level it would serve little purpose to discuss, for example, @COUNT as a logic function. In fact, this particular subject has received little attention anywhere, because most other spreadsheets have a larger set of logic functions.

Fourth, AppleWorks was written for a 128K system. Several firms now offer extended-memory cards in the 256K–1536K range, along with software to modify the AppleWorks Startup and Program disks. These modifications make it possible to exceed specific limits described in the AppleWorks Reference

Manual, enabling you to use AppleWorks in a broader range of applications. It also changes the ways in which the AppleWorks programs most effectively complement one another.

The tips, techniques, and cautions in this book have been arranged in ways that complement the AppleWorks Reference Manual most efficiently. At the beginning of each chapter I have provided an overview of the information that follows, as well as an explanation of why some options are more useful than others. At the beginning of each section within a chapter, I have provided a more detailed overview. If you are reading the book from cover to cover, I think you will appreciate these overviews. If you are simply looking for an answer to a specific question, they are not required reading.

ORGANIZATION OF THE BOOK

However you approach the book, the following overview should be helpful. Almost everyone will want to read the Desktop chapter, because its tips and cautions are broadly useful in AppleWorks. Beyond that, there is no preferred way to approach the book.

Chapter 1 covers the Desktop and related subjects. Everything in AppleWorks goes through the Desktop—sometimes once, often repeatedly. The closely related subjects include ProDOS, the clipboard, and key commands.

Memory expansion for the Desktop has greatly increased the range of AppleWorks. Many readers will want to pay special attention to this subject, because a small investment in memory makes AppleWorks perform much more efficiently.

Chapter 2 covers the Word Processor, which has particular strengths and limitations that serious users should be aware of. The tips and cautions in this chapter cover form letters, printing, editing, proofreading, and extended report writing. Many readers will be surprised to find solutions to minor undocumented problems that sometimes occur without being noticed.

Chapter 3 covers the Data Base. This program has assumed new importance because additional memory can so greatly extend its capabilities. The chapter includes tips on using large databases and cautions on undocumented problems in the record-selection rules.

Chapter 4 covers the Spreadsheet. No other part of Apple-Works offers more flexibility for applications development. Readers interested in the Data Base will want to study the section on using the Spreadsheet for database management.

Chapter 5 is probably the most challenging in the book. It covers methods for transferring information between AppleWorks programs, to AppleWorks from other sources, and from AppleWorks to other sources. Before you read about transfers between any two AppleWorks programs, you should understand the two programs individually. Advanced Apple users will particularly appreciate the many complementing options offered by the Data Base, Apple-Works Mailing Program, Spreadsheet, and SuperCalc 3a.

AppleWorks can also serve as an editor for BASIC programs. Programming and external data transfers sometimes require disk format conversions from ProDOS to DOS 3.3 or vice versa. This subject has been covered in detail.

Chapter 6 covers printers. I have tried to distinguish between printing and printers. If you are having problems with your printer, read this final chapter first. Printer problems include such curious things as an "80N" printed at the beginning of a Word Processor file, or too many spaces between lines. When you have configured the printer correctly, you can then use the standard printing options described in the first five chapters.

This chapter also includes some control code techniques, but be sure you understand the basic options before you attempt these techniques.

Appendix A discusses a logical development path for the Apple II series and AppleWorks, as well as additional approaches to studying the programs. Appendix B provides insights on using the keyboard for configuring printers, entering text, entering numbers, and editing data. Here you will find a table of ASCII values and some keyboard templates that you may find useful. Appendix C reviews the general subject of sources, while Appendix D provides a bibliography of publications directly related to AppleWorks.

CONVENTIONS USED IN THE BOOK

In writing this book, I have used some conventions that are consistent with AppleWorks. If you make note of them now, you will be able to use the book more efficiently.

AppleWorks uses capital letters for specific purposes. The three programs within AppleWorks have generic names, but they begin with capitals so that you will know, for example, the difference between the Spreadsheet in particular and spreadsheets in general. The same convention applies to the Desktop and some other generic words with particular meanings in the context of Apple-Works. The spelling of clipboard is an exception to the rule.

I have also used capital letters to begin names of keys, such as Return, Escape, and so on. Arrow keys are indicated by arrows, as in →. Key sequences are sometimes noted parenthetically as brief reminders. For example, in the Word Processor you can underline text (Control-L) without accessing the Printer Options menu. For our purposes ProDOS volumes will be synonymous with disks. ProDOS volumes have names preceded by a slash mark. In this book all disks will be designated /P (for ProDOS) unless otherwise noted.

The commands in AppleWorks use the key with an outline of the Apple logo on it. Almost everyone calls this key the Open-Apple key, and the AppleWorks Reference Manual consistently uses terms such as Open-Apple-S and Open-Apple-1. In Apple-Works, the Open-Apple and Solid-Apple keys are interchangeable, so I have used terms such as Apple-S and Apple-1 instead. The Solid-Apple key is often more convenient for commands that include letters on the left side of the keyboard. (However, it may take some time to overcome old habits.)

It is important to understand the meaning of specific words used throughout the book. For our purposes, these are the most important terms: command, option, function, number, value, arrange, sort, category, field, layout, format, standard, global, and utilities. The following paragraphs define these terms briefly; some of these words will be defined in greater detail in related tips and cautions.

AppleWorks includes commands, options, and functions. For our purposes a *command* begins with an Apple key, as in Apple-S for the Save command, or a Control key, as in Control-L for underlining. In many cases a command accesses a menu of *options*. The longest list of options appears on the Word Processor Printer Options menu. Note in this context that underlining can be either a command (Control-L) or an option within the Printer Options menu. *Functions* are confined to the Spreadsheet. They include arithmetic and logical functions. Many begin with @, as in @SUM.

Numbers are numerals, the characters 0–9. In the Spreadsheet they can be labels or values. *Values* can be added and subtracted. Remember that simple rule of thumb, because it will serve you well throughout the book, especially in Chapter 5 ("Transferring Information").

AppleWorks uses several terms that are not well known. If you have used other spreadsheets and database managers, it may take some time to get used to the new terms. *Arranging* in Apple-Works is the same as *sorting* in other programs. Likewise, a Data Base *category* would be called a *field* in many other database managers. In AppleWorks you choose *layouts* instead of *formats,* and you specify *standard* values instead of *global* values.

Utilities are programs or files that perform useful functions in support of larger systems, in this case the Apple II, AppleWorks, and applications being developed on AppleWorks. In each case, I have tried to give the utility in question a descriptive title.

GENERAL APPLEWORKS TIPS

Some tips are generally applicable, beyond the boundaries of any single chapter, perhaps even beyond the boundaries of Apple-Works. Most of the tips that follow are reinforced with specific variations in one or more chapters.

Tip: *Learn about AppleWorks in bite-size pieces, according to your own needs and interests.*

There is much information in this book, and there will probably always be more to learn from other sources. If you take all this on at once, you can be overwhelmed. Take it in bite-size pieces, starting with whatever interests you most. If that is what you already know best, so much the better.

If you need AppleWorks for writing reports, spend your time with the Word Processor first. Then consider possible interactions with the Spreadsheet and Data Base. If you want to create reference tables for management reports, learn enough about the Spreadsheet to do just that. No one has to know everything about AppleWorks. It is important to define what you should and should not attempt to learn. Set priorities.

Tip: *Read about AppleWorks and encourage others to read.*

Some people own relatively few programs, but they accomplish much with what they have. They read the manuals, write in the margins, note undocumented problems, consult Apple journals, and study advanced books. Many otherwise competent people somehow forget about the manuals. The fact is that everyone needs at least the manuals, and Apple wrote good manuals for AppleWorks.

Those of us who read the manuals are often the ones who teach AppleWorks to those who don't. When you teach, explain the basics and strongly encourage your students to read enough to teach others something useful. It makes everyone more confident, and you avoid becoming a question-answerer forevermore.

Knowing that many teachers will be using this book, I have attempted to provide some examples and illustrations that can be adapted easily for beginning students.

Tip: *Add to the book.*

Throughout the book I have made brief suggestions about additional applications and possibilities for further study. It is my way of encouraging you to go beyond the book in using Apple-Works in your own field. For example, a technique abstracted from an environmental design application can later serve a completely different purpose in a scientific research application.

Write in the margins, highlight the text, and add tabs to the pages you use most. Abbreviate and modify wherever necessary. Remember that my comments may sometimes be inappropriate to your specific needs. Above all, have as much fun adding to the book as I had writing it.

Tip: *Start an AppleWorks notebook.*

Your notebook can hold the most important information you collect about AppleWorks beyond this book. It should be your own specialized reference. Include the following:

- Two copies of your printer control codes

- Samples of available character sets from your printer

- Hard copies of all the menu screens in AppleWorks

You get the point: this is where you keep what you use most often. Include documentation for the applications you develop. When you have too much for one notebook, start a hanging file system in a file cabinet, but keep the most important information in the notebook.

Time and time again you will need to consult your notes. You will often be able to use applications completed months ago, and you will always be thankful that you organized the information in a logical way.

Tip: *Use the hardware that makes AppleWorks function most efficiently.*

If you have an Apple IIe, use two disk drives and an 80-column extended-memory card. If you have an Apple IIc, get a second disk drive. Although AppleWorks can function with one disk drive and as little as 64K memory, that configuration compromises the smooth operation that sets this software apart.

On the other hand, there is no need to acquire more hardware for AppleWorks than you really need. If you enter information with two fingers, the bottleneck in your system is probably right at the keyboard. Learning to type is the wisest investment you can make. After you learn to type, four dollars worth of chips for the printer buffer may be the most prudent choice. Think about what you really need. Ask yourself what you would do with additional hardware.

This book was written on a 192K Apple IIe with two Apple-compatible disk drives, an amber monochrome monitor, a buffered Okidata 92P printer, and AppleWorks version 1.2. There were some variations: I eventually installed the Apple IIe enhancement kit and tested larger memory cards, but the basic system was two years old.

Tip: *Use the most recent version of AppleWorks.*

If you use any program regularly, use the most recent version, because that version is generally the most dependable. At least know which version is current, because Apple generally offers software upgrades on reasonable terms. In fact, Apple dealers provide the disk upgrade to ProDOS version 1.1.1 and AppleWorks version 1.2 without charge. Both upgrades are highly recommended.

On the other hand, every rule has its exception. Some experienced Spreadsheet users prefer version 1.1 because it can effectively blank a cell with one less keystroke than version 1.2

requires. This means they can develop templates slightly faster on the earlier version, even though the completed template will be used on version 1.2.

Tip: *Use product descriptions as reference points.*

This book includes specific descriptions of hardware and software related to AppleWorks. These descriptions can provide generic insights about products of similar design. Use any given product note in this book as a reference point for judging other products that may be more recent or more appropriate to your needs. Study current issues of Apple journals, and look for specific information in reviews and advertisements.

Tip: *Make hard copies of the screens.*

AppleWorks has a command (Apple-H) for printing the contents of a screen to your printer. Use it for everything you can imagine: menu screens, Printer Options menus, error messages, lists of files on disk, key Spreadsheet formulas, quick Data Base record printouts. In fact, this book has been illustrated with hard copies printed with a daisy-wheel printer. (It prints the @ sign in place of the Open-Apple.) Specific versions of this tip appear throughout the book, because the concept can never be stressed enough.

1
The Desktop

*T*he Desktop is the AppleWorks file-handling area. On it, you can load up to 12 files, access and display them quickly, create new files, save some to disks, discard others, and keep tabs on the status of each file. The Desktop can display an Index of available files, enabling you to change between files quickly, but it cannot display two files at the same time. The AppleWorks Reference Manual introduces the Desktop and clearly illustrates its functions, but it does not document the available shortcuts.

The overall performance of the Desktop is impressive, and it is very much an extension of ProDOS, Apple's fast and dependable operating system. Experienced users have run AppleWorks for thousands of hours without losing any information. You can learn how to use the Desktop on two levels: it guides beginning users safely with logical menu sequences, and it offers several file-handling shortcuts for experienced users. If you feel comfortable with the menus, it is time to start using the shortcuts.

The tips in this chapter address the problems that tend to slow people down most often: misplaced files, uncertainty about what to do next, and second thoughts about choices just made. They are among the most important tips in this book, simply because you can use them so often.

This chapter is divided into eight sections. The first section introduces general, broadly useful tips on using the Desktop. The second section concerns using the Desktop menus more efficiently. Everyone should read the sections on managing files and using the clipboard, because they contain essential information and a few surprises.

The fifth section describes options for expanding Desktop memory. No innovation has been more important to AppleWorks than memory expansion. The section on common AppleWorks commands covers previously undocumented options. The ProDOS section explains what experienced users need to know about the operating system and its utility programs.

The last section covers the problems of managing your own desktop—the one with real pencils and papers. Because Apple-Works lets you work more productively, you may have to manage more disks and paper.

GENERAL DESKTOP TIPS

The following tips are valuable for anyone using AppleWorks. The techniques will help you use the available Desktop options more efficiently. If you are an experienced Apple user, you may be surprised by the ease with which AppleWorks uses lowercase letters and prints copies of the screen display.

Tip: *Print and annotate hard copies of the Desktop menu screens.*

You can print a hard copy of any monitor screen by using Apple-H when the screen is displayed. Start by printing the Main Menu screen, then the Add Files menu screen, then the Word Processor, the Data Base, and the Spreadsheet menu screens. Highlight your most common choices with a yellow marker, and write notes about when to use each option. Keep the hard copies of the screens nearby so you can see the Desktop menus at any time. Figure 1.1 shows the Main Menu screen.

Tip: *Use lowercase letters wherever appropriate.*

AppleWorks will always accept lowercase letters for finding text, for setting layout options, for Spreadsheet formulas, and so on. Experienced Apple users who just winced may continue using uppercase letters forever, but the fact is that lowercase letters are easier to enter, simply because there is no need to depress the Shift key.

More importantly, lowercase letters are easier to read. We tend to make certain visual mistakes consistently, confusing the characters S and 5, for example. The Apple II creates each letter within a 56-dot matrix on the monitor screen. In contrast, some other personal computers use dot matrices with more than twice that

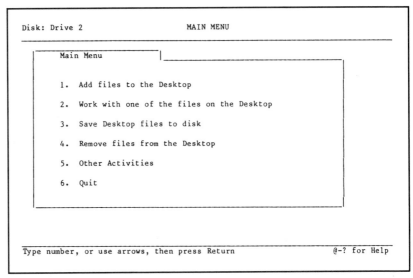

```
Disk: Drive 2                      MAIN MENU

    ┌─────────────────────┐┌──────────────────────────────
    │ Main Menu           ││
    │                     │└──────────────────────────────
    │   1.  Add files to the Desktop
    │
    │   2.  Work with one of the files on the Desktop
    │
    │   3.  Save Desktop files to disk
    │
    │   4.  Remove files from the Desktop
    │
    │   5.  Other Activities
    │
    │   6.  Quit
    │
    └──────────────────────────────────────────────────


  Type number, or use arrows, then press Return          @-? for Help
```

Figure 1.1: Main Menu

density, thereby permitting more fully formed screen characters. Given the Apple II screen character matrix, it is important to use a logical blend of capital and lowercase letters that makes text easier to read. It is rarely a good idea to use all capitals. I will note specific exceptions to this rule in other tips and cautions. (For example, you may choose to use all capitals for report headings and other circumstances where it is more important to differentiate between word groups than between letters.)

When you are searching for text in a Word Processor document, you can enter lowercase letters for the desired word or phrase, even if it begins with a capital letter (unless you choose case-sensitive text selection). In Spreadsheet formulas, lowercase letters are automatically converted to capitals when the formula has been completed.

Tip: *Find things to do while the disk drives are running.*

The Startup Disk takes a little more than ten seconds to load—more than enough time to insert your data disk in drive 2 and too long to wait around doing nothing. As a rule of thumb, an AppleWorks file requires less than a second per thousand bytes to load from or save to disk. You will be saving files far more often than loading them, and each time you save a 30K file, you have 25–30 seconds to do something else. (For example, it takes about that long to look up a word that you suspect you might have misspelled.)

Tip: *Use the file utilities provided with AppleWorks.*

AppleWorks has three important utilities: two for disk cataloging and one for disk formatting. You can obtain a catalog of only AppleWorks files from option 1 on the Main Menu. You can obtain a complete catalog of all ProDOS files from option 2 on the Other Activities menu. Figure 1.2 shows the Other Activities menu.

Disk formatting is particularly convenient with AppleWorks. It can be used at any time, even when you have 12 files on the Desktop and information on the clipboard waiting to be moved to another file.

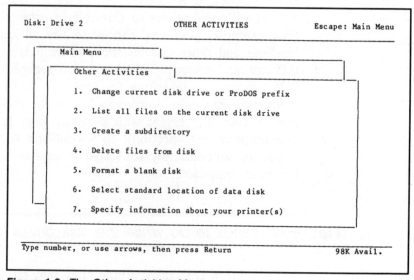

```
Disk: Drive 2                    OTHER ACTIVITIES            Escape: Main Menu
_____

    ┌─ Main Menu ──────────────┐
    │    ┌─ Other Activities ──────┐
    │    │  1.  Change current disk drive or ProDOS prefix
    │    │  2.  List all files on the current disk drive
    │    │  3.  Create a subdirectory
    │    │  4.  Delete files from disk
    │    │  5.  Format a blank disk
    │    │  6.  Select standard location of data disk
    └────│  7.  Specify information about your printer(s)
         └─────────────────────────────────────────────────┘

_____
Type number, or use arrows, then press Return                      98K Avail.
```

Figure 1.2: *The Other Activities Menu*

Although a file copying utility has not been included, you can effectively copy AppleWorks files by loading one or more files on the Desktop and then saving them to other disks. You cannot use this technique to copy other kinds of ProDOS files, however.

Tip: *Use the Desktop to run a cleaning disk in drive 2.*

Many disk manufacturers recommend running a specially designed cleaning disk in both drives every two weeks or so. To run a cleaning disk in drive 1, simply insert the disk, turn the Apple on for about 30 seconds, and then turn it off.

There are two traditional methods for running a cleaning disk in drive 2. The first method is to change drives on the controller card and run the normal drive 2 in the drive 1 position. The second uses a BASIC utility program to activate drive 2.

Here is an easier method. Load AppleWorks, place the cleaning disk in drive 2, proceed as if to add files to the Desktop from drive 2, and hold down Return for the period of time needed for cleaning (usually about 30 seconds). AppleWorks attempts to catalog files from a data disk for about five seconds, finds no files, and sends an error message as shown in Figure 1.3. By holding down Return, you essentially ask AppleWorks to keep trying.

WORKING ON THE DESKTOP

The menu options and commands can work differently for beginners and experienced users. In this section we will take a closer look at the choices. The tips and techniques in this section define limits more precisely, so that you can work efficiently within those limits. Several tips explain why some options are more appropriate than others for specific purposes. You will find, for example, that the Apple-Q command offers many ways to move quickly within AppleWorks.

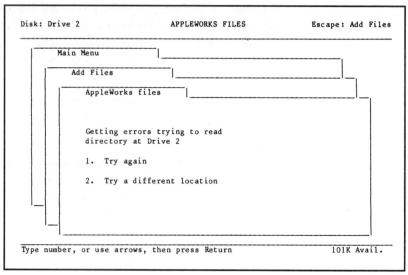

```
Disk: Drive 2                  APPLEWORKS FILES          Escape: Add Files

      ┌──────Main Menu─────────────┐─────────────────────────────┐
      │   ┌────Add Files───────────┐─────────────────────────────┐
      │   │   ┌──AppleWorks files──┐─────────────────────────────┐
      │   │   │                                                    │
      │   │   │     Getting errors trying to read                  │
      │   │   │     directory at Drive 2                           │
      │   │   │                                                    │
      │   │   │     1.  Try again                                  │
      │   │   │                                                    │
      │   │   │     2.  Try a different location                   │
      │   │   │                                                    │
      │   └───┤                                                    │
      │       │                                                    │
      └───────┤                                                    │
              └────────────────────────────────────────────────────┘

  Type number, or use arrows, then press Return              101K Avail.
```

Figure 1.3: *Try again option used for cleaning drive 2*

Tip: *AppleWorks loads as much of a program as it thinks you will need, and you can choose commands accordingly.*

When changing to a file that requires a different program, as from a Word Processor document to a Spreadsheet template, AppleWorks loads enough of the new program to get you started, more when you use additional functions. This is a good design choice, because you may want to load an application simply to check information on a file in that application.

In the Spreadsheet, for example, AppleWorks will load more of the program when you attempt to blank a cell. Using the Apple-B command usually indicates that you intend to spend some time revising the worksheet. If you actually intend to leave right away, use ", the Space bar, and Return to blank the cell.

Caution: *When Desktop files use enough memory, file changes slow down.*

It is fast file handling that makes AppleWorks a workhorse for professional applications. But if you have, for example, 24K of files loaded on a 55K Desktop, the Apple-Q command accesses the Program disk for more than four seconds before going to the Desktop Index, and then again for another four seconds before going to the new file.

By expanding the Desktop with extra RAM memory, you can maintain instant file access at much higher memory-use levels. For example, the Apple-Q command can provide instant access to more than 60K of files on a 101K Desktop. That makes a significant contribution to overall efficiency on a project such as this book. The options for memory expansion are covered in detail later in this chapter.

Even when file changes slow down, everything keeps working dependably. The Main Menu options for removing files from the Desktop, checking on what must be saved, and loading new files continue to work as efficiently as ever.

Tip: *Use Apple-Q instead of option 2 on the Main Menu.*

No matter how long you have been using AppleWorks, start thinking through your strategies. When would you use option 2 on the Main Menu? Probably never, because it gives you the Desktop Index, which is accessible with Apple-Q from anywhere. After loading two or more files, what do you do when the screen message tells you to press the Space bar? Use Apple-Q again, because the Space bar just takes you back to the Main Menu to select option 2.

Tip: *Use Apple-Q to return to the Desktop Main Menu.*

Whenever you press Apple-Q, the next Escape takes you back to the Main Menu. There are times, particularly in the Data Base, when you would otherwise need to press Escape four times to return to the Main Menu. That means waiting for each new screen to appear on the way. Use Apple-Q to save time.

Tip: *Use Apple-Q to check the remaining available memory.*

Apple-Q serves another useful purpose. When the Desktop Index appears, the Apple-? message disappears from the lower-right corner of the screen, and you can then see how much memory is available on the Desktop. The Desktop Index always highlights the file you are using, so if all you want to do is check the available memory, Return takes you directly back to the same cursor position in your document.

Tip: *Use Apple-C to check the remaining available memory.*

Most experienced users would probably rather see the available memory than the Apple-? reminder for the Help file. You can see the available memory quickly by pressing Apple-C and then Return. Note the number, then press Escape to come back to the previous status. This method works equally well in each Apple-Works program, as does the Apple-Q method described in the previous tip.

To see the amount of memory used by any given file on the Desktop, press Escape to get to the Main Menu and choose option 3 to save Desktop files to disk, even though you have no intention of actually doing that.

Tip: *Use Apple-S to save files.*

If you recently purchased AppleWorks, this is so obvious that you may wonder why it has to be mentioned. The answer is simple: the Tutorial Manual for AppleWorks version 1.0 gave Apple-S a bad name. It was specifically called the "Ultimate Quick and Dirty Save Shortcut." In reality, it is quick and clean. Unless you need to check the status of your file at the end of a session, use Apple-S to save.

Use Apple-S often, at least every twenty minutes. Use it when you have just solved a difficult problem, such as a complex sentence construction, a Data Base report layout, or a long Spreadsheet formula. Use it instinctively when you will spend the next half minute away from the keyboard, because that is when a save costs the least time.

Tip: *Use the Main Menu Add Files option to see what is on the data disk.*

The Add Files option provides the easiest and safest method for finding out what you have on your data disk, how much space you have left, and so on. It is useful even when you have no intention of adding files to the Desktop. The Add Files option addresses such questions as the following:

Do I have enough free space on the disk? Proceed as if you are adding files from the primary data disk, but simply note the amount of disk memory available. The formatted disk began with 136K, so the files plus the remaining memory should add up to 136K, give or take a little. If they don't, you may have some unwanted non-AppleWorks files on the data disk. To find them, first select the Other Activities option on the Main Menu and then the option to list all files. If you find any unwanted Other (non-AppleWorks) files, delete them from the disk. These might include ASCII or DIF files that you used to transfer information and then forgot about. Figures 1.4 and 1.5 illustrate a discrepancy caused by an ASCII file.

Did I save the file to both the primary and backup disk? Proceed as if you are adding files from the primary data disk, read the catalog, find the date for the file in question, note the file size, and press Escape. Then remove the primary disk, insert the backup disk, press Return, and compare your notes with the catalog information for this disk.

Do the primary and backup disks have the same files? This is an extension of the last procedure. It is not unusual to save a file to the data disk that happens to be in drive 2, even though that

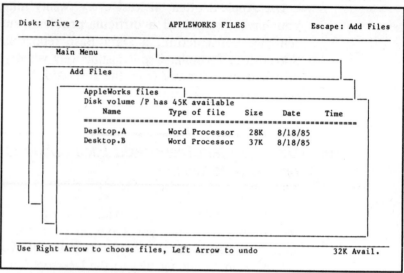

Figure 1.4: *All AppleWorks files listed*

file may actually belong on some other disk. Print a hard copy of the catalog for the primary disk. Then remove the primary disk, insert the backup disk, press Return, and compare your hard copy with the catalog information for this disk.

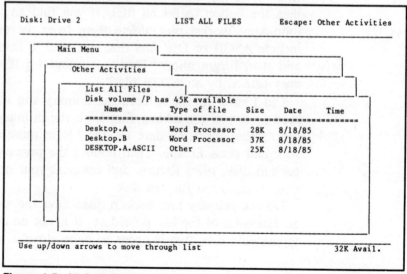

Figure 1.5: *All ProDOS files listed*

Of course, there are times when you merely want to know which disk you have in drive 2. Then you can just open the disk drive door and look at the disk label, provided, of course, that the drive is not running.

Caution: *The act of printing causes the file to be listed as Changed.*

When you check the status of a file that has been printed, the file is listed as Changed (even if you simply pressed Return to use the printer proposed). If you encounter a case like this, there is no need to save the file again before removing it from the Desktop. With large files this is well worth remembering.

How does the file change just by printing it? When you print a file, you actually select a printer that up to that point was merely highlighted. In the unlikely case that you save the file after printing and then print it exactly the same way again, the file will indeed be listed as Unchanged.

There are times when you will make file changes simply for one printout. You may have no reason to save a file with the changes, so choose the option to "throw out" the changes when you remove the file from the Desktop.

Tip: *The Save Desktop files option is generally more useful than the Quit option.*

The Quit option (6 on the Main Menu) will tell you which files have been saved, which files have changed, and which remain unchanged (and hence need not be saved). The problem is that if a file needs to be saved, you will usually want to save it to a backup disk as well. The Quit option shows only one file at a time and provides for only one save.

By selecting option 3 (Save Desktop files to disk), you can see the status of all the Desktop files at once, and you can also save any file as many times as you wish. Figures 1.6 and 1.7 show information screens of the Quit and Save Desktop files options.

Figure 1.6: Quit option

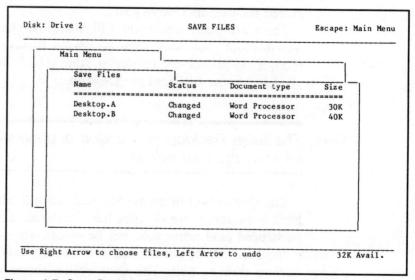

Figure 1.7: Save Desktop files option

MANAGING FILES

Few of us think about how we manage files, so this is another place where it is time to take a closer look at work habits.

The most important tip here is the advice about using small files. This book was assembled from dozens of files that were about 30K in size, despite the ready availability of large extended memory cards. Once you are comfortable with file management methods, using small files will clearly be the most sensible way to work.

This section also provides additional documentation on methods of cataloging and saving files. Pay special attention to file naming, because the rules will be important later.

Caution: *AppleWorks uses an indirect save that requires more disk space than you might expect.*

AppleWorks saves files in a two-step process that I call the indirect method. When you press Apple-S, AppleWorks first saves the file to available free space on the disk, and then it deletes the previous file of the same name. If you attempt to save a 70K file to the disk from which it came, AppleWorks will tell you that there is insufficient room, because a disk holds only 136K.

When there is insufficient room for an indirect save, you can first delete the previous file of the same name. That creates some additional risk, but you do have a backup disk—right?

Tip: *Use small files whenever possible.*

AppleWorks can save small files faster; they require less free space on a disk and use less memory on the Desktop. More importantly, small files let you take maximum advantage of the Desktop.

Think of the chapters in a book or report. If you keep a whole chapter in one file, what happens when you want to write in two different sections as you think of related information? If the chapter is in two files, you can use Apple-Q to flip back and forth between two related cursor locations. This method is generally faster and easier than setting markers within a single file.

How small is small? A small Word Processor file is something under 30K. Even at that size some of the commands, such as Apple-M, slow down noticeably. You can always assemble small files into large files for special printing needs. You can do this by moving 250 lines to the clipboard at a time, which is the maximum number permitted. In the case of a Word Processor file of 490 lines, which can be about 30K, that means two moves to the clipboard. You can find the approximate halfway point by pressing Apple-5.

A small Spreadsheet file is also something under 30K. At that size the recalculation times generally approach 30 seconds. Modular construction methods permit you to assemble small files into large files when you really need a large integrated model. Again, multiples of 250 lines (or rows in this case) can be moved to the clipboard.

Database applications generally use more memory than other kinds of applications, simply because they generally contain more information. In this relative sense, a small Data Base file is something under 60K. None of the commonly used Data Base functions have slowed down much by then, but it does take longer to save the file.

Some intermediate users think that they need to build at least one large spreadsheet template. Focus instead on small files and subtle craftsmanship—less is more, particularly when less is just enough.

Tip: *Learn how AppleWorks lists files.*

It is helpful to know where to start looking for files on AppleWorks catalogs. When you see a list of AppleWorks files on the current disk, the file grouping is always Word Processor, Data Base, and Spreadsheet, in that order. When Other files are listed from option 2 on the Other Activities menu, they are listed after Spreadsheet files. "Other" means ProDOS but not AppleWorks.

Within each file group, file names are arranged alphabetically, more precisely in an ASCII order that recognizes all letters as uppercase letters. You can use capitals and lowercase letters any way you want, but note that spaces and periods come before letters in ASCII order. See Appendix B for a complete ASCII table.

You can also use a prefix to group your file listings. For example, suppose you assign the prefix "A." to all Word Processor files in a project (A.Appendices, A.Index, and A.Text, for instance). They would then be listed together, in alphabetical order, before any files beginning with a "B." prefix. Figure 1.8 shows an example.

Tip: *The Desktop Index lists files in the order that they were loaded.*

Files are never listed alphabetically in the Desktop Index unless they were loaded in that order. You can easily load the Desktop

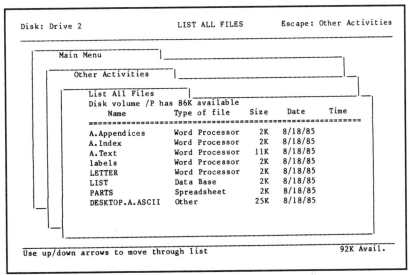

Figure 1.8: Alphabetical file listing showing use of the prefix "A."

in alphabetical order from one program group on a single disk by selectively loading the files.

Tip: *You can move the cursor backwards in the Desktop Index.*

If the cursor is on the first file and you want it on the last file, press ↑ once to move the cursor to the bottom of the list. To go back to the top of the list, press ↓. This technique saves time when you have four or more files on the Desktop. Note that it does not work with disk file catalogs.

Tip: *AppleWorks file naming rules are more liberal than those of other ProDOS files.*

AppleWorks file names can have blank spaces within them, but other ProDOS file names cannot. When Rupert Lissner wrote AppleWorks, he created three special ProDOS file types: AWP for AppleWorks Word Processor, ADB for Data Base files, and ASP for Spreadsheet files. You will see those file type names when you catalog a disk from ProDOS BASIC.

Note, however, that Data Base report names have nothing to do with file names, even though a report name can be the same as a file name. A report always exists as part of an ADB file. Rules for naming Data Base reports are far more liberal than rules for naming ProDOS or AppleWorks files. Table 1.1 shows the differences in rules. We will discuss Data Base report and category names in greater detail in the Data Base chapter.

Tip: *Learn how to change Desktop file names.*

In AppleWorks, this option is as useful as the option for printing hard copies. By changing the name of a file on the Desktop,

Table 1.1: *Rules for file and report names*

Options	ProDOS Files	AppleWorks Files	Data Base Reports
Maximum characters	15	15	19
Lead numerals			X
Internal numerals	X	X	X
Lowercase letters	X	X	X
Symbols			X
Blank spaces		X	X

you isolate it from the previous version on disk. That means you can make all kinds of changes without worrying about destroying the previous file by accidentally saving the Desktop file. Specific applications of this tip appear throughout the book. The concept is broadly useful, and it cannot be stressed enough.

To change a file name, press Apple-N to put the cursor on the file name. Press Control-Y to clear the existing name, enter a new name, and press Return.

When you change a file name, the previous file name disappears from the Desktop, but the previous file of that name remains on the disk. If you do irreparable damage to the Desktop file, discard it, load the previous version again, and change the name again. If you make changes and want the new version to replace the previous version on the disk, change back to the original name before saving the file to disk.

Caution: *Never use the same name for two different files.*

If you name a Word Processor file Farm.Report and save that file on a disk named /P, AppleWorks will not let you overwrite it with a Spreadsheet (or Data Base) file that uses exactly the same name. An error message will appear telling you why you can't use that file name, and you will have to change the name. Figure 1.9 shows the error message screen.

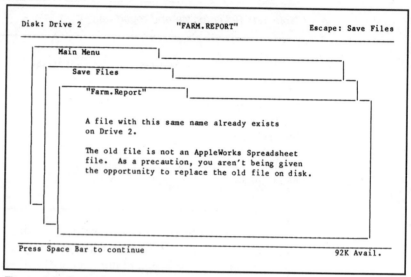

```
Disk: Drive 2                      "FARM.REPORT"              Escape: Save Files
------------------------------------------------------------------------------
    ┌──────────────────────────────┐
    │   Main Menu                  │─────────────────────────────────────
    │  ┌───────────────────────────┴──┐
    │  │    Save Files                │───────────────────────────────
    │  │  ┌───────────────────────────┴──┐
    │  │  │     "Farm.Report"            │─────────────────────────
    │  │  │
    │  │  │  A file with this same name already exists
    │  │  │  on Drive 2.
    │  │  │
    │  │  │  The old file is not an AppleWorks Spreadsheet
    │  │  │  file.  As a precaution, you aren't being given
    │  │  │  the opportunity to replace the old file on disk.
    │  │  │
    │  │  │
    │  │  │
    │  └──┤
    │     │
    └─────┤
          │
------------------------------------------------------------------------------
Press Space Bar to continue                                      92K Avail.
```

Figure 1.9: *Same file name, different program*

If you name an ASCII or DIF file Farm.Report, AppleWorks will not prevent you from overwriting the AppleWorks file when you enter the path name /P/Farm.Report. That alone is reason enough to add special suffixes to ASCII and DIF files.

When loading files, you will be warned when a file name is identical to one already on the Desktop. However, AppleWorks will always let you do it, even if you have substantially changed the file already on the Desktop.

Lastly, you should know that AppleWorks considers FARM.REPORT and Farm.Report to be the same files. If you save Farm.Report to a disk that contains FARM.REPORT, AppleWorks will delete the file named FARM.REPORT.

Caution: *You can accidentally format the Program disk.*

Because AppleWorks writes date information on the Program disk each time you load AppleWorks, you cannot use a write-protect tab on the Program disk. When you begin using a new Program disk, you might forget to select drive 2 as the standard location of the data disk (with option 6 on the Other Activities menu). If you forgot to select drive 2 as the standard location of the data disk, drive 1 will remain the standard location by default. If you begin formatting disks without looking at the data drive location specified in the upper-left corner of the screen, AppleWorks *will* format its own Program disk.

Caution: *Desktop files generally require more space than disk files.*

Data in Desktop files is often further compressed when you save the file to disk. The corollary to this rule is that the Desktop will not always have room for a file, even if it seems to be small enough on the disk. When you attempt to load a file onto the Desktop, you may need to remove another file first.

Any discrepancy between Desktop file size and disk file size is understandably a matter of concern. Here are two examples of file size discrepancies that should make you feel more comfortable with AppleWorks.

A Data Base file named Members.List requires 90K on the Desktop, but only 76K on the disk. Discrepancies of this magnitude are common with Data Base files. When you load the file, make certain the Desktop has enough remaining memory.

A Spreadsheet file named Projections requires 16K on the Desktop and 17K on the disk. It is not unusual to find minor exceptions to the rule, particularly for Spreadsheet files with many copied formulas.

Caution: *When the Desktop has insufficient memory, remove the file AppleWorks requests you to remove.*

If you are close to the Desktop memory limit, the Desktop may run out of memory while you are entering information. (This may have happened to you already.) AppleWorks will tell you that you should save and must remove a specific file from the Desktop Index. It may not be the largest file, and it is almost never the one you would like to remove, but you have no choice. Figure 1.10 shows the screen message.

There is an easy way to avoid this problem: keep track of the remaining available memory. You may be wasting memory by leaving information on the clipboard.

USING THE CLIPBOARD

Apple-C permits you to copy information to the clipboard. The clipboard provides a temporary storage place where up to 250 lines of a file can be stored until retrieved. The clipboard borrows Desktop memory as needed, but AppleWorks never gives you direct information about how much memory the clipboard is using.

The clipboard is far more useful than the AppleWorks Reference Manual suggests. For example, it can efficiently move and copy information within documents, because it allows you to do

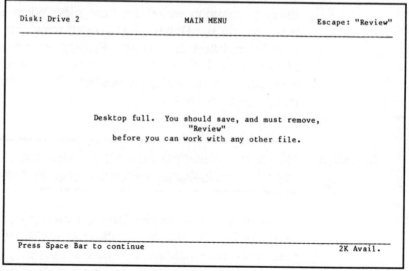

```
Disk: Drive 2                    MAIN MENU              Escape: "Review"
-------------------------------------------------------------------------




              Desktop full.  You should save, and must remove,
                                  "Review"
                    before you can work with any other file.






-------------------------------------------------------------------------
Press Space Bar to continue                                  2K Avail.
```

Figure 1.10: Request to remove a specific file

other things while text is in temporary storage. The designated options for moving and copying within the document do not provide that capability.

In each chapter we will discuss specific additional applications for the clipboard. Some are surprising, while others are more obvious. Here we will review general approaches applicable throughout AppleWorks.

Tip: *Moving to the clipboard is often the most efficient way to move sections of information within a document.*

Place the cursor on the first line to be moved. Press Apple-M to access the Move menu, and then press T to indicate that the move will be to the clipboard. Move the cursor to highlight the desired lines, and press Return.

By using the clipboard you are free to do other things before deciding where to put the information. When you decide, place the cursor where you want the text to begin, and press Apple-M to access the Move menu again. Press F to move the lines from the clipboard. Copying lines to the clipboard is similar to moving, except that the text also remains in its original position.

If you use the designated option to move lines within the document, you cannot perform other operations until the move has been completed. If you move text to the clipboard, you can do almost anything before the move is completed. In fact, you can even move text within the document.

Tip: *By using the clipboard, you can copy two separate sections of information at once.*

If you copy one section of information to the clipboard, then immediately copy another section to it, the second section will replace the first. There is no way to keep two separate sections of information on the clipboard simultaneously, unless you first join the sections within the source document.

However, you can still copy another section within the document, while one section of information remains on the clipboard. Simply press Apple-C and select the first option to copy within the document. This option has no effect on the clipboard, but you must unload the "within" section before unloading the information on the clipboard.

Tip: *When you need to transfer anything between files, move to and from the clipboard whenever possible.*

The move and copy commands require different amounts of memory. Copying to the clipboard creates two copies of the text in memory. Copying from the clipboard leaves a copy on the clipboard (for a total of three). Moving simply changes the location of one segment, requiring almost no additional memory. Moving from the clipboard empties the clipboard.

Therefore, when you copy to the clipboard, move from the clipboard to empty it. When you move anything to the clipboard, you can still make multiple copies in the new document by copying from the clipboard more than once. The last use of the clipboard should be a move, again to empty it.

Tip: *You can empty the clipboard by moving or copying an empty space to it.*

There may be times when you copy lines from the clipboard and then realize that you really should have moved them from the clipboard instead. Suppose the clipboard has a 15K segment that you want to throw out. To do that, copy an empty space or line to the clipboard. The one-byte segment will replace the 15K segment, essentially emptying the clipboard and returning the needed memory to the Desktop. Figure 1.11 shows how the available Desktop memory decreases when 250 lines of text are copied to the clipboard.

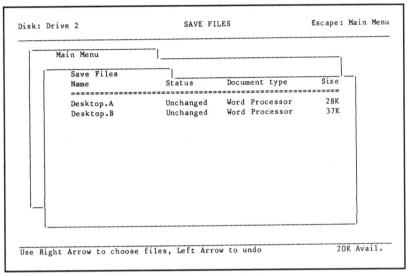

```
Disk: Drive 2                    SAVE FILES              Escape: Main Menu
_____

     Main Menu
                          |_____
       Save Files         |
       Name               Status       Document type      Size
       ================================================================
       Desktop.A          Unchanged    Word Processor       28K
       Desktop.B          Unchanged    Word Processor       37K








    __
_____
Use Right Arrow to choose files, Left Arrow to undo         20K Avail.
```

Figure 1.11: *101K Desktop, clipboard with 250 lines of text*

Leaving copied information on the clipboard may bring you above the memory-use level at which file changes start to slow down. The copied information may even fill all the remaining available Desktop memory, forcing you to remove a file from the Desktop before proceeding further. The smaller the Desktop memory, the more important it is to use the clipboard efficiently.

EXPANDING THE DESKTOP

AppleWorks was designed to operate within 128K of RAM in both the Apple IIe and the Apple IIc. Several firms have recently offered 80-column extended-memory cards in the 128K–1536K range, however, and they also provide software that modifies AppleWorks so it can take advantage of the extended memory. We will look at representative 192K and 384K Apple IIe systems to understand the practical implications of this important innovation.

The descriptions that follow should be considered generically, because memory-expansion technology is evolving rapidly and innovations are appearing almost every month. Applied Engineering and Checkmate Technology have led the way in developing memory cards and in modifying AppleWorks to use additional memory. (Both cards were used in the writing of this book.) The Applied Engineering card can be expanded to 512K, while the Checkmate card expands to 768K. Both firms offer optional piggyback cards that double their respective memory capacities.

Many experienced users already have the RAMWORKS card and Super Desktop Expander software from Applied Engineering. Several tips that follow include details about this software, because it can benefit from additional documentation. In contrast, the newer and less well-known Checkmate MultiRam card and related software come with remarkably thorough documention; in fact, the Checkmate manual is a very useful technical reference for AppleWorks.

Extended-memory cards speed up the overall performance of a given task, which is often more important than the extended-memory capacity itself. The speed improvements come from two changes in the operation of AppleWorks: the improved performance of Apple-Q, and the option to run AppleWorks from a RAM drive.

In a previous caution we noted that with 24K of files loaded on a 55K Desktop, the Apple-Q command accesses the Program disk for more than four seconds before going to the Desktop Index, and then again for another four seconds before going to the new file. By adding enough RAM to the Desktop, you can change files within the same program almost instantly up to much higher memory-use levels.

When changing to a file that requires a different program, as from a Word Processor document to a Spreadsheet template, AppleWorks loads enough of the new program to get you started, more when you use additional functions. With the AppleWorks program also in RAM, the programs themselves change almost instantly. At this stage there is virtually no lag time on the Desktop.

Incidentally, there are two other possibilities for minimizing the time required for a given task:

1. With AppleWorks program files and data files on a hard disk, you can bring program segments and files to the Desktop in much less time than it requires to load them from a floppy disk. Hard disks for the Apple II generally come in five- and ten-megabyte sizes, and although they greatly extend disk memory, they have no effect on Desktop memory capacity.

2. With an additional card that uses a 65C02 processor running at a faster clock speed, AppleWorks can execute processing operations faster. Because that option is important mainly for Spreadsheet recalculation, we will review it in the Spreadsheet chapter.

Tip: *Increase the Desktop memory.*

You can buy an Applied Engineering (AE) extended-memory card with 64K installed for considerably less than the cost of Apple's own 80-column extended-memory card. Moreover, the basic Apple card cannot be expanded beyond 64K, whereas the AE card can be expanded to 512K and beyond. If you already have an Apple extended memory card, remove the 64K chips and install them in the empty banks of the AE card. Better yet, sell the Apple card and buy a set of nine 150-nanosecond 64K chips for less than eight dollars. In either case, the added 64K gives you a 128K card, or a 192K system when you include the memory already on the Apple IIe motherboard.

Inserting chips is simple enough, but there is one probable complication: you may find that the pins are slightly wide for the socket. To correct this problem, lay one side of pins on a firm, flat surface and apply just enough pressure to bend them slightly inward, all together. This should make them fit. Follow directions about where the notched end of the chip should be.

The AE card comes with Super Desktop Expander (SDE) software that modifies the AppleWorks Startup disk, increasing the Desktop capacity to 101K. Because this more than doubles the memory-use level at which the Apple-Q command accesses the Program disk, it is the single most significant improvement you can make to AppleWorks.

If you so choose, the SDE software will also modify the routine for saving files. AppleWorks normally saves a Desktop file to the disk before deleting the previous file of the same name. For example, if you want to save a 70K file, you need at least 70K of free space on the disk. If the previous version of the file is on the disk, you must go through the Main Menu to the Other Activities menu to delete it before you can save the updated file from the Desktop.

The Applied Engineering software modifies the Program disk so that AppleWorks saves the Desktop file in a direct way, overwriting the previous file. If you press Escape during the save, the save is terminated as always, but the previous file has been deleted. Because the Desktop file remains intact, there is little risk. However, if the power happens to fail for a split second during the save, you will be completely dependent on your backup disk. Incidentally, the SDE software changes all the save routines available through the Desktop menu from indirect saves to direct saves.

Tip: *Consider replacing one bank of 64K chips with 256K chips.*

As costs decrease, you may want to consider using 150-nanosecond 256K chips instead of adding 64K chips. Most chips come in sets of nine, providing a spare in case of any problem. With a simple chip puller, available from electronics stores, you can remove one bank of 64K chips and replace them with 256K chips. They are the same size as 64K chips, with the same socketing, and the memory card recognizes them. This revision gives you 320K plus 64K on the motherboard, for a 384K system. The

SDE software then increases the Desktop capacity to 229K—enough to do almost anything you can imagine.

The larger memory capacity allows the SDE software to make additional modifications to AppleWorks. These are summarized in Table 1.2, and discussed in detail in several tips that follow.

Tip: *You can save a file to more than one disk with a 256K memory card.*

With 183K of memory on the Desktop, it is obvious that files can grow too large for standard 136K Apple disks. The SDE software modifies AppleWorks to save such files to more than one disk in sequentially numbered segments.

If the file name is Budget, the second segment is automatically named Budget.2. When you reload, you load the segmented file in an orderly sequence. If your file already ends with the suffix .2 to denote the second version of the budget itself, the second segment is automatically called Budget.3. That may not be exactly what you had in mind. If you save very large files consistently, consider naming them differently. For example, a file named Budget.B would then be neatly segmented as Budget.B.2.

Table 1.2: Super Desktop Expander 4.0 modifications to AppleWorks

	RAMWORKS Card				
	64K	**128K**	**256K**	**320K**	**512K**
System Memory	128K	192K	320K	384K	576K
Desktop Memory	55K	101K	183K	229K	367K
Direct Save	X	X	X	X	X
Multidisk Save			X	X	X
RAM Drive			X	X	X
5114 Records			X	X	X

Limit the names of large files to 13 characters, because segmenting will truncate file names to fit the segment identification number within the ProDOS limit of 15 characters. Figure 1.12 shows some segmented file examples.

There is another possible complication with the segmenting process. If you try to save a new 20K file on a disk with room for only 10K, the modified AppleWorks will save what it can and ask for another disk to continue the save. In this case you should Escape from the save, find a disk with more room, and save the file as a single entity.

Tip: *You can expand the Desktop by adding memory to your Apple IIc.*

Apple IIc owners have not been ignored by firms offering memory expansion. Applied Engineering and Checkmate also offer extended memories of 256K and 512K for the Apple IIc, along with software to modify AppleWorks. The RAM drive

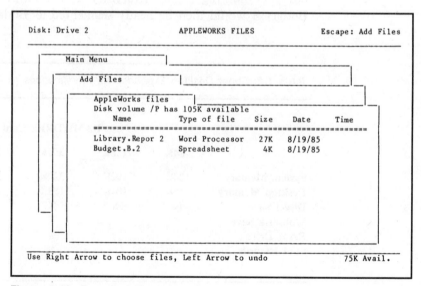

Figure 1.12: Renamed file segments

option described in the following tip is particularly useful for Apple IIc users who want to use AppleWorks efficiently with one disk drive.

Tip: *You can load AppleWorks into a RAM drive with a 256K memory card.*

The SDE software can modify AppleWorks so that it automatically loads into a RAM drive, providing instant access to each component program. It takes about 75 seconds to load everything from the Program disk to the RAM drive, so there may not be a net benefit for short sessions.

The RAM drive has no effect on the available Desktop memory. If you have a 384K system, the Desktop has 229K whether you use the RAM drive or not. In general, it makes sense to use the RAM drive option when shifting back and forth between programs (for example, to add several Spreadsheet tables to a Word Processor report). Rapid program access makes it easier to remember how to respond in one file to information you have just seen in another file.

Apple IIc owners will appreciate the RAM drive option because it allows you to efficiently use drive 1 as the standard data disk location. However, you should understand that if the Desktop is loaded to near capacity, the RAM drive may allow a file segment to replace a program segment. After that point AppleWorks will need to access the Program disk in drive 1 for the necessary program segment. The more memory you have, the less likely it is that this will happen.

Tip: *The SDE software dramatically increases the Data Base record capacity.*

The standard Data Base can manage up to 1350 records. With the SDE software that capacity increases to 5114 records. This is probably the most important AppleWorks innovation to date, but it has not been widely advertised. The complete Data Base file is stored in RAM all at once, so record selection and arranging are incredibly fast. The modified Data Base gives the Apple II series a significant advantage over other personal computer systems in a broad range of professional applications.

Incidentally, the SDE software also increases the Word Processor capacity from 2,250 lines to more than 5,000 lines. This is equally impressive, but it is has fewer practical advantages in applications development.

Tip: *You can minimize the number of AppleWorks disks needed if you know where the SDE modifications reside.*

Because the SDE software makes many modifications, you will want to avoid unnecessary permutations requiring additional AppleWorks Startup and Program disks. It is not necessary to have a complete set of disks for every option if you know where the modifications reside.

Table 1.3 shows the location of each modification in the Super Desktop Expander version 4.0. You will want to list the relevant modifications on each disk, along with the total system memory and Desktop memory (written as 384/229, for example).

Table 1.3: *Location of Super Desktop Expander 4.0 modifications*

	Startup Disk	Program Disk	Comments
Desktop Expansion	X		Begins with 128K card
Direct Save		X	Overwrites previous file
Multidisk Save	X		Segments files
RAM Drive	X		No effect on Desktop size
5114 Records	X		Increased from 1350 limit

With a 64K or 128K RAMWORKS card, you need only one Startup disk. The direct-save modification goes on the Program disk, so you will probably want one Program disk with the direct-save modification and one without. It is prudent to have a separate disk with the indirect save for any beginning users who share an Apple and AppleWorks with experienced users. (Ideally, of course, it would be best to have an option to select either an indirect or direct save, depending on your understanding of available disk space and potential risks.)

With 256K and larger cards, you will probably want to have two Startup disks, one with the RAM drive option for long sessions and one without it for short sessions. You must thereafter decide which Startup disk to use when you load AppleWorks. Note, however, that you can always override the RAM drive option shortly after entering the date: simply press Escape when segments from the Program disk begin loading into memory.

With 256K and larger cards, you get the direct save automatically, and therefore need only one Program disk.

Tip: *You can make time-clock modifications to the Apple-Works disks.*

Several firms offer clock cards that can be used to add the date and time to any ProDOS file, including AppleWorks files. If you have installed a clock, the correct date will automatically appear when you load the AppleWorks program, and you will never have to consult a calendar.

Applied Engineering includes software with its clock card that can modify AppleWorks in two additional ways. First, the lower-right corner of the screen can show the date and time in place of the Help message. This modification has no particular advantage over a wind-up watch, and some people may prefer not to be constantly reminded about time. Second, another modification allows you to enter the actual time and date into Data Base time and date categories by simply entering an at sign (@). This can be particularly useful in specialized time-conscious applications, such as record-keeping for shipping and receiving operations.

Both the Startup and Program disks are modified with the AE clock card software, but you can subsequently use the modified disks with or without the clock card installed.

Caution: *There are no standards for memory cards yet.*

Software for one memory card will not necessarily work with another. Bank-switching methods may vary from card to card. When Apple releases a card of its own in the 256K–1536K range, that card will probably become the accepted design standard.

For our purposes, AppleWorks file integrity is the most important issue. The Checkmate and Applied Engineering systems described in this section can recognize each other's segmented AppleWorks files. If you have one system, you can use segmented files created by someone using the other system.

COMMON APPLEWORKS COMMANDS

About a dozen commands work the same way in each of the three component programs. These commands are as central to the operation of AppleWorks as the Desktop itself. The following tips supplement the information in the AppleWorks Reference Manual.

Tip: *AppleWorks has undocumented control commands.*

As with many programs, AppleWorks can use additional control commands that duplicate documented AppleWorks commands. One offers a particular advantage: Apple-Y functions exactly as Control-Y does, deleting the rest of a Word Processor line, Data Base category, or Spreadsheet cell. Apple-Y is often more convenient, because you use the Apple keys so often. You should also know that if your finger slips while using Apple-U to edit a Spreadsheet cell, you might clear the cell with a mistaken Apple-Y.

Some other control commands are standard commands on the Apple: Control-I for Tab, Control-J for ↓, Control-K for ↑, Control-H for ←, Control-U for →, and Control-M for Return. These offer no particular advantage, but if the cursor moves unexpectedly when you thought you pressed Control-B, Control-L, or Control-Y, you will know that it happened because you used an Apple rather than an AppleWorks command.

Tip: *When a screen message requests you to hit the Space bar, Return will do as well (but not vice versa).*

This tip is most worth remembering when you format a box of disks; using nothing but Return improves your response time. Space bar messages are generally used to make you slow down and think about your response. If you have been there a hundred times before, you may not need to think it over again.

Caution: *The Ruler is really a divider.*

The Ruler in AppleWorks divides a file into eight vertical parts. It is therefore really a divider, not a ruler. While it finds relative locations well, it cannot be used to locate precise positions within a file.

Apple-1 marks the beginning of the first section; Apple-8 marks the beginning of the eighth; Apple-9 marks the very end of the file. The locations of section markers 2 through 8 change as the file becomes longer or shorter.

To find precise locations, use fixed markers in the Word Processor and cell coordinates in the Spreadsheet. For locating precise points in Data Base files, there is no obvious all-purpose choice.

USING PRODOS

The Desktop is, in a functional sense, the operating system for AppleWorks. It depends on and extends ProDOS. AppleWorks performs efficiently because of the operating system, and ProDOS has gained wide acceptance because AppleWorks has become the most widely used Apple software package.

ProDOS loads and saves files quickly by any standards. It can load an 18K Spreadsheet file in less than ten seconds, which is less than 20 percent of the time required for a similar file using the DOS 3.3 version of VisiCalc. If you use only AppleWorks files, you can probably get by without knowing much more about ProDOS. Everyone else should read on.

If you have an Apple IIe, you probably have the ProDOS User's Disk Utilities. If you have an Apple IIc, you have a disk called the ProDOS System Utilities. In this book I will refer to both as the ProDOS utilities. They are used most often to copy disks.

Tip: *Learn the differences between DOS 3.3 and ProDOS files.*

DOS 3.3 and ProDOS differ in many ways, but one difference is particularly important here: a disk formatted for ProDOS has a volume name preceded by a slash (/) mark. That name is separated from any file name by another slash. The name can be brief, such as the /P used throughout this book. ProDOS volume names cannot be longer than 15 characters. The same rule applies to ProDOS file names. Volume names precede file names, as in /P/Filename. Together they are called the path name.

Tip: *Think of a ProDOS volume as a disk.*

For most AppleWorks purposes, a ProDOS volume is the same as a standard 136K floppy disk. Although a ProDOS volume can have subdirectories, there is really no need to use them with a two-disk-drive system. An AppleWorks data disk seldom has more than 20 AppleWorks files, so there is rarely any confusion. If you have a hard disk or a high-capacity floppy disk, subdirectories provide branching paths for finding your way through many files.

Tip: *If you use standard 136K disks, give each data disk a standard volume name.*

A brief standard volume name (such as /P) is easier to remember and enter when you write path names for ASCII and DIF files or for segmented Data Base files.

Formatted data disks can then be interchangeable on an Apple system with two standard disk drives. If you use the ProDOS utilities to compare or copy files or volumes, you can quickly rename one volume to avoid confusion or error. Note, however, that in most cases you will be copying files by loading them to the Desktop and saving them to another disk.

Note that this tip is limited to 136K AppleWorks data disks. Program disks should have distinct names. Each copy of an AppleWorks disk should also be named /APPLEWORKS.

Tip: *The ProDOS User's Disk Utilities can compare Apple-Works files and volumes.*

If you question whether two identically named AppleWorks files are in fact identical, the ProDOS Filer can compare them. Use the Filer first to quickly rename one of the volumes.

When should you compare files? Suppose you saved two important Spreadsheet files. You might want to make certain that both saves were perfect. Suppose you checked one Word Processor file for spelling errors, made corrections, and saved the file to two disks. You might want to make certain that both saves were perfect. In general, it is a test for perfection. If you simply doubt whether a file has been backed up, just save it from the Desktop again.

The ProDOS Filer will also run on the Apple IIc, even though it is not included with the ProDOS System Utilities.

Tip: *The ProDOS utilities can lock AppleWorks files.*

There are good reasons to lock AppleWorks files. For example, you may eventually use templates as the source for 80 percent of all new AppleWorks files. Sooner or later you will save a completed file over the template because you forgot to change the file name. If you lock the template file, that cannot happen.

The ProDOS utilities can lock any ProDOS file. Then, if you try to save a file to a disk that contains a locked file of the same name, AppleWorks will not permit it. You will see the screen message shown in Figure 1.13. If you later want to unlock the file, return to the ProDOS utilities.

MANAGING PROJECTS

This section covers the problems of managing your own desktop—the one with real pencils and papers. Because AppleWorks lets you work more productively, you may have more to manage.

If you want to work efficiently with AppleWorks, group your tasks into clearly defined projects. Give each project its own disks, notebook, hanging files, and so on. You can undertake many projects in the same time period, provided everything remains neatly partitioned.

If you spend time searching for papers lost in heaps, pay particular attention to this section. AppleWorks will eventually straighten you out, whether you want it to or not, but everything will be easier if you make a conscious effort to cooperate.

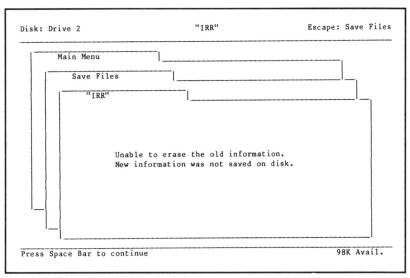

Figure 1.13: *Screen message indicating locked file*

Tip: *Learn to manage disks efficiently.*

The important concept is to keep related files on the same disk. Use key words to describe the contents of the disk. For example, Ames Project Letters could describe a disk of letter files, even though no single file uses that specific name. The key words on the label need have nothing to do with the ProDOS volume names (all of which might be /P, for example).

Keep related disks in the same box. Some disks come in a hard box that can store up to 12 disks, and they last a long time. Use key words to describe the box. For example, Ames Project could describe a box of disks, even though no single disk has that label.

Neatly typed file names on the label mean little in themselves. Twenty unrelated files on a disk will always be something of a jumble, even if the file names are typed alphabetically on the disk label—logical grouping is the key.

Tip: *Make a "working disk."*

At any given time you may be working on several projects, transferring information, and saving unrelated files on the same disk. A "working disk" allows anyone to break the rules in a controlled way.

The disk should include at least three files we will design later: a Word Processor template, a Spreadsheet parts file, and a multi-purpose Data Base template. All of these together take about 6K on the disk, leaving another 130K free for the day's work. Figure 1.14 shows the catalog of a typical "working disk."

During the day, save files to the "working disk" if they cannot conveniently be saved to the proper disk. At the end of the day, save everything to its proper disk and delete any unnecessary files.

Tip: *Print hard copies of the screen to document your work.*

Documentation is, without question, the most tedious part of applications development; few people do it thoroughly. When you design a template, make copies of key screens and annotate them. In many cases your documentation will be a collection of these annotated copies.

Tip: *Use keyboard templates and make notes.*

Keyboard templates offer a simple but effective way to remember the things that count most, such as commands and formulas. You can design a template sheet, print it on utility bond paper, and have it copied onto card stock. Highlight specific commands in yellow, and write comments in pencil in the margins. You can and should make your own templates for specific applications, or use self-adhesive Post-It notes for simple reminders.

The most common kind of keyboard template is for people who are learning AppleWorks or using it only occasionally. It should be designed for using the Word Processor and for working with exist-

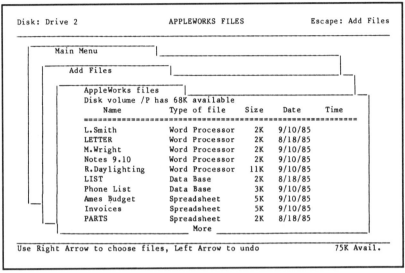

Figure 1.14: Partial catalog of a "working disk"

ing Spreadsheet and Data Base applications. The commands in AppleWorks use the letter keys wisely for mnemonic purposes, but some people need time to adapt, particularly if they have used other programs. For example, VisiCalc users may have difficulty remembering Apple-L for layout (rather than F for format).

Specialized templates are also helpful for experienced users who design Spreadsheet or Data Base applications. Include what you need most: engineering formulas, selected commands, and so on. After several days away from AppleWorks you may need a template to remember obscure command sequences, such as the one to reset manual recalculation in the Spreadsheet.

No matter how experienced you are with AppleWorks, you will always be learning something new that you have not quite mastered. This is the kind of information that belongs on a keyboard template. There is no point in remembering information such as the number equivalent to column N in the Spreadsheet, even though you sometimes need to know that when designing applications. This kind of information also belongs on a template.

There are some patterns for templates in Appendix B. Before you spend as much as $20 on a plastic template, think about making one yourself (and make some copies for your friends).

Tip: *Put a note board on the wall near your Apple.*

You need a place to post information, especially hard copies of the AppleWorks menu screens. After a hundred hours on Apple-Works, when you can see the screens in your mind's eye, you can use the space for new information. People always need more surface area for information, and note boards conveniently provide that.

What else belongs on the note board? An Apple II reference chart is particularly helpful. Beagle Brothers, a firm specializing in utility software, publishes one such chart that is a classic in graphic design. The chart comes with many Beagle Brothers programs, including Extra-K, a program noted in Appendix A.

Tip: *Develop a method for differentiating programs, templates, and data files just by glancing at the disk label.*

One way to do this is to use different-colored pens to write the disk labels. For example, use a red soft-tip pen to write disk labels for programs. A ProDOS volume name may be different from the program name, so it is usually best to include both names on the disk label. Use a black soft-tip pen for templates and common data files, or use any color combinations that makes sense to you.

To differentiate template files from common data files, you can write and enter the template file names entirely in uppercase letters. Though uppercase letters are harder to read, this is a case where it may be more important to differentiate between word groups than between letters.

Tip: *Assign a prefix to note the purpose of an Apple-Works file.*

Choose a prefix for denoting files of similar type (for example: LTR or L for letter). Use short prefixes to leave more space for descriptive names. The idea is to choose prefixes that make sense to you. Above all, be consistent. Include your own standard abbreviations on an editorial style sheet, and post that sheet on your note board.

Tip: *Add time records to critical files.*

AppleWorks provides an option to enter the correct date when the Program first loads. Use that option faithfully, because you will often need to compare file dates.

Sometimes you will need to know which of two files is the most recent when both have the same date stamp. A clock card can place a time stamp on a file, but rather than buying a clock card, why not write the date and time at the beginning of the file, so that you can find it with Apple-1. Use a consistent form, such as the AppleWorks convention (Oct 1 85 5:30 PM).

Printouts likewise need date and time stamps. We have all mistakenly used the wrong printouts as often as the wrong files. By entering the time in the file itself, you also print it on paper copies—something a clock card does not do.

Tip: *Use the Escape key to hide your work.*

If someone needs to talk to you while you are using Apple-Works, their eyes will inevitably be attracted to the flashing cursor on the screen. You may have some work displayed that you would rather not have others see. Simply press Escape to go to the Main Menu. Your work is off the screen, and pressing Escape again will bring it back just as quickly.

Tip: *For archival storage, use both sides of your disks.*

To write to the opposite side of any disk, lay another disk on it face down, outline the notch location, then use a common paper punch to make a new notch. Verify the blocks with the ProDOS utility disk.

Use the two-sided disks mainly for archival storage, even though many people use them every day. In theory, using both sides can expose the magnetic surfaces to more dust particles; in practice this has not been a recurring problem.

Tip: *Use the plastic case that comes with AppleWorks.*

The AppleWorks plastic case carries up to six disks. Peel the label off the spine and put your own address label on the front. The case fits neatly into a briefcase. When it wears out, buy something similar.

Tip: *When available time on your Apple is limited, consider the things you can do by hand.*

In many cases, two or more people share an Apple for personal and professional uses. Sometimes it would be nice to use AppleWorks when someone else is using it, but it may not be all that necessary. Consider what can be done with a pencil and paper.

Preliminary report outlining can be done as efficiently on paper as on the Word Processor. Spreadsheet design can be done efficiently on graph paper, and you can make preliminary back-of-the-envelope calculations with a $15 scientific calculator. Database design can be done on hard copies of record layout, report format, and printer options screens.

SUMMARY

In this chapter I have addressed the common problems that tend to slow people down by presenting many tips and techniques that you can use repeatedly.

As you understand more about Desktop operation, you can work more efficiently with the Word Processor, Data Base, and Spreadsheet. In the next three chapters, you can draw upon what you have learned in this chapter. There will be tips for changing file names, copying to the clipboard, and using AppleWorks commands for unexpected purposes. The tips and techniques in this chapter will help you build component parts that can be used again and again in many useful applications.

2

The Word Processor

ost AppleWorks users spend more time with the Word Processor than with the other programs, and for good reason. We generally exchange information by putting our thoughts into words and sentences, which we then use to construct letters, reports, manuals, and even books. In doing so we become, in effect, wordsmiths, for whom the Word Processor can be a valuable tool.

As word processors go, the AppleWorks Word Processor is easy to learn and teach, because what you see on the screen is essentially what you get printed on paper (especially if you keep the formatting simple). Most people feel comfortable enough with the Word Processor to begin typing without much instruction. If you are teaching others, encourage them to start writing on their own. AppleWorks has good error-trapping routines, so no one will get lost.

Although the Word Processor may lack some commands, it is large and fast. (In fact, one can make that comment about all the AppleWorks programs.) When you compare it to another respected word processor for the Apple, Screenwriter II, AppleWorks does not look quite as powerful. But in day-to-day work, AppleWorks holds its own. Although the AppleWorks Word Processor does not have Screenwriter II's capability to generate complex form letters, a related AppleWorks Mailing Program meets most common needs. AppleWorks does not provide exact word and character counts, but its line and character counts suffice for approximations. AppleWorks cannot use macros to substitute one keystroke for a block of text, but its screen response is faster, it has better file-handling routines, and it has larger file capacity in RAM. Most people will find the Word Processor good enough, even for writing a book.

This chapter provides tips in eight sections for getting the most from using the AppleWorks Word Processor. The first section provides some general tips. The section on entering text provides some important insights about efficient use of the keyboard. The section on writing letters includes useful information on using letter templates, writing form letters, and printing mailing labels. In the large section on printer options, you should particularly note the Word Processor rules for paragraph and page integrity, as well as techniques for managing margins and character columns.

The fifth section provides some tips for using the copy command in ways you may not have considered. The following section introduces some useful applications for the find and replace commmands. The next section covers methods for handling problems presented by long files with complex formats. The final section in this chapter provides tips for using spelling checkers with the Word Processor.

GENERAL WORD PROCESSOR TIPS

This section contains general insights about how the Word Processor works. You will usually begin your work from scratch or by loading a file onto the Desktop. Writing is only as good as the thought and editing behind it. By using this program efficiently, you can have more time to do the work that counts. Figure 2.1 shows the Word Processor menu.

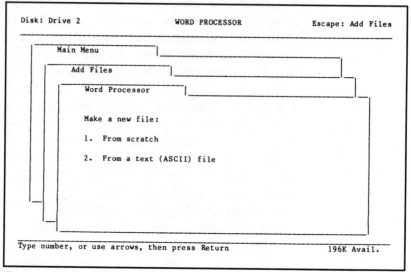

```
Disk: Drive 2                 WORD PROCESSOR          Escape: Add Files
  ┌──────────────────────┐
  │    Main Menu         │
    ┌──────────────────────┐
    │    Add Files         │
      ┌──────────────────────┐
      │  Word Processor      │

           Make a new file:

           1.  From scratch

           2.  From a text (ASCII) file




  ──────────────────────────────────────────────────────
  Type number, or use arrows, then press Return        196K Avail.
```

Figure 2.1: *Word Processor menu*

Tip: *Print and annotate hard copies of the Word Processor menus.*

You will need a hard copy of the Word Processor menu and the Printer Options menu, as well as the command menus for Apple-Tab, Apple-F, Apple-R, and Apple-P. If you have not yet done so, print copies of all these screens using Apple-H, and post the copies on a note board near your Apple. Pencil in notes about when you use each option. A hard copy of the Printer Options menu appears in Figure 2.2. Use a yellow marker to highlight the line showing the main printer options in effect.

Tip: *The cursor always appears at the beginning when you reload a file.*

A file is also always displayed in the normal display mode when you reload it, regardless of whether you were previously using the

```
 File: Options                 PRINTER OPTIONS      Escape: Review/Add/Change
 =====|====|====|====|====|====|====|====|====|====|====|====|====|====|====|===




            PW=8.0  LM=1.0  RM=1.0  CI=10  UJ  PL=11.0  TM=0.0  BM=2.0  LI=6  SS
          Option:              UJ: Unjustified    GB: Group Begin       BE: Boldface End
                               CN: Centered       GE: Group End         +B: Superscript Beg
          PW: Platen Width     PL: Paper Length   HE: Page Header       +E: Superscript End
          LM: Left Margin      TM: Top Margin     FO: Page Footer       -B: Subscript Begin
          RM: Right Margin     BM: Bottom Margin  SK: Skip Lines        -E: Subscript End
          CI: Chars per Inch   LI: Lines per Inch PN: Page Number       UB: Underline Begin
          P1: Proportional-1   SS: Single Space   PE: Pause Each page   UE: Underline End
          P2: Proportional-2   DS: Double Space   PH: Pause Here        PP: Print Page No.
          IN: Indent           TS: Triple Space   SM: Set a Marker      EK: Enter Keyboard
          JU: Justified        NP: New Page       BB: Boldface Begin
```

Figure 2.2: Printer Options menu

layout mode. (The Data Base follows similar conventions, but in the Spreadsheet the cursor remains where you left it.)

While the file is on the Desktop, the cursor and the display mode always remain as you left them, which is exactly as it should be. Make a note of this, because when you make a quick change to another file, you may return with text on the clipboard, and you almost always need to come back to precisely the same place.

Tip: *Format option values are saved with each file.*

When you save a file, you save all the specified printer options with it. When you load a file, use Apple-Z to make these options visible in the stack at the beginning of the file. Notice that when an option has been superceded, it nevertheless remains in the stack. You can delete the ones you no longer need with Apple-D.

Tip: *Printers are listed in the order you added them.*

When you first tell AppleWorks you want to print, the proposed printer is always the one at the top of the list. To have your printer there you must configure it first, even if that means removing the Apple Dot Matrix Printer and the Imagewriter that Apple has already added. It helps to have your standard printer on top, so you can use Return to step through the printing menu sequence.

ENTERING TEXT

Most of your time with the Word Processor will be spent entering text, so it helps to know everything you can about working efficiently. With AppleWorks you spend more time on the lower rows of the keyboard than you would on a typewriter. That is where the arrow keys are located, along with the Apple-C, Apple-M, and Apple-Z commands.

Tip: *Move the cursor as efficiently as possible.*

Each method of moving the cursor has advantages in specific situations. Your choice of method depends on where you are in a document and where you want to move.

When moving the cursor most of a line forward or backward, hold down an Apple key and press → or ← to jump one word at a time. On wide lines, try this variation: hold down → or ← to start the cursor moving one character at a time, then press an Apple key to increase speed as needed; you will quickly get the feel of it.

Apple-← will move the cursor to the left across a large space in a line with one move. You can use such moves often, because you will normally enter text at the end of a document, where the line below the cursor is empty. To move the cursor from anywhere in the last line of a document to the first letter of the last line, you can move down into the empty space with ↓, left all at once with Apple-←, and up to the first letter of the last line with ↑. Use these open-space moves whenever you can.

There is another way to move quickly from the end to the beginning of the line your cursor is on. Press ↑ to go to somewhere near the end of the previous line, then press Apple-→ one or more times to reach the first letter of the line.

Tab and Apple-Tab also move the cursor quickly back and forth across lines of text. These keys are particularly useful for reaching a specific column in an empty line or empty part of a line. Try working with fewer tabs, so that the ones you have set are useful not only as tabs but also for moving the cursor quickly.

Tip: *Make a note of when you use the insert and over-strike cursors.*

The insert cursor is a blinking underline that inserts characters—place the cursor on a character, type in another character, and the original character is pushed to the right. The overstrike cursor is a blinking rectangle that types over characters—place the cursor on a character, type in another character, and the new character replaces the old. You can switch between cursors using Apple-E, and you will undoubtedly develop preferences for each in different circumstances.

You may find that you generally use the insert cursor for draft writing, because you need to add information and push text ahead of the cursor. The overstrike cursor works well for editing, particularly for changing individual characters within defined spaces, as in tables, for example. In overstrike mode you can use the Space bar to blank out characters with spaces.

Tip: *The overstrike cursor is useful for creating small tables.*

The overstrike cursor types over letters instead of pushing letters to the right. Use it to maintain alignments on small tables that you build in the Word Processor.

Use the insert cursor with the Delete key and Space bar to push entire rows back and forth within tables. Note also that you can copy spaces from the clipboard to create a whole new column. This technique is described in the section on moving and copying text.

For large tables designed and built by trial and error, use the Spreadsheet. We will discuss this "build-and-transfer" technique in Chapter 5.

Tip: *Delete characters as efficiently as possible.*

Apple-Y deletes everything from the cursor to the end of the line. For large deletions, place the cursor on the first or last character to be removed. Press Apple-D, move the cursor to highlight the text to be erased, and then press Return to complete the deletion. Note that when you highlight lines of text from the first character of a line using ↓, the highlighting continues one character beyond the final line specified. Therefore, you must remember to press ← once before you press Return to delete the material.

The Delete key works well for deleting one or two words, but Apple-D is more efficient for deleting more than two words (to the left or right of the cursor). Again, however, the highlighting goes one character too far when you use Apple-→ to highlight whole words, so remember to press ← once before you press Return.

One Delete will traverse all of the open space to the left of a carriage return marker and remove that marker if it is the first and only thing in the line. To delete any other carriage return marker, move one space to the right of it and press the Delete key to eliminate it. Make certain the return markers are visible when you do this.

Tip: *Delete any spaces preceding carriage return markers.*

Spaces between sentence-ending periods and carriage return markers can cause mischief in printing, notably by adding unexpected empty lines. You need to see the markers in order to find and delete the unwanted spaces; Apple-Z takes you to the display mode that shows those markers. In most cases, you will be writing text with simple formatting and the markers will not be obtrusive.

If you use many printer options embedded in your text, you may not want to see all the markers all the time. In that case you can check carriage returns and other markers all together just before printing.

Tip: *Minimize word-wrapping distraction.*

If the last word on a line does not quite fit, that entire word moves down to the beginning of the next line. It will move back up to the previous line only if you delete enough of the characters in front of it. This process is called word wrapping; it can be confusing to watch continuously.

There is an easy way to prevent words from wrapping during writing and editing. If you plan to insert a sentence or more in the middle of a paragraph, press Return and type on an empty line until you finish that sentence. Then press Delete to eliminate the carriage return marker and close up the space that separates new text from what follows.

Tip: *Use the clipboard efficiently.*

Read all the clipboard tips in Chapter 1 if you have not already done so, because with the Word Procesor it is especially important to use the clipboard efficiently. Where the tips refer to lines, think of text. In the Word Processor, you can move or copy as little as one character or as much as 250 lines. The 250 lines are counted in the source document, even if the source document has wider lines than the destination document or vice versa.

Tip: *Sticky spaces serve two important purposes.*

Sticky spaces are normally used to keep two words together on a line. For example, Apple II would look peculiar if Apple and II were split apart, so you can replace the space with a sticky space (Apple-Space bar) to keep them together. You will often need to do this for words with associated numbers.

Sticky spaces can also be used independently to make the Word Processor recognize an otherwise empty line. Two following tips explain the use of sticky spaces with page calculations and double spacing.

WRITING LETTERS

Business letters are generally less than one page long, with simple formatting and printing requirements. You may want to use the same thought in more than one letter, or produce a dozen or more letters of almost exactly the same form. The following tips present useful information for those who write business letters.

Tip: *Left-justified letters are the easiest to format.*

Left-justification (or blocked style) is an efficient letter form for both the word processor and the reader. There is no need to spend time centering headings and closings (in fact, people who do so are now considered dated). Leave at least three line spaces for the signature before the typed name.

Figure 2.3 shows a sample letter. You may want to enter the letter as a Word Processor document so you can try out some of the techniques discussed below.

Tip: *Use a letter template.*

A letter template need contain no more than an address heading, a greeting, a closing, and a signature name, along with some basic format settings (for example, tabs and margins) and any necessary printer option settings. You can save copies of the template on several disks, wherever it is needed. Use an uppercase file name, such as LETTER, for the template.

A basic letter template can be used for reports as well. Just add a footer that will begin printing on page 2. Then delete the address heading and related text.

Figure 2.4 illustrates a basic letter template without showing carriage return markers.

Tip: *Learn how to transfer paragraphs from letter to letter.*

A broad range of friends and associates can often benefit from the same information, although you may not say things exactly the same way to each of them; you can copy paragraphs from letter to letter when appropriate.

Suppose you want to include the paragraph about the Apple table (Figure 2.3) in an informal letter to a friend who also owns an Apple. Begin writing the letter and note the place where you

```
September 21, 1985

Dear Bob:

Here's a suggestion for using AppleWorks.  Maybe you can include
it in the next edition of the book.

A regular kitchen table is too high for the Apple.  After
refinishing our old table, we decided to saw more than two inches
off the legs and make it the Apple table.  The top is now less
than 28" high.  We also found a reasonably-priced secretarial
chair with pneumatic height adjustment. Everyone in the family
works with the Apple, each using a different seating height.
Workspace comfort is important, and this is an affordable design
solution.

Sincerely,



Susan Smith
```

Figure 2.3: *Left-justified letter*

want to include the previous thought. Insert the data disk with the previous letter into drive 2. Then proceed as follows:

1. Load the file with the previous letter onto the Desktop.

2. Find the paragraph you need and copy it to the clipboard.

```
File: LETTER                    PRINT MENU         Escape: Review/Add/Change
=====|===========================|=========================================
--------Right Margin:  0.5 inches
--------Pause Each page
January 1, 1986

Susan Smith
34 Meetinghouse Rd.
Jefferson, RI 02845


Dear




Sincerely,



Susan Smith
--------New Page
-----------------------------------------------------------------------
Print from?  Beginning  This page  Cursor
```

Figure 2.4: *Letter template*

3. Press Apple-Q to change files.

4. Place the cursor on the name of the file containing the new letter, and press Return.

5. Place the cursor on the line and column where the paragraph is to begin.

6. Move the paragraph from the clipboard.

7. Check to make certain that there are no unwanted spaces.

8. Save the new letter.

The beginning of the new letter might appear as shown in Figure 2.5. Notice that the first sentence of the copied paragraph has been moved to the end of the previous paragraph, and that several changes have been made to the wording of the copied paragraph.

Tip: *If you want to repeat more than two lines of text, transfer the text rather than rewrite it.*

The deciding issue on whether to transfer or rewrite is really not length but difficulty in reconstructing the thought. With practice you should be able to make transfers quickly enough to justify copying as little as two lines from almost any file already on the Desktop.

Sometimes it is faster to modify an existing letter. When you want to repeat almost all of a long letter, add it to the desktop, change the file name (with Apple-N), delete the unwanted parts, add the parts you need, and save the new file.

Tip: *The best way to proofread is from hard copy.*

When you finish writing a letter or any document, check it for mistakes by reading the printed draft. You can annotate printed copy, and it is much easier to read than text on the screen, especially if it is printed on a letter-quality printer or a high-quality dot-matrix printer.

```
September 30, 1985

Dear Jeff:

When are you coming this way again?  We have been steadily
converting the old farmhouse into workspace and have much to show
you.

Your father tells me you bought one of those classic old IIe's
with the white-letter keyboard.  Make sure you find a good place
for it.  A regular kitchen table is too high for the Apple.

After refinishing our old table, we decided to saw more than two
inches off the legs and make it the Apple table.  The top is now
not quite 28" high.  We bought a secretarial chair with pneumatic
height adjustment for less than ninety dollars.  Three of us work
with the Apple, each using a slightly different seating height.
Workspace comfort is important, and this is an affordable design
solution.
```

Figure 2.5: Paragraph copied into a second letter

Tip: *You can write form letters without a mail-merge program.*

There are several mail-merge programs available for use with AppleWorks. We will discuss one, the AppleWorks Mailing Program, in Chapter 5.

You can partly automate letter writing without using a mail-merge program. If you have a buffered printer, this method is efficient for up to a dozen letters at a time (some would say more). Consider the example of a letter announcing a meeting and agenda to ten members of a library association building committee.

Write inside addresses for each of the committee members, or load your file if you have previously written them. They should be stacked on top of one another, as shown in Figure 2.6. These small lists need not be kept in the Data Base. However, they can be produced from existing Data Base reports printed to the clipboard, a subject covered in Chapter 5.

Save the file if you have not previously done so. Then use Apple-N to change the file name, because you will be making significant changes to this file.

Enter the date at the top of the list, then copy it to the clipboard. Copy it from the clipboard repeatedly, above each name

```
File: Address List              COPY TEXT        Escape: Review/Add/Change
=====|====|====|====|====|====|====|====|====|====|====|====|====|====|====|===
--------Left Margin:  1.0 inches
--------Right Margin:  0.5 inches


Susan Smith
81 Main Rd.
Jefferson, RI 02845

Arnold Wright
52 Mill Rd.
Jefferson, RI 02845

Thomas Farmer
12 Field Rd.
Jefferson, RI 02845

Edward Joiner
19 Mill Rd.
Jefferson, RI 02845


--------------------------------------------------------------------------
Copy Text?  Within document   To clipboard (cut)   From clipboard (paste)
```

Figure 2.6: *Address list in the Word Processor*

on the list. Then write the letter at the end of the file, including a general greeting, closing, and signature name, followed by a new page marker (NP). Copy that letter to the clipboard, then copy it from the clipboard repeatedly, below each name on the list. The file will then contain a series of identical letters beneath different addresses. When the file is printed, the new page option places each letter on a separate page, as shown in the partial printout in Figure 2.7.

There is another variation to the method described above that works well with a buffered printer. Write the body of the letter, beginning with a standard greeting and ending with the signature name. Type in the date at the top of the stack of headings and copy it to the clipboard.

Copy the date from the clipboard repeatedly, before each address in the stack. Set the cursor just above the lowest date in the stack, print from the cursor, and then delete that date and heading. Move the cursor just above the next date and repeat the process. Keep repeating it until the printer buffer is full.

With either of these methods, you might want to include specific greetings, such as "Dear Mr. Farmer," in the address stack and omit the general greeting from the body of the letter.

```
September 8, 1985


Susan Smith
81 Main Rd.
Jefferson, RI 02845

Dear Friends:

The Building Committee will meet on Thursday, September 19, at
7:00 PM in the library meeting room.  The agenda will include the
following items:

Arnold Wright will tell us what he has learned about possible
modifications to the building that will increase available
daylight.  He will also discuss related lighting controls.

The working group on handicapped access will have copies of their
most recent progress report.  Thomas Farmer will discuss
additional improvements that will benefit all library users.

If you think of additional agenda items, please call me at
888-1182.

Sincerely,



Ellen Cooper




September 8, 1985


Arnold Wright
52 Mill Rd.
Jefferson, RI 02845

Dear Friends:

The Building Committee will meet on Thursday, September 19, at
7:00 PM in the library meeting room.  The agenda will include the
following items:

Arnold Wright will tell us what he has learned about possible
modifications to the building that will increase available
daylight.  He will also discuss related lighting controls.

The working group on handicapped access will have copies of their
most recent progress report.  Thomas Farmer will discuss
additional improvements that will benefit all library users.

If you think of additional agenda items, please call me at
888-1182.

Sincerely,



Ellen Cooper
```

Figure 2.7: *Two copies of a form letter*

Tip: *Use address lists to print addresses on envelopes.*

There are several different ways to print addresses for envelopes. For more than a dozen envelopes, print from a Data Base labels report onto mailing labels. (See Chapter 3 for more on mailing labels.)

For fewer than a dozen envelopes, return to the list of addresses shown in Figure 2.6. Load the original address list file, because you will need the addresses together again.

For addressing envelopes you need wide left margins. Assuming ten characters per inch, specify 2.5 inches for small envelopes and 4 inches for business envelopes. Specify a new page after each address on the list and a pause for each page. Load the envelope as you would a sheet of paper, so that the print head is on the line where you want the address to begin. Remember that the default top margin is 0 inches.

The printer will print the address and eject the envelope. In fact, the roller will move far enough to eject an 11-inch sheet of paper. You may want to specify a shorter page length and tell the printer not to accept top-of-page commands when printing envelopes, but that is not absolutely necessary.

The formatted file for printing business envelopes appears in Figure 2.8 (without showing carriage return markers). Note that you can also print addresses on continuous 4 × 6-inch post cards, which are available for tractor-feed printers. Print the address on one side and the message on the other. In this case it is necessary to specify a page length of 4 inches, and to make certain that your printer is configured to accept no top-of-page commands.

PRINTER OPTIONS

Using the printer options requires some thought. Press Apple-O to review the Printer Options menu. It may appear confusing at first, but the 37 printer options are logically grouped. You will normally use only about half a dozen of these options anyway.

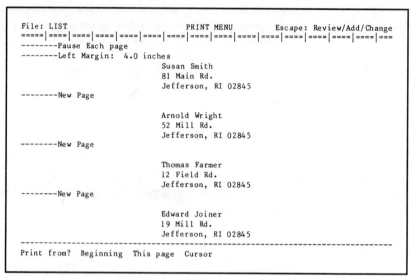

```
File: LIST                          PRINT MENU            Escape: Review/Add/Change
=====|====|====|====|====|====|====|====|====|====|====|====|====|====|====|===
--------Pause Each page
--------Left Margin:  4.0 inches
                                     Susan Smith
                                     81 Main Rd.
                                     Jefferson, RI 02845
--------New Page

                                     Arnold Wright
                                     52 Mill Rd.
                                     Jefferson, RI 02845
--------New Page

                                     Thomas Farmer
                                     12 Field Rd.
                                     Jefferson, RI 02845
--------New Page

                                     Edward Joiner
                                     19 Mill Rd.
                                     Jefferson, RI 02845
-------------------------------------------------------------------------------
Print from?  Beginning  This page  Cursor
```

Figure 2.8: *Format for business envelope addresses*

The printer options are logically grouped from top to bottom in columns, but they are not arranged alphabetically. The tips and cautions in this section refer to specific options; they follow the order on the Printer Options menu.

Press Apple-H to print a hard copy of the menu screen if you have not already done so. Use a yellow marker to indicate the groups of options on the menu; the groups are defined in Table 2.1.

Table 2.1: *Printer option groups*

Group	Option	
Line Length, Print Density	PW	Platen Width
	LM	Left Margin
	RM	Right Margin
	CI	Characters per Inch
	P1	Proportional-1
	P2	Proportional-2
Text Positioning	IN	Indent
	JU	Justified

Table 2.1: *Printer option groups (continued).*

Group	Option	
	UN	Unjustified
	CN	Centered
Page Length, Line Density	PL	Paper Length
	TM	Top Margin
	BM	Bottom Margin
	LI	Lines per Inch
	SS	Single Space
	DS	Double Space
	TS	Triple Space
Page Controls	NP	New Page
	GB	Group Begin
	GE	Group End
Page Calculation	PH	Page Header
	PF	Page Footer
	SK	Skip Lines
	PN	Page Number
Place Markers	PE	Pause Each Page
	PH	Pause Here
	SM	Set a Marker
Print Enhancements	BB	Boldface Begin
	BE	Boldface End
	+B	Superscript Begin
	+E	Superscript End
	−B	Subscript Begin
	−E	Subscript End
	UB	Underline Begin
	UE	Underline End
Variable Text Entry	PP	Print Page number
	EK	Enter Keyboard

Line Length and Print Density

Printing requires some mechanical understanding of where everything goes on a page. Spend some time watching the print head move across the paper. Where does it start and end? Is your paper running even with the left side of the platen? This is the kind of information that lets you print with predictable accuracy.

Tip: *You can adjust the margin settings to have visually equal margins.*

The platen width is the distance the print head travels across the printer roller. Most printers have a platen width of 8 inches, although standard paper is 8½ inches wide. Paper is usually aligned so that the left-most character just barely fits on the paper when the left margin is set at 0 inches.

When you enter the first line of text, you will see that the default margins leave space for only 60 characters. When printing with the default margins and the paper aligned as described above, the right margin will appear to be about three-quarters of an inch wider than the left margin. You can change the left and right margins to make them appear equal. For example, if the printer is set for ten characters per inch (the Word Processor default setting), left and right margins can be set to 0.8 and 0 inches respectively, allowing you to print 72 character spaces.

Why have we chosen such a narrow right margin? Given the platen width and paper location, the left margin is exactly 0.8 inches wide. The right margin is actually half an inch wide, because it includes the half inch beyond the platen width. The right margin will be uneven, with few characters extending to column 72, hence the actual half inch on the right is enough to balance 0.8 inches on the left.

Caution: *The Word Processor uses 77-character lines.*

The screen shows 80 character columns per line, but even with no margins, the words will wrap at column 78. The maximum line length on the screen is 77 characters. You should know all this when you set wide margins.

Because the margins are set in tenths of inches rather than character spaces, only the 10 CI setting matches the screen to the printer. If the printer option settings allow more than 77 characters, the printer will not print the text exactly as you see it on the screen. Given the screen's effective 77-character width, margin settings of 0.3 on the left and 0 on the right will print the text as it appears on the screen. The maximum margins for other print densities are problematic: there may be no perfect match, so it's best to use a conservative line length.

Tip: *You can print more than 77 characters on a line.*

To print more than 77 characters on a line, select more characters per inch or change the platen width if your printer can accommodate this. The page calculations still work, though the lines will not break as shown on the screen. In fact, you may not see the first page break until beyond screen line 66.

Caution: *You can use only one character size per line.*

Word processors use available printer font capabilities much more than most other programs, but the Word Processor in AppleWorks is limited in this respect. In general, you can use only one character size per line. If you want to know about the few exceptions to this rule, see the advanced printer techniques in Chapter 6.

Caution: *Proportional printing can produce unwanted results.*

Proportional printing adjusts the amount of space between characters, depending on the width of each character. For example, an "i" requires less space than an "m" does. P1 and P2 were designed primarily for the Apple Dot Matrix Printer (DMP), although five other listed printers have one proportional mode. Proportional 1 prints on average about 15 characters per inch on the DMP, and it is probably the most attractive font on that printer. Some DMP users prefer to use it whenever possible. The Proportional 1 option can produce a couple of unwanted results, however.

For some reason, spaces are not considered to be characters of a fixed size. When paragraph indentations are created by tabs, some paragraphs may be printed with a greater indentation than others. Indentations created with spaces, even sticky spaces, are treated the same way. For the same reason, proportional printing does not work with aligned columns—the columns almost never remain aligned during printing. These problems effectively limit proportional printing to text with block paragraphs.

Text Positioning

You will sometimes want to center text and use other text positioning options. Read the following tips and cautions carefully, because these options can produce unwanted results.

Caution: *The indent option cannot indent the first line of a paragraph.*

The indent option indents everything but the first line of a paragraph, thereby creating what the AppleWorks Reference Manual calls hanging paragraphs. The indent option is functionally similar to increasing the left margin, except that indenting counts character spaces instead of tenths of an inch.

Tip: *Use the default setting for left-justified text.*

You will almost always use left-justification for letters and text. Left-justification is built in (the term "unjustified" in the default setting refers to the right margin). With typeset text, as in this book, adjustments are made to spaces between letters as well as spaces between words to produce an aligned (flush) right margin.

In the Word Processor, however, right-justification and proportional printing work independently, and neither works very well.

Caution: *Right-justification can produce unwanted results.*

Right-justification is simply called justification in AppleWorks, because left-justification is built in. Justification aligns the right margin by adjusting spaces between words, whereas P1 and P2 adjust spaces between letters. Justification has the same problems as proportional printing with indentation and aligned columns, because spaces are adjustable characters.

If you use a long print line, 14–17 CI print, and few long words, justification can look good. If you use a short print line, 10–12 CI print, long words, aligned columns, or indented paragraphs, justification will make decisions about spacing that may disorient readers.

Page Length and Line Density

This is one group of options that you can ignore most of the time. The default settings were wisely chosen for normal use. However, it may take some practice to insert double-spacing marks correctly.

Tip: *When you specify less than 11 inches for paper length, make certain your printer does not accept top-of-page commands.*

For 4 × 6-inch continuous post cards, you will need a paper length of 4 inches; with mailing labels you may need a paper length of 1 inch. On the Change a Printer menu, make certain that the response to option 2, for accepting top-of-page commands, is No.

Many printers allow you to enter control codes to change the paper (or form) length, but the Word Processor offers no option for entering special codes. The Data Base and Spreadsheet do have this special code (SC) option.

Tip: *The top and bottom margin settings really do make sense.*

Notice that the default margin settings are 0 for the top and 2 inches for the bottom. Most people prefer to insert paper in the printer up to the intended first line. This allows room to sight the paper and set the roller bar on friction-feed printers.

The default margins give you the flexibility to allocate actual top and bottom margins by adjusting the starting point on the paper up or down. For example, you may prefer a little more than an inch of margin for the top and a little less than an inch for the bottom.

Caution: *The spacing options can be inserted only in front of paragraphs.*

To begin double spacing, insert the DS code on the line before the line where you want it to take effect. (Note that an empty line does not count in this rule, although a line with nothing more than a sticky space does count.) You cannot change spacing in the middle of a paragraph; if you access the printer options in the middle of a paragraph, the DS will be placed in front of that paragraph. Remember all this well, because if you forget, double spacing will start sooner than you expect. The same rules apply to triple spacing, and to single spacing when you return from double or triple spacing.

Page Controls

The page controls are surprisingly dependent on the Word Processor rules for paragraph integrity. Pay special attention to the techniques for working around these rules.

Tip: *To use page control options effectively, learn the rules for text integrity.*

The Word Processor has an inherent respect for paragraph integrity. It will never print only one line of a paragraph on a page (if that paragraph has at least two lines), and it will not allow the new page option to break a paragraph in any way.

Any text group that ends with a carriage return is a paragraph. Remember that rule and consider the implications. It means that a table can be divided between pages, because each line ends with a carriage return (to preserve column alignment). A section title can be printed all alone at the bottom of a page, because it is considered a one-line paragraph.

Given these rules, the trick is to designate text groups that cannot be divided between pages. Use the GB (group begin) and GE (group end) options to mark these groups. You can insert them as you write, preparing for any eventuality. Or you can wait until the end of your writing, calculate the pages (with Apple-K), and then insert group designations where you need them.

Tip: *Use carriage returns within paragraphs to accommodate page control options.*

If you are certain of margins and pitch settings and that the text lines will be less than 77 characters wide, you can insert carriage returns where a line would normally wrap. This makes separate paragraphs in the Word Processor rule book, even though the text is still printed as a single paragraph. Once you insert a carriage return, you can insert NP, GB, GE, and DS where they would not otherwise be permitted.

Page Calculation

The Apple-K command calculates pages, but there are some minor calculation problems you should understand. Pay special attention to the following caution and the caution on printing from the cursor.

Caution: *Empty lines are generally not counted in page calculations.*

After page 1, when a calculated page begins with an empty line, that line is not included in the remaining calculation. This is rarely a problem, because in practice most return markers occur between single-spaced paragraphs. But how do you begin a page with enough empty lines to allow for a drawing to be pasted in later? Put a sticky space just in front of the first return marker you want counted.

Incidentally, AppleWorks correctly calculates empty lines when you use the printer option to skip lines (SK), but that option does not display the space on the screen.

Tip: *Printer options require lines of their own on the screen.*

A printer option such as Double Space requires a line of its own on the screen, but not on the printed page. The line is always counted on the screen, even when the option is hidden in normal display mode. Word Processor files often have several printer options stored at the beginning of the file. In normal display mode it is therefore common to see the first displayed line listed as line 5 or beyond.

Tip: *Page calculations may show partial lines at the end of each page, but those calculations are invariably correct.*

After calculating page breaks, you may see partial lines just before the page-dividing line. This is because 80-character columns may be available to the printer, but only 77-character columns are available on a screen line. The page break calculations are invariably correct. Figure 2.9 shows an example of a page break with a partial line preceding it, and Figure 2.10 shows how the lines appear when the document is printed.

Partial lines may also appear when printer option markers fill character spaces that are not actually printed. Again, the page-break calculations are invariably correct.

Caution: *When you print from the cursor or from the page on which the cursor is positioned, use Apple-K first.*

Although AppleWorks calculates the pages after you request printing, that may not be good enough. You must calculate the pages yourself with Apple-K before entering the print command sequence with Apple-P. If you forget to do this, your printout may include text from the previous page.

```
File: Word.Process.A               PRINT MENU          Escape: Review/Add/Change
=====|=====================|=============================|====================
so we can replace the space with a sticky space (Apple-Space bar) to keep
them together. You will often need to do this for words with associated
numbers.
     Sticky spaces can also be used independently to make the Word Processor
recognize an otherwise empty line. As we will later see, this can be
important for page calculations and double spacing.

A)WRITING LETTERS(A
     Business letters are generally less than one page long, with simple
formatting and printing requirements. You may want to use
- - - - - - - - - - - - - End of Page 5 - - - - - - - - - - - - - - -
the same thought in
more than one letter, or produce a dozen or more letters of almost exactly
the same form. The following tips present useful information for those who
write business letters.

TIP: Left-justified letters are the easiest to format.
     Left-justification (or blocked style) is an efficient letter form for
both the word processor and the reader. There is no need to spend time
centering headings and closings (in fact, people who do so are now considered
-------------------------------------------------------------------------------
Print from? Beginning  This page  Cursor
```

Figure 2.9: Partial lines in page calculations

Tip: *Consider the header and footer lines in planning pages.*

Page headers and footers take up lines on the screen only once, at the beginning of the file, but they take up space on every page during printing. Headers and footers are printed within the specified text depth, not within the top or bottom margins.

A header or footer will use at least three lines per page. This means that if you use single spacing and the default top and bottom margins, you will have room for 51 lines per page aside from the header or footer.

Because headers and footers are usually brief lines, they can make a standard margin look too large. You may therefore want to decrease the bottom margin setting.

Caution: *You can get locked out of AppleWorks if you press Return at the wrong time while finding a page.*

Try making this mistake when you can afford to start over. The correct sequence for finding a page is listed below, followed by a note on the error.

1. Press Apple-K to calculate the pages.
2. Press Apple-F for the Find menu.
3. Press P to select the page option.
4. Enter a page number, and press Return.

The cursor moves to the bottom of the page selected. However, if you make the mistake of pressing Return *before* entering the page number, AppleWorks may lock you out and you will have to reboot with the Startup disk.

The error cannot occur unless the pages have been calculated, and there is no problem when you enter a Return incorrectly while attempting to find text or markers.

```
A)WRITING LETTERS(A
      Business letters are generally less than one page long, with
simple formatting and printing requirements. You may want to use


Word Processor 2.5




the same thought in more than one letter, or produce a dozen or
more letters of almost exactly the same form. The following tips
present useful information for those who write business letters.
```

Figure 2.10: *Printout showing the page break indicated in Figure 2.9*

Caution: *If you calculate pages and then immediately delete the last page break line, you can get locked out of AppleWorks.*

This can occur in earlier versions of AppleWorks. It is likely to happen only if you add carriage return markers to the end of a file to see how many more lines would fit on the last page. If you instinctively delete return markers after calculating pages, you may delete the page break line by mistake.

Tip: *Page numbering is controlled by three different options working together.*

The header or footer option controls the line location of the page number, the print page option (PP) controls the character location of the page number within the line, and the page number option (PN) controls the actual number printed.

The page number automatically increases by one with each new page, but you can begin numbering pages with any number up to 512. For example, Section 2 of a report may be a separate file, but the first page of that section can be page 26.

The ^ symbol indicates the PP option, the specific character location for printing the page number. It is usually located in the header or footer. The actual page number 1 is designated with the PN option anywhere prior to the PP option, which means that footers allow more flexibility than headers.

Place Markers

The most important place markers are the pause markers used to control printing. With them you can print specific ranges of text. The set-a-marker option (SM) identifies fixed points, something that the AppleWorks Ruler cannot do.

Caution: *The pause here option (PH) cannot break a paragraph.*

As with the page control options, you may need to insert a carriage return in order to use PH within a paragraph. If you are using PH simply to stop at the end of a page, use PE (pause each page) instead, because it avoids the need to insert a carriage return.

Tip: *Pausing at the end of each page offers several advantages.*

The option to pause at the end of each page allows you to manually insert single sheets into a friction-feed printer. However, the PE option can also be used to control text loading into a printer.

AppleWorks provides no option to print just part of a document, such as the first four pages of a 25-page report. If you want to print only the first four pages, calculate the pages (with Apple-K), enter a PE anywhere on page 4, and print from the beginning. When the flashing cursor reappears on the screen, press Escape to return to the document.

You can use a similar technique to print a specific range of pages, such as pages 12 through 15 of a 25-page report. If you want to print only this range, calculate the pages, insert PE anywhere on or before page 12, move the cursor to page 12, and choose "This page" on the printer menu. When the flashing cursor reappears on the screen, press the Space bar and release another page to the printer. Continue the process until all the required pages are released.

If you want to print just part of the last page of a specified range, insert PH in the appropriate place on that page. It is important to keep a count of the pause markers and pages if you have a large printer buffer, because you can load several pages in less than a minute.

Print Enhancements

Boldfacing, superscripting, subscripting, and underlining are the most important print enhancements used in writing. Eight printer menu options provide these. Underlining and boldfacing can also be used with control commands. Italics are not listed on the Printer Options menu. If your printer can produce italics, see Chapter 6 for tips on accessing them.

Tip: *Character-control markers take up space on the screen but not on the printed page.*

The presence of character-control markers for such print enhancements as underlining and boldfacing can make a significant difference between what you see on the screen and what you get from the printer. For example, if you have six character-control markers on a line, that can be enough to push a five-letter word onto the next line on the screen, but not on the printed page.

Unfortunately, you cannot turn off the display of character-control markers to see how your text will appear on the printed page.

Caution: *Superscripts and subscripts may not print properly on some tractor-feed printers.*

Almost all printers have friction feeds that allow superscripts and subscripts to be printed correctly. But if you plan to use these options often in printing long reports, you will want to use a tractor feed so that you can walk away from the printer—just make certain the tractor is bidirectional.

A unidirectional tractor pulls the paper up over the roller but cannot pull it back down. This means that the print line will not return to the normal position after a superscript or subscript.

Tip: *Use Control-L for underlining and Control-B for boldfacing.*

Moving back and forth from the Printer Options menu can be time-consuming. Instead, you can begin and end underlining with Control-L, and begin and end boldfacing with Control-B. The convenience of this method may tempt you to use it as well to access italics or alternate character sets. It can be done: the mechanics of installing additional character controls are explained in Chapter 6.

Variable Text Entry

The Word Processor has two options for entering variable text. The page number option enters numbers, and the enter keyboard option allows you to enter text from the keyboard during printing.

Tip: *Make the most of the page number option.*

The page number option (PN) allows you to enter a different number on each page, and it has several additional uses that may surprise you.

The first page of Chapter 2 can be page 2.1, provided that 2.^ is entered in the header or footer. If you want to begin the numbering with 2.2 on the second page of a chapter, the header or footer should be moved to the second page. The actual page number 2 is then designated with the PN option anywhere on the second page prior to the header or footer.

The highest page number permitted is 512, which is probably enough for any document you want to print. You can skip page numbers by inserting another PN option on another page. For example, you may want to jump from page 14 to page 18 to accommodate illustration pages.

The page number option can also be used to print sequential identification numbers for such things as invoices. The number can be entered more than once on a page. Figure 2.11 shows an interesting example.

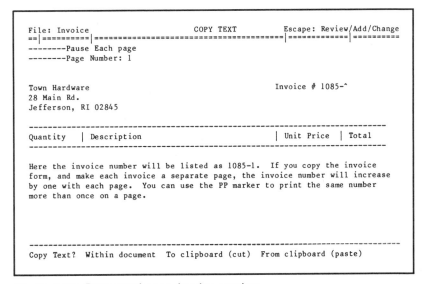

Figure 2.11: *Page number as invoice number*

Tip: *You can enter more than 50 characters with the EK option.*

To enter more than 50 characters of text from the keyboard while the printer pauses, select the EK option more than once, leaving no spaces between the marks. (You can provide any needed spacing in the text you enter.) For example, text with the EK option indicated by ^ ^ ^ ^ will accept up to 200 inserted characters.

MOVING AND COPYING TEXT

If you have used the Word Processor a great deal, you may already appreciate how much time you can save by taking advantage of its capabilities for moving and copying text. This section includes tips for using the copy command in ways that you might not have considered.

Tip: *When moving or copying text, highlight the space or spaces following the last sentence.*

If your sentences usually end in a period followed by two spaces, include those two spaces when you highlight a block of text. This way, everything will fit perfectly when you insert the block of text later. When moving or copying text from the clipboard, place the cursor on the first character that will follow the inserted sentence.

Tip: *Use the copy command to repeatedly insert text.*

Copy a repeated phrase to the clipboard and then copy it from the clipboard as often as needed. The phrase remains on the clipboard until you replace it with another. Although you can have only one block of text on the clipboard at a time, it is easy to store several more blocks of text at the beginning or end of your working document. By using Apple-1 and Apple-9, you can retrieve and insert blocks of text quickly.

Tip: *Use the copy command to copy printer options.*

Zoom to the display mode that shows printer options at the beginning of the file. Copy the options to the clipboard and copy from the clipboard as often as needed to any number of files. (Delete the existing options in those files first.) This works well when you use many printer options in one section of a report and want the other sections to match. Figure 2.12 shows a complete range of printer options waiting to be copied.

The same process works within a file. Instead of using Apple-O to access printer options each time you need to insert a new page marker, copy an existing new page marker to the clipboard. Then copy the marker from the clipboard wherever you need one.

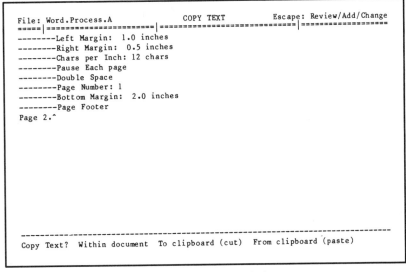

```
File: Word.Process.A              COPY TEXT           Escape: Review/Add/Change
=====|=========================|==============================|==================
--------Left Margin:  1.0 inches
--------Right Margin:  0.5 inches
--------Chars per Inch: 12 chars
--------Pause Each page
--------Double Space
--------Page Number: 1
--------Bottom Margin:  2.0 inches
--------Page Footer
Page 2.^




-----------------------------------------------------------------------
Copy Text?  Within document  To clipboard (cut)  From clipboard (paste)
```

Figure 2.12: Printer options waiting to be copied

Tip: *Move text to the clipboard to delete it.*

Sometimes you think you should delete a section of text, but you are uncertain, and you know the decision will be irreversible. (There is no Undo command in AppleWorks, as there is in some other word processors.)

If you have any doubts about deleting, move the text to the clipboard and attempt a rewrite. If that works, forget about the clipboard, because you will overwrite it whenever you copy or move to it again. If you still think you might need the copy later, move the text from the clipboard to the end of the file.

Tip: *Use the copy command to copy blank spaces.*

A specific number of blank spaces can be treated just as any other text. For example, suppose you want to insert 28 spaces into each of 12 lines in a table, between the first and second columns. Copy 28 spaces to the clipboard, then repeatedly copy the spaces from the clipboard.

In creating tables, you will want to do this when you forget a column. You can enter information into the new column using the overstrike cursor, so that nothing is misaligned.

The same general technique applies to characters used for borders, such as repeated hyphens or asterisks. It also applies to dotted and solid lines used in contracts.

Tip: *When you copy from a file to the clipboard, the file remains unchanged.*

If you load a file onto the Desktop for the single purpose of copying text to another file, copy to the clipboard rather than move. When you copy, the file remains unchanged, and you can remove it from the Desktop quickly, without having to respond to menu questions in the option for removing files from the Desktop.

FINDING AND REPLACING TEXT

It takes time and practice to discover the many uses of the powerful find and replace commands in the Word Processor. If you are new to using these commands, pay special attention to the tip on replacing words one at a time.

Tip: *The Word Processor has the most powerful find and replace commands in AppleWorks.*

Table 2.2 shows the differences between the find and replace commands in each AppleWorks program. The Word Processor alone has the ability to replace text and identify case-sensitive text. You can use Apple-R rather than Apple-F when you want to find only case-sensitive text—simply choose not to replace and then move on to the next instance.

The first entry in the normal replace command appears in uppercase letters, no matter how you enter it. The second entry

Table 2.2: Options available for find and replace functions

Option	Word Processor	Data Base	Spreadsheet
Finds text	X	X	X
Finds case-sensitive text	X		
Finds numbers	X	X	as labels only
Finds page numbers	X		
Also finds	markers		coordinates
Searches from	cursor	beginning	cursor
Replaces one instance	X		
Replaces all instances	X		
Maximum number of characters	30	30	25

appears as you entered it, with any capitalized letters you speci-fied. Replacement words are always case-sensitive.

When finding text, AppleWorks always proposes the last text you used, unless you leave the file and then return. This is one way to start with a fresh slate. The other way is to use Apple-Y before entering any new text to be found or replaced.

Caution: *The find and replace commands search from the cursor for text, pages, and markers.*

If you want to search through a whole file, use Apple-1 first, to return to the beginning of the file. If you have a header or footer line, the cursor will return to that line. If you don't use Apple-1 first, you will be searching through only the part of the file that follows your current cursor position.

Tip: *When you replace words, replace them one at a time.*

You may be tempted to replace all instance of a word or phrase. Consider the word *I* about to be replaced by *you* in a report. Unless you specify case-sensitive text and include the pre-ceding and trailing space, you can cause yourself much grief, because there is no neat way to convert unwanted *you* entries back to *I* entries.

When you replace characters, words, or phrases, replace them one at a time for the first twenty times you use the command. Keep notes on unexpected results and lessons learned. When you feel confident, start replacing all instances in routine cases. If you have any doubts whatsoever, replace one at a time.

If you replace misspelled words one at a time after your spell-ing checker lists them, you can see them in a larger context. This can improve your proofreading, because you may have made other mistakes in the same vicinity.

Tip: *There is a way to check spacing following sentence-ending periods.*

If you proofread a letter or brief report on the screen, it is difficult to make certain that exactly two spaces follow each sentence-ending period. The most common errors are three spaces or just one. There is a way to check this, however, that's a little easier on your eyes.

First, switch to the overstrike cursor, because it makes extra spaces stand out. Use Apple-R to replace all instances of a period followed by three spaces. Replace them one at a time with a period followed by two spaces. There will generally be few or no instances of a period followed by three spaces.

Next, use Apple-R again to replace all instances of a period followed by one space. Again, replace them one at a time with a period followed by two spaces. This will find every sentence-ending period, but each occurrence will then appear vividly as either one space or two. You can move through the file quickly by alternately pressing the N and Y keys as appropriate. You should be able to correct the spacing in a 10K file in less than a minute.

If you use one space after each sentence-ending period, life is much easier. Use Apple-R to replace all instances of a period followed by three spaces, then all instances of a period followed by two spaces.

Tip: *There is a simple way to verify spacing between words on different lines.*

In the process of editing text, you may occasionally forget how many spaces there are between the last word of a line and the first letter of the following line. If that happens, put the cursor on that first letter, delete back until the two words meet, and then insert the space or spaces you need.

When a sentence ends with a period in the last usable character column, column 77, this technique can sometimes cause the following line to indent one space. If that happens, go back to the previous line, enter the two required spaces on that line, and then delete the indented space on the next line. Columns 78 and 79 will hold functional spaces, but not characters.

If you want to confirm that there are two spaces at the end of a line, you can place the cursor just before the end of that line and use Apple-F to find the next occurrence of two spaces.

Tip: *The replace command can be used for writing macros.*

Some word processors insert a larger word or phrase at the time a designated character combination is typed. This is often called macro writing, and although AppleWorks does not have this capability, it can be simulated using the replace command.

For example, you can type *xx* everywhere *AppleWorks* is intended, then replace all occurrences of *xx* with *AppleWorks*. Although *aw* would also be a good substitute, the replacement instructions in that case would have to include the spaces before and after the *aw*. You do not want to replace an occurrence of *awesome* with *AppleWorksesome*.

Although no double letter occurs as rarely as xx, several others are at least improbable enough to use for additional words. These include hh, ii, jj, qq, uu, and yy. Double letters can be entered quickly, but you run the risk of accidentally entering triple letters. When you replace double letters, search for triples just in case. Note also that these are all lowercase letters—capitals simply take too long to enter.

Combinations of letters and numbers, such as a1 and a2, can be used to replace commonly used long words such as *application* and *architecture*. You can make a complete list of equivalents for your own writing purposes. Include commonly used phrases as well. Figure 2.13 shows a text screen with macro codes instead of complete words.

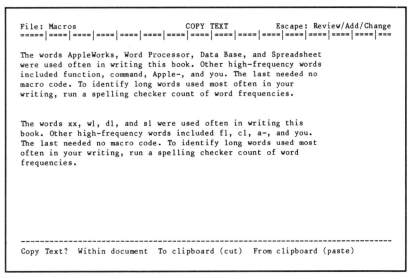

File: Macros   COPY TEXT   Escape: Review/Add/Change
=====|====|====|====|====|====|====|====|====|====|====|====|====|====|====|===

The words AppleWorks, Word Processor, Data Base, and Spreadsheet
were used often in writing this book. Other high-frequency words
included function, command, Apple-, and you. The last needed no
macro code. To identify long words used most often in your
writing, run a spelling checker count of word frequencies.

The words xx, wl, dl, and sl were used often in writing this
book. Other high-frequency words included fl, cl, a-, and you.
The last needed no macro code. To identify long words used most
often in your writing, run a spelling checker count of word
frequencies.

Copy Text? Within document To clipboard (cut) From clipboard (paste)

Figure 2.13: *Macro codes instead of complete words*

WRITING LONG REPORTS

If you write extended reports with complicated formatting, you
need to know more about the Word Processor. Reports often
extract information from other sources, including spreadsheets,
databases, and information services such as CompuServe. In
Chapter 5 we will discuss transfer methods; here we will deal with
internal problems related to the length and complexity of Word
Processor files.

Tip: *The Word Processor can handle up to 2,250 lines per
file.*

The 2,250 lines amount to 40–45 pages of single-spaced text—
normally enough for one section of a report. Sections tend to
make logical files, so there is rarely a need to chain files for

printing purposes. Page numbering presents no problem, because the second section of your report can start at any designated number from 1 to 512.

The Super Desktop Expander software that comes with the RAMWORKS card can extend the Word Processor's capacity to more than 5,000 lines per file. That allows for 90–95 pages of single-spaced text, which can be useful for printing complete reports from one file.

Tip: *You can "chain" files for printing purposes.*

There is no facility for chaining files as such, but there is a way to have files print with consecutive numbers and keep all the pages full. Follow these steps:

1. Calculate page breaks using Apple-K.

2. Move the cursor to the last page.

3. Note the page number of the last complete page.

4. If the last page is incomplete, move that text to the clipboard.

5. Move the text from the clipboard to the beginning of the next file.

6. Use PN to specify the page number from which the next file should start printing.

Use this method for final drafts only, because insertions and deletions will change the page breaks.

Tip: *Use rules of thumb for approximate word counts.*

The Word Processor lacks character and word counts, but the lower-right corner of the screen shows the line and column numbers. Multiplying the line count by the line-ending column number gives an approximate character count, and dividing the character count by eight gives an approximate word count. In AppleWorks a Word Processor file occupying 10K on a disk will have about fifteen hundred words.

If you need accurate word counts, most spelling checkers can provide them. For example, Sensible Speller can tell you the total number of words, the number of unique words, and the frequency distribution for each unique word.

Tip: *When a Return takes too long to insert a blank line, your file is too long.*

When you become impatient waiting for a Return to take effect, that is a good indication that your file is too long. If you have more to write, consider dividing the file into two or more smaller files. You can merge the two files later for printing.

Tip: *Make a file of commonly used sentences and paragraphs for use in other documents.*

Every once in a while you read a report or article that explains a point better than you have ever been able to do it yourself. Rewrite the best paragraphs in your own style, and store them in a file called Writing. Review and rewrite them again from time to time.

If you like to quote Shakespeare or Homer, store your favorite lines in the Writing file. If you have standard contract text, store that in a Contract file. The idea is to have the necessary components on hand.

Caution: *Word processors have increased the chances of telltale revisions.*

Sometimes the most embarrassing words get left behind: extra verb tenses, extra adjectives, and so forth. Word processors can work from templates and revise text quickly, which makes it simple to assemble text and test different constructions. In the process, it's easy to overlook details, and spelling checkers cannot identify the problem.

Here are some examples of the tell-tale revisions word processing can produce:

- A sentence begins "The good excellent report . . ."

- The date is September 12, 1985, but the date on the letter is January 1, 1985.

- A letter to Ellen Hayes includes two inappropriate paragraphs from a letter to someone else.

- A revised phrase reads "We would be are willing . . ."

Furthermore, we have had little experience proofreading these kinds of errors, and they remain largely outside our focus. Tell-tale revisions require preventative maintenance. When you complete a revision, reread it at that time with special attention to verbs and adjectives. If you write letters from a template, make the template changes right away. Above all, read anything you have assembled as if you had just written it.

Tip: *After writing a report outline, save the outline file.*

Once you have saved the outline file to disk, rename the file on screen and develop the report directly from the outline. If you need to see the outline itself again for an overview of the report structure, you can always add the original outline file to the Desktop.

Outlines begin as lists, and most have only two levels, except perhaps for selected sections where you have to go into greater detail. This book began as a list of tips and cautions entered in a Spreadsheet file. For more about this method of writing outlines, see Chapter 5.

Tip: *If you make calculations for reports, keep a scientific calculator and note pad nearby.*

An inexpensive scientific calculator remains an indispensable tool. Keep one nearby for any back-of-the-envelope calculations you need to make while writing reports. Your scientific calculator may even include a reference manual of applied math formulas for everything from finance to engineering.

If you have added memory to your Apple and use AppleWorks in a RAM drive, keep a Spreadsheet Calculator file on the Desktop. As you will see in Chapter 4, that worksheet can serve several additional purposes.

USING SPELLING CHECKERS

In this section several tips and techniques are provided for using spelling checkers with AppleWorks. Some tips demonstrate techniques for using the Sensible Speller program with Word Processor files. These techniques generally apply to other spelling checkers used with AppleWorks, such as MegaWorks and Spellworks.

Tip: *Correct spelling adds to your credibility.*

Many competent people have great difficulty spelling words, and they frequently do not even know when they have erred. Others make typing mistakes, transposing letters when they know very well how to spell the words. Some of us omit letters in haste. These are three different problems, but each can be at least partly managed.

For problems with spelling, the best approach is to buy a good paperback dictionary and keep it on top of your monitor. When you start spelling words correctly the first time, copy is easier to proofread and correct no matter what tools you use.

For problems with typing errors, the find (Apple-F) or replace (Apple-R) commands can help. When you find an error, enter the same spelling to find additional occurrences, because such errors tend to recur. For example, if you find an occurrence of *spreadhseet* instead of *spreadsheet,* the chances are that you typed it incorrectly more than once—mistakes with transposed letters are predictable.

Tip: *Spelling checkers work quickly and accurately.*

Checking spelling is part of proofreading, which also includes identifying mistakes in punctuation, capitalization errors, incorrect words, improper constructions, and editorial inconsistencies. These tasks require more time than most of us want to commit. People who never check like to assume that everything came out right. Those who proofread know otherwise—corrections always take more time than expected.

By using a spelling checker, you can save time. A spelling checker can narrow the focus for proofreading, and that improves your accuracy in finding nonspelling errors.

Sensible Speller for ProDOS installs easily and works quickly with AppleWorks files. It processes files in three stages, collecting the words, attempting to match them to a dictionary, and listing any that cannot be matched.

Tip: *Add words to the dictionary.*

The most important option in any spelling checker is the one for adding specialized words (for example, product names such as VisiCalc). Add words carefully, because you can compromise your word list with mistakes. Your entries should come directly from published sources, including specialized dictionaries.

The following example provides some understanding of how spelling checkers work. Sensible Speller spent 126 seconds processing a 2,400-word file about AppleWorks. It then sent 52 unmatched words to the printer. Of those words, 2 were indeed misspelled and 18 were specialized words. Another 10 were abbreviations and such things as Spreadsheet cell coordinates. One of the unmatched words was a questionable choice, later replaced.

Sensible Software based its word list on a Random House dictionary. The two sides of the Sensible Speller dictionary disk contain 43,000 and 37,000 words respectively. The second dictionary contains the less commonly used words, and you will probably use that word list sparingly. For the file mentioned above, the second dictionary matched 17 of the 52 previously unmatched words, including the one later replaced, but none of the specialized words. Searching through the second dictionary required an additional 68 seconds. Adding specialized words to the basic dictionary is generally at least as effective as using the second word list, and it is considerably faster.

Science, medicine, and law have thousands of specialized words, too many to enter individually. Sensible Software offers specialized dictionary disks in these fields. They can be used effectively in place of the second side of the standard dictionary.

Tip: *Use AppleWorks commands to correct misspelled words.*

Only two words were misspelled in the 2,400-word file, but Sensible Speller sent 52 unmatched words to the printer. That kind of ratio is common for people who spell reasonably well. Instead of using the spelling checker to display every word in context, read the printed list of unmatched words. Highlight the misspellings with a yellow marker, and make the corrections from AppleWorks.

Suppose you typed *spreadhseet* instead of *spreadsheet*. With Apple-F, you can find the first occurrence and answer No when the message asks if you want to find the next occurrence. That leaves the cursor on the word, where you can make the correction. When you press Apple-F again, AppleWorks proposes the last word you searched for, and you are back in the hunt.

Apple-R works best when you know that a word was spelled incorrectly in the same way several times.

Tip: *Learn and respect the limitations of your spelling checker.*

Spelling checkers cannot flag words such as *there* when *their* is intended. Also, most spelling checkers live in a world of upper-case letters (think of the complications if it were otherwise). That means they cannot tell the correct spelling of *AppleWorks* from the incorrect *Appleworks*. If you buy a spelling checker, read the manual and take advantage of any options that will minimize the number of suspect words. For example, Sensible Speller offers the option to ignore acronyms.

Spelling checkers cannot generally keep track of last names, many of which are often misspelled. However, you should add names that you use repeatedly to the dictionary. You should also enter place names and brand names that you use frequently.

Tip: *Not everyone needs a spelling checker, at least not all the time.*

If you spell accurately, take proofreading seriously, recognize misspellings, and write fewer than four single-spaced pages at a time, a good paperback dictionary may be an adequate resource.

SUMMARY

This chapter has reviewed a broad range of options and problems in the Word Processor. You will be able to use many of the tips and techniques repeatedly.

As you understand more about the Word Processor, you will find that you can write and edit more efficiently. The next two chapters will draw upon what you have learned about printer options in this chapter. While exploring the Data Base and Spreadsheet, you will continue to change file names, copy to the clipboard, and use AppleWorks commands for unexpected purposes. You will continue building component parts that can be used again and again in many useful applications. In Chapter 5 some of those parts will be transferred back to the Word Processor.

3

The Data Base

any people first use the Data Base to make lists. With each list, they learn more about the Data Base's capabilities for selecting records, creating report formats, printing labels, and so on. Some of these things can also be done on the Spreadsheet, so there is additional information on database management in Chapter 4. Chapter 5 includes tips for using the Data Base and Spreadsheet together.

As database managers go, the AppleWorks Data Base is easy to learn and teach. You can see the records individually during data entry or in a table for an overview. Most people find the Data Base simple enough for them to begin entering information into existing files without much instruction. When you teach others, let them work with an existing file on their own. AppleWorks has good error-trapping routines and clearly marked escape routes, so it is difficult to get lost.

The Data Base offers convenient reporting options. These reports can also be edited on the Word Processor, and when the Data Base is used in conjunction with the AppleWorks Mailing Program, you will find that you have greatly extended reporting capabilities, including the ability to generate form letters. In fact, some experienced users think AppleWorks is the most efficient database manager available for common applications with up to 5,000 records.

Additional memory capacity makes the Data Base unusually large and fast. Data Base files tend to need more memory than Word Processor files or modular Spreadsheet applications. Although it is possible to divide Data Base files by some category into A–M and N–Z sections, this compromises arranging and selection capabilities. Additional memory capacity allows you to undertake projects that can have more than 5,000 records. When you exceed the limits of the 128K Apple, simply add the memory you need.

This chapter provides tips for using the AppleWorks Data Base in thirteen sections. Everyone who uses the Data Base, or plans to, should read the first section of general tips.

The section on building lists includes basic information on designing templates for multiple purposes. It introduces tips on choosing categories and developing a simple database as a basic component for other databases. In the next three sections, tips are given for using the available options for finding, selecting, and arranging records. The topics have been divided in this way to focus on the logic of record-selection rules. Pay particular attention to the undocumented problems in these rules. Sections on creating report formats cover both labels-style and tables-style reports. The section on printing text includes important information on techniques for working with small cards and labels.

Database applications require considerable attention to design. Three sections cover advanced techniques for designing and developing Data Base applications. The following section explains how to merge records from one file with those of another. The last section outlines the design and use of inventory and citation databases. All this taken together should make the Data Base easier to use for large applications.

GENERAL DATA BASE TIPS

The tips below apply throughout the Data Base, and include minor cautions. The Data Base requires attention to detail, and you should pay special attention to the need for documenting everything you do.

The Data Base encourages development of templates that can be modified for many different purposes. If you know when and how to change file names, you can develop applications more efficiently. If you appreciate the cost of acquiring data, you can develop applications within your budget.

Tip: *Print and annotate hard copies of the Data Base menus.*

You will need a copy of the Data Base menu and the Data Base Printer Options menu, as well as menus for the Apple-F, Apple-N, Apple-R, and Apple-P commands. If you have not yet done so, print copies of all these screens using Apple-H, and hang the copies on a note board near your Apple. Pencil in notes about when you use each option. A hard copy of the Data Base menu is shown in Figure 3.1.

Tip: *The cursor appears on the first record when you reload a file.*

A file with records is also always displayed in multiple-record layout when you reload it, regardless of whether you were previously using single-record layout.

While the file is on the Desktop, the cursor and the display mode always remain as you left them, which is exactly as it should be. Make a note of this, because when you make a quick change to another file, you may return with records on the clipboard, and you almost always need to come back to precisely the same place.

There is one exception to the above: if you leave the file from a report format, the cursor returns to multiple-record layout.

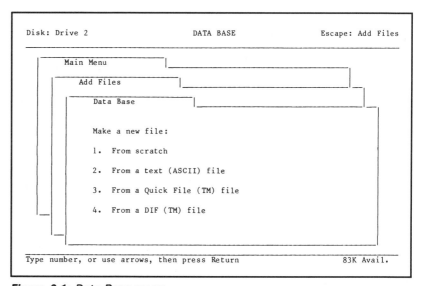

Figure 3.1: *Data Base menu*

Tip: *Use uppercase letters for Data Base category names.*

Many database managers distinguish category names from actual data with inverse video. AppleWorks does not, so use uppercase letters for category names, and the appropriate combination of upper- and lowercase letters for the data. (This is another case in which it is more important to differentiate between word groups than between letters. By the time you have entered the tenth record, you will probably know the category names by heart and in order.)

Tip: *Category and report format naming rules are more flexible than file naming rules.*

Category and report format names can begin with numbers and include symbols (such as # and *). In addition, a category name can be up to five characters longer than a ProDOS file name. A report format can have a name up to 19 characters long. It can also be exactly the same as an AppleWorks file name if you so choose. Table 3.1 shows the differences in the rules.

Tip: *Once you change the name of a Data Base file that has been saved, you can do almost anything with it.*

This is an important tip, and the concept will be adapted for specific purposes throughout this chapter. Once a file is saved to primary and backup disks, you can change the name on the Desktop and make any changes you like without changing the files on disk. You can copy, delete, replace, and rearrange data for any purpose. If you make a serious mistake, simply remove the file from the Desktop, load the original file again, and change its name on the Desktop once more.

Table 3.1: *Rules for file, report, and category names*

Option	ProDOS Files	AppleWorks Files	Data Base Reports	Data Base Categories
Maximum characters	15	15	19	20
Lead numerals			X	X
Internal numerals	X	X	X	X
Lowercase letters	X	X	X	X
Symbols			X	X
Blank spaces		X	X	X

Tip: *Data Base design can be done with pencil and paper.*

When two or more people use the same Apple, there will be times when one person wants to use AppleWorks and cannot. That is a good time to start working with pencil and paper. For example, you can design Data Base record layouts using graph paper. You can design report formats using a hard copy of a report format screen that includes all the categories. Print a hard copy of the Printer Options menu showing all the default values, like the one in Figure 3.2. Pencil in proposed changes for a specific report format.

Tip: *Document all your work.*

When you write a report on the Word Processor, you rarely need directions when you load it again several weeks later. When you develop a database application with several report formats, you may get lost later unless you have previously made notes.

The documentation you write should explain why you developed the application. It should include step-by-step instructions on how to load and use the Data Base file, and should note any

```
File: Everyone                    PRINTER OPTIONS            Escape: Report Format
Report: CARDS
================================================================================

------Left and right margins--------      ------Top and bottom margins------
PW: Platen Width           8.0 inches     PL: Paper Length          11.0 inches
LM: Left Margin            0.0 inches     TM: Top Margin             0.0 inches
RM: Right Margin           0.0 inches     BM: Bottom Margin          0.0 inches
CI: Chars per Inch         10             LI: Lines per Inch         6

    Line width             8.0 inches         Printing length       11.0 inches
    Char per line (est)    80                 Lines per page         66

         --------------------Formatting options-------------------
         SC:  Send Special Codes to printer                         No
         PD:  Print a Dash when an entry is blank                   No
         PH:  Print report Header at top of each page               Yes
         OL:  Omit Line when all entries on line are blank          Yes
         KS:  Keep number of lines the Same within each record      Yes


------------------------------------------------------------------------
Type a two letter option code                                 79K Avail.
```

Figure 3.2: *Data Base Printer Options menu*

problems encountered with the data. Your documentation should
be filed along with hard copies of important screens and formats
(a multiple-record display screen, a single-record display screen, a
list of the report formats, each report format, and the respective
printer option settings for each).

Every application should have its own manila file folder or
something functionally equivalent. Print a tables-style report of
all the data in the file.

Tip: *Data acquisition costs more than you think.*

Databases need specific information. Think of all the missing
ZIP codes and all the misspelled last names in your rotary card file
at work. What happens if you plan to enter these names and
addresses into a database and generate mailing labels from it? You
simply have to find the correct information before you begin.

The time spent on the simple application presented in the next
section will give you some idea of how much data acquisition
costs in large applications. In fact, the cost of obtaining,

reviewing, entering, and updating data should be a primary consideration in the design of any AppleWorks application. Appendix C includes more on reference information and the costs of data acquisition. When you understand how to search for information, you can often save time and expense.

BUILDING LISTS

If letters are the most common Word Processor files, lists are probably the most common Data Base files. Good planning and design can save considerable time in the building and use of databases. For this section I have constructed a LIST template (see Figure 3.3), from which I built an "Everyone" list as an example database (see Figures 3.4 and 3.5). From such a list you can create card files, mailing labels, form letter headings, and telephone lists. The Everyone list keeps information on the people and institutions you need to remember from day to day—it can be filled with the names and addresses in your current business card collection.

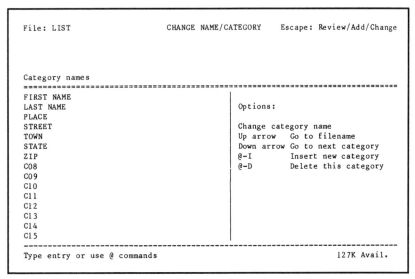

```
  File: LIST                    CHANGE NAME/CATEGORY      Escape: Review/Add/Change



  Category names
  ================================================================================
  FIRST NAME
  LAST NAME                             Options:
  PLACE
  STREET                                Change category name
  TOWN                                  Up arrow    Go to filename
  STATE                                 Down arrow  Go to next category
  ZIP                                   @-I         Insert new category
  C08                                   @-D         Delete this category
  C09
  C10
  C11
  C12
  C13
  C14
  C15
  --------------------------------------------------------------------------------
  Type entry or use @ commands                                       127K Avail.
```

Figure 3.3: *LIST template showing category order*

```
File: Everyone                    MOVE RECORDS           Escape: Review/Add/Change

Selection: All records


FIRST NAME   LAST NAME   PLACE        STREET              TOWN       STATE ZIP
================================================================================
Joanne       Martinelli  -           25 Brook Rd.        Jefferson  RI    02845
Robert       Smith       -           28 Bayberry Rd.     Esterly    CT    06414
Roberta      Miller      -           14 Brook Rd.        Jefferson  RI    02845
Edward       Joiner      -           19 Mill Rd.         Jefferson  RI    02845
Rob          Martin      -           22 Meadow Rd.       Jefferson  RI    02845
William      Venn        -           24 East Rd.         Jefferson  RI    02845
Robin        Jones       -           33 Field Rd.        Jefferson  RI    02845
Joan         Smith       -           72 Jefferson Pike   Westbrook  MA    02731
Thomas       Farmer      -           12 Field Rd.        Jefferson  RI    02845
Susan        Smith       -           81 Main Rd.         Jefferson  RI    02845
Arnold       Wright      -           52 Field Rd.        Jefferson  RI    02845




----------------------------------------------------------------------------
Move records?  To clipboard (cut)   From clipboard (paste)
```

Figure 3.4: *Everyone list in multiple-record layout*

```
File: Everyone                  REVIEW/ADD/CHANGE              Escape: Main Menu

Selection: All records


Record 10 of 11
================================================================================
FIRST NAME: Susan
LAST NAME: Smith
PLACE: -
STREET: 81 Main Rd.
TOWN: Jefferson
STATE: RI
ZIP: 02845
PHONE: (401) 888-3311
NOTE: Town Librarian
CODE: F1
KEYWORD: SMITH
R1: -
R2: -
R3: -
R4: -
----------------------------------------------------------------------------
Type entry or use @ commands                               @-? for Help
```

Figure 3.5: *Single-record layout from the Everyone list*

Tip: *Make a LIST template that contains 15 categories and two basic report formats.*

Name your basic Data Base template LIST. It should have at least 15 categories, a tables-style report, and a labels-style report. Most applications use fewer than 15 categories, and most are lists of names and addresses. The first seven template categories can be named FIRST NAME, LAST NAME, PLACE, STREET, TOWN, STATE, and ZIP. AppleWorks uses no precommitted category forms, so the name of any category can be changed and used for any kind of information.

Empty categories require little memory, so if you do not need all the categories in your template for a particular application, there is no need to delete the extra ones. Figure 3.3 shows the category-order screen for the LIST file.

Tip: *Spend time thinking about the categories you will need.*

You can quickly convert the basic LIST template into an Everyone list. First, think about the additional categories you will need, based on the information you want to enter as records. The categories described below should suffice for most purposes. Figures 3.4 and 3.5 show the list in multiple- and single-record layouts.

I chose to have FIRST NAME as the first category because it is easier to create report formats—almost all labels-style reports have the first name first.

Some people prefer to enter the last name before the first name in the category order, because lists are often sorted by last name. However, it is probably more important to read names in the order you say them: first name first.

Some people like to use a separate category for the form of greeting. Such a category could be used to enter a preferred name, where a legal name appears in the FIRST NAME category. For example, someone named Mary Smith may prefer to be greeted by her middle name, Lynn. A form-of-greeting category could also be used for noting gender and professional credentials and titles. In the Everyone list, you can use the NOTES section to note gender and any discrepancies between legal and preferred names. Professional credentials and titles can be entered after the name in the LAST NAME category.

The PLACE category is for the name of the institution for which the address follows. You can sort records by this category when it is more appropriate for your needs. If you most often deal with similar types of institutions, you may want to rename this category COMPANY, for example.

The NOTE category can be used to store brief notes on what you need to remember, if anything. For example, "President?" might indicate that you are not certain whether the person is in fact the president of the firm.

It is sometimes necessary to include a separate category for institutional titles, for example, Dean, Associate Director of Finance, or whatever is appropriate. (Correct titles are sometimes difficult to track down.) If you have relatively few titles to worry about, there is no need for such a category. Simply enter titles in the NOTE category as needed.

The CODE category allows you to divide the people in the list into several groups (for example, clients, friends, relatives, and suppliers), for finding or selecting records later. (See a following tip on using this category effectively.)

The KEYWORD category will be used for either a duplicate last name, a duplicate company name, or a subject word that you can later use to select records from the database.

Tip: *Try to be accurate and consistent when you enter data.*

Consistent data entry rules make it easier for two or more people to enter and find information in a database. Consistent rules also make it easier to proofread and edit records. Following are some commonly used rules; you will probably want to add some of your own.

FIRST NAME: Such as Ralph, Rolf, Dr. Bob, or R.J., as the person prefers. Include a middle initial only if the person uses one in a signature. In general, use the simplest form for first names.

LAST NAME: Such as Wright, Smith AIA, or other abbreviations for professional credentials and titles. Pay special attention to the spelling, because everyone deserves to have their name spelled correctly.

PLACE: Some institutions have names that are two lines long, for example, David Taylor Engineering Laboratory, Department of Mechanical Engineering. Shorten the name if such cases are rare on your list; otherwise use an extra category. You might shorten the name in this example to Taylor Lab, Mech. Engineering.

STREET: Use standard postal abbreviations for Boulevard, Avenue, Street, Road, Lane, Circle, Place, etc. This category is also for Post Office box numbers and rural delivery route box numbers.

TOWN: Use standard abbreviations for East, West, South, North, etc.

STATE: Use two-letter postal abbreviations, such as MI for Michigan. States that begin with A and M are the most difficult to remember. (Arizona is AZ, Arkansas is AR, and Alaska is AK. Missouri is MO, Montana is MT, and Mississippi is MS.)

ZIP CODE: Five digits (02881) or nine (02881-4356). Use one form or the other consistently if you plan to transfer information with DIF files.

If the address is for a foreign country, include any postal code used in that country in the STATE category. Then enter the country name in the ZIP CODE category. When you arrange the ZIP codes using the A–Z option, all country names will be arranged in alphabetical order after any American addresses. When you enter country names, use consistent spelling.

PHONE: The form (401) 989-2714 covers most possibilities. The telephone company generally places the area code in parentheses. By a happy coincidence, that makes it easier to transfer telephone numbers in DIF files. This point is discussed in greater detail in Chapter 5.

The form x1234 can designate an extension number with one to four digits. Put the extension in a separate category or add it to the right of the phone number. The Data Base can arrange entries of variable length because it left-justifies them.

Tip: *One CODE category can do the work of two or more.*

Suppose you have divided the people in your Everyone list into several groups, including clients, friends, relatives, and suppliers, and have chosen codes for each as follows:

- C (clients)

- F (friends)

- R (relatives)

- S (suppliers)

Suppose you have also classified each person according to frequency of contact, with these codes:

- 1 (weekly)

- 2 (monthly)

- 3 (quarterly)

- 4 (annually)

- 5 (less frequently)

By combining the two codes, you can make one category do the work of two. For example, R4 might include relatives in another country; S5 might include a parts supplier for equipment that has worked perfectly for years.

These codes allow for four variables with letters and five with numbers. The single-letter part of the code can represent as many as 26 variables. The single-number part of the code can represent up to 10 variables (if you include zero).

Only the first character of a combined code can be sorted effectively, so place the character of the code you would be most likely to sort by (for example, relationship or frequency of contact) first. This is a significant limitation in the Data Base. You will see in Chapter 4 that this limitation is not so significant in the Spreadsheet, where arranging can be done by rows within selected ranges.

Tip: *Limit the number of records in your lists.*

If you want to run your life without a secretary, 280 records is a reasonable limit for an Everyone list. If you have fewer records, good for you. If you have more, think about thinning out records.

Tip: *Develop consistent standards for thinning out records.*

The tedium of data entry will invariably encourage you to do this. Be careful, though, because it gets more boring as you go along. Give as much consideration to records near the end of the list as you did to those at the beginning. Or, to put it another way, set rigorous standards from the start.

Tip: *When you revise a single category entry in the Data Base, remember to press Return after completing the entry.*

Make it a habit to press Return after you make an entry, especially when you are in multiple-record layout. In that layout, you can press Escape without triggering a reminder beep, and your revisions will be lost.

Notice the message in the upper-right corner of the screen when you make a change:

Escape: Restore former entry

Even if you have replaced all the characters in an entry, pressing Escape restores the previous entry perfectly.

FINDING RECORDS

Sometimes you want to find a record to see if it is in the database, to see whether it is a duplicate record, to reassure yourself of its content, or to revise it. If you already know some of the text in the record, you can use Apple-F to find it. If you know the general area it is in, you may simply want to scan multiple-record layout in that area. If you are just plain lost and need to find a familiar record, such as the first or last, you can use Apple-1 or Apple-9.

The tips that follow cover the general process of finding records and finding your way around. You already know Apple-F from the Word Processor. It searches for anything that contains specified text. In this sense it can be considered as a record-selection rule that searches all categories at once. The Data Base has no replace command, but this section describes a useful replacement technique.

Apple-F and the record-selection rules often do similar things equally well. The record-selection rules appear in a separate section because they require an introduction to Boolean logic, and because they have some serious undocumented problems.

Caution: *Returning from a file save can be confusing.*

If you save your file from single-record layout, the cursor may come back to some record preceding the one you had been working on. Although this can be disorienting, there is no need for concern.

Here is an example of what can happen. Suppose you want to enter new records at the end of an existing file. You load the file, select single-record layout, and attempt to move beyond record 222, the last current record. The message screen that appears in Figure 3.6 is a significant dividing line in the Data Base.

Suppose you answer Yes and subsequently enter a dozen new records. After you save the file while in record 234, the cursor returns to record 222, the last record in the file before you started the session. The Data Base does this consistently.

Apple-9 will take you back to record 234. If you save the file from somewhere other than the last record, remember the record number if you want to find it again. If you subsequently go beyond record 234, add a dozen more records, and save the file from record 246, the cursor will return to record 234.

Tip: *If you are in single-record layout and cannot get to the record you need, switch to multiple-record layout.*

This tip is related to the caution above. Suppose you want to enter new records at the end of an existing file. You load the file,

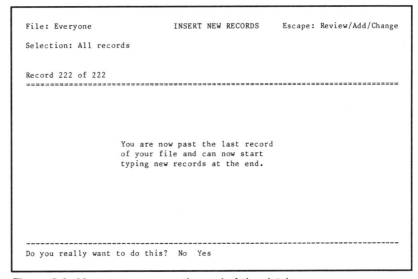

```
File: Everyone              INSERT NEW RECORDS      Escape: Review/Add/Change

Selection: All records


Record 222 of 222
==============================================================================




                    You are now past the last record
                    of your file and can now start
                    typing new records at the end.






         ----------------------------------------------------------------------
Do you really want to do this?  No  Yes
```

Figure 3.6: Message screen at the end of the database

select single-record layout, and attempt to move beyond record 222, the last current record. The message screen shown in Figure 3.6 appears. You answer Yes and then enter one record.

Next, you need to see an entry five records back, but in single-record layout you cannot step back into the previous file area. Use Apple-Z to zoom to multiple-record layout, find the record you need, and then change back to single-record layout with Apple-Z again.

Tip: *If you are in multiple-record layout and cannot see a category, use Apple-Z or Apple-L.*

Multiple-record layout shows only as many categories as will fit on the screen. (Many people find this hard to believe, because scrolling to the right is so simple in the Spreadsheet.) If you need to see only a few entries in a category that is not visible in multiple-record layout, switch to single-record layout. For example, multiple-record layout displays five categories, but not the NOTE category you want to see. If you need to see the NOTE entry for one record, place the cursor anywhere on that record and press Apple-Z to view the record in single-record layout.

If you need to see and compare NOTE entries for 80 records, press Apple-L to rearrange the categories. You can move the NOTE category onto the multiple-record screen and remove some other category. This can be tedious, and it explains why some people prefer to use the Spreadsheet, where you can scroll the screen to see all the information.

Tip: *Use Apple-F as an effective record-selection rule.*

Apple-F can be used to find records that contain specified text and numbers, and it searches through all categories at once. For this purpose it works faster than the more defined record-selection rules. For example, if you want to find a specific ZIP code, that five-digit number probably exists in no other category.

Another example of a good case for using Apple-F would be searching the database for all the addresses in Vermont. Simply search for the letter combination VT—it is unlikely that the letters VT will appear together otherwise. It would not work so well with MO, the postal abbreviation for Missouri. The letters MO appear often in other words, as in Morris, mountain, almond, etc. Apple-F makes no distinction between uppercase and lowercase letters. Note that you cannot specify MO with leading and trailing spaces to isolate the two characters, as you can in the Word Processor.

When two letters are likely to appear together often in a Data Base file, use the record-selection rules to confine the search to a single category.

With Apple-F you can gather records quickly, copy them to the clipboard, and use them for other purposes, including starting a new Data Base file.

Tip: *Apple-F searches the entire database, regardless of where the cursor is located when the search begins.*

Apple-F in the Data Base differs from Apple-F in the Word Processor and the Spreadsheet. Table 3.2 shows the differences in the find and replace commands within the three programs. You cannot search part of a database using only the find command.

Tip: *To search part of a database, move unwanted records to the clipboard temporarily.*

One efficient way to search part of a database is to move unwanted records to the clipboard temporarily. For example, suppose a tool supplier wants to find all the people from Vermont who ordered items during the first half of 1985. The supplier can arrange by date category, and move all of the records from Jul 1 85 through Dec 31 85 to the clipboard, then use Apple-F to find all of the remaining records with the postal abbreviation VT.

Table 3.2: Options available for find and replace functions

Option	Word Processor	Data Base	Spreadsheet
Finds text	X	X	X
Finds case-sensitive text	X		
Finds numbers	X	X	as labels only
Finds page numbers	X		
Also finds	markers		coordinates
Searches from	cursor	beginning	cursor
Replaces one instance	X		
Replaces all instances	X		
Maximum number of characters	30	30	25

Tip: *Use Apple-F from multiple-record layout.*

Even when you want to find one record, you may retrieve more than one, so it is helpful to see them displayed on the multiple-record screen. If you use Apple-F from single-record layout, only the first retrieved record is displayed. By using Apple-F from multiple-record layout, you can immediately scan up to 15 records at once. Pressing Escape will return you to all the records in multiple-record layout.

Caution: *The Apple-" command should be Apple-'.*

The Reference Manual rightly calls this the ditto command, so it made sense to refer to it with ditto marks (otherwise known as quotation marks). However, to create the ditto marks you would also have to press Shift, which is not part of the command. So Apple simply added "do not press Shift" in their instructions. In this chapter I will write the command as Apple-'.

Tip: *Apple-' can substitute for the replace command lacking in the Data Base.*

The Word Processor has a replace command (Apple-R) but the Data Base does not, even though this is a commonly used feature in other database managers. However, there is a way to use Apple-' as a substitute:

1. In multiple-record layout, use Apple-F or the record-selection rules to retrieve all the records with the information you want to replace.

2. Enter the new information in the first retrieved record.

3. Place the cursor in the same category of the next record and hold down Apple-' to quickly change the information.

4. Move through the remaining records, using Apple-' to replace the old information with the new.

This method gathers the required records together before you make the changes, and allows you to see each change as you make it. Even if the Data Base did have a global replace command, it would be risky to replace information without seeing it in context.

SELECTING RECORDS

Most people select records just before printing, but record selection works equally well in the Review mode. That is where experienced users make decisions about what to report and print.

There are some serious problems in the AppleWorks record-selection rules. Every program has undocumented problems, but it hurts most to find problems with logical functions, because they are difficult enough to master anyway. If you have depended on the Data Base to track accounts receivable or send legal notices, some of the tips and cautions that follow may prompt you to review your previous work.

Tip: *Use the record-selection rules from multiple-record layout.*

Even when you want to select one record, you may retrieve more than one, so it is helpful to see them displayed on the multiple-record screen. If you use the rules from single-record layout, only one selected record is displayed. By using the record-selection rules from multiple-record layout, you can immediately scan up to 15 records at once. Press Apple-1 to begin the display with the first selected record.

Using Apple-R again will return you to all the records in multiple-record layout. Simply answer Yes to the question, "Select all records?"

Caution: *The "equals" criterion in the record-selection rules may retrieve unwanted records.*

The easiest way to describe this problem is with specific examples. Suppose your database includes two people with the first name of Roberta. You select all records in which the first name "equals" Roberta, but the records you retrieve also include everyone with the first name of Robert.

Suppose your database also includes one person named Rob and another named Robin. You select all records in which the first name "equals" Rob, but the records you receive also include everyone with the first name of Robert, but not Robin.

The Data Base appears to match six letters at a time. When the match word has fewer than six letters, it also takes six-letter words that begin with the match word. (But it will not take words of fewer than six letters that begin with the match word.) For match words with more than six letters but fewer than twelve, it seems to be satisfied with a match on the first six letters alone.

It is sometimes difficult to foresee the effects of this problem in specific applications. Suppose your database includes a last name of Martinelli. You select all records in which the last name "equals" Martinelli, but the records you receive also include someone with the last name of Martin. However, when you select Martin, Martinelli is not retrieved. Figures 3.7 and 3.8 illustrate this.

Although the Data Base will sometimes retrieve more than you want, it apparently does not retrieve less. There appears to be no problem matching numbers.

Tip: *The "contains" rule can sometimes get you around the "equals" problem in the record-selection rules.*

It helps to use the "contains" rule more often. For example, the rules will not select Martin when you specify last names that "contain" Martinelli, as shown in Figure 3.9. Note that this is a prudent choice anyway. There may be an occasion when some last

```
File: Everyone              REVIEW/ADD/CHANGE          Escape: Main Menu

Selection: LAST NAME equals MARTINELLI


FIRST NAME  LAST NAME  PLACE       STREET         TOWN       STATE ZIP
==================================================================================
Joanne      Martinelli  -          25 Brook Rd.   Jefferson  RI    02845
Rob         Martin      -          22 Meadow Rd.  Jefferson  RI    02845










----------------------------------------------------------------------
Type entry or use @ commands                               @-? for Help
```

Figure 3.7: "Equals" rule: Martinelli

```
File: Everyone                    REVIEW/ADD/CHANGE              Escape: Main Menu
Selection: LAST NAME equals MARTIN

FIRST NAME  LAST NAME   PLACE        STREET         TOWN        STATE ZIP
===================================================================================
Rob         Martin      -           22 Meadow Rd.  Jefferson   RI    02845




                        






-----------------------------------------------------------------------------------
Type entry or use @ commands                                      @-? for Help
```

Figure 3.8: *"Equals" rule: Martin*

name you thought equalled Smith was actually Smith with a mistaken empty space in front of it or Smith, AIA. The "contains"
rule works accurately in either case.

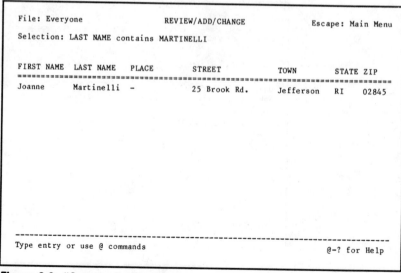

```
File: Everyone                    REVIEW/ADD/CHANGE              Escape: Main Menu
Selection: LAST NAME contains MARTINELLI

FIRST NAME  LAST NAME   PLACE        STREET         TOWN        STATE ZIP
===================================================================================
Joanne      Martinelli  -           25 Brook Rd.   Jefferson   RI    02845






-----------------------------------------------------------------------------------
Type entry or use @ commands                                      @-? for Help
```

Figure 3.9: *"Contains" rule: Martinelli*

Caution: *The "does not end with" rule does not work.*

If you ask for any last name that "does not end with" S, the Data Base returns Anderson, Barnes, and Collins. The rule simply does not work: not for letters, not for numbers, not for punctuation marks. Figure 3.10 shows an example.

If you started using "does not end with" statements before learning that they are worthless, you may have developed serious doubts about your understanding of logic. Have faith in yourself— it was Apple's problem all along.

Caution: *The "ends with" rule can produce unwanted results.*

In earlier versions of AppleWorks, the "ends with" criterion in the record-selection rules sometimes failed to retrieve requested records.

```
File: Logic                REVIEW/ADD/CHANGE          Escape: Main Menu

Selection: LAST NAME does not end with S


FIRST NAME  LAST NAME  PLACE      STREET        TOWN       STATE ZIP
==================================================================
Jeff        Barnes     -          18 Westbrook Pike Jefferson  RI    02845
Ann         Collins    -          12 Highland Rd.   Jefferson  RI    02845
William     Anderson   -          48 Main Rd.       Jefferson  RI    02845






------------------------------------------------------------------
Type entry or use @ commands                       @-? for Help
```

Figure 3.10: *"Does not end with" rule*

Suppose you are working with the Everyone list (shown in Figure 3.4), which has two last names ending in the letter n. (One last name is Martin and one is Venn.) When you ask the Data Base to retrieve all last names ending in the letter n, you get Martin but not Venn (see Figure 3.11). When the character preceding the last character is the same as the last character, this record-selection rule ignores the record.

The problem includes numbers. For example, suppose you have made a CODE category for a two-digit number, hoping that it can do the work of two CODE categories. (A two-digit number in the form of 92 can indicate ten different cases that "begin with" 0–9, and ten more independent cases that "end with" 0–9.) However, the record-selection rule ignores the record if the preceding digit is identical. Thus, in order to select all cases that "end with" 1, you must also specify the criterion "or equal 11".

With AppleWorks it is preferable to use one letter and one number, as in an earlier tip; with a code in the form of C2, the problem cannot occur.

Although this problem does not occur with version 1.2, remember the people who never upgraded their AppleWorks disk. If you have AppleWorks version 1.2, consider the possibility that your template may some day find its way to someone using an earlier version.

Tip: *When you use more than one positive record-selection rule, "or" increases the number of records selected.*

As you would therefore expect, "and" decreases the number of records selected. The logic of this is easy to understand.

Suppose you have three records with the respective last names of Anderson, Barnes, and Collins. If you ask for any last name that "begins with" A, the Data Base selects Anderson. If you ask for any last name that begins with A or B, you get Anderson and Barnes, as shown in Figure 3.12.

If you ask for any last name that begins with A and B, you get nothing, as shown in Figure 3.13, because a name cannot begin with both A and B at the same time.

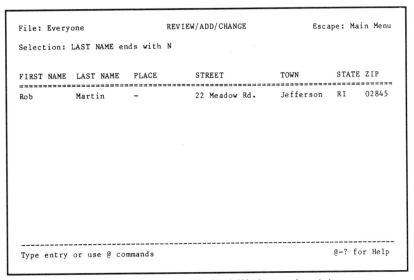

Figure 3.11: *"Ends with" criterion in AppleWorks version 1.1*

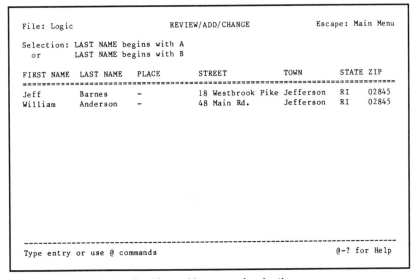

Figure 3.12: *Using "or" with positive record selection*

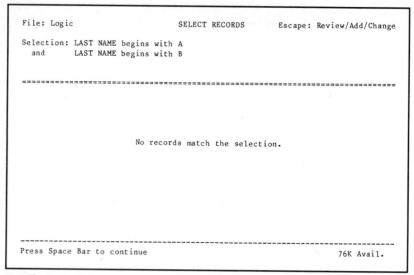

```
File: Logic                    SELECT RECORDS       Escape: Review/Add/Change

Selection: LAST NAME begins with A
   and     LAST NAME begins with B

==============================================================================



                        No records match the selection.




------------------------------------------------------------------------------
Press Space Bar to continue                                     76K Avail.
```

Figure 3.13: *Using "and" with positive record selection*

Tip: *When you use more than one negative record-selection rule, "or" increases the number of records selected.*

As you would expect from the above tip, "and" decreases the number of records selected. The logic of this requires some thought.

Suppose you have three records with the respective last names of Anderson, Barnes, and Collins. If you ask for any last name that "does not begin with" A, the Data Base selects Barnes and Collins. This is easy enough to understand.

If you ask for any last name that "does not begin with" A *or* "does not begin with" B, the Data Base retrieves all three names, as shown in Figure 3.14. Why? In this case Barnes and Collins fit the first rule because they do not begin with A, while Anderson and Collins fit the second rule because they do not begin with B.

The way to exclude both Anderson and Barnes is to ask for any last name that "does not begin with" A *and* any last name that "does not begin with" B, as shown in Figure 3.15.

```
File: Logic                REVIEW/ADD/CHANGE          Escape: Main Menu

Selection: LAST NAME does not begin with A
  or       LAST NAME does not begin with B

FIRST NAME  LAST NAME  PLACE      STREET            TOWN       STATE ZIP
======================================================================
Jeff        Barnes     -          18 Westbrook Pike Jefferson  RI    02845
Ann         Collins    -          12 Highland Rd.   Jefferson  RI    02845
William     Anderson   -          48 Main Rd.       Jefferson  RI    02845




----------------------------------------------------------------------
Type entry or use @ commands                          @-? for Help
```

Figure 3.14: *Using "or" with negative record selection*

Try the examples at least once yourself. Note that it is less confusing to use positive record-selection rules whenever you have a choice.

```
File: Logic                REVIEW/ADD/CHANGE          Escape: Main Menu

Selection: LAST NAME does not begin with A
  and      LAST NAME does not begin with B

FIRST NAME  LAST NAME  PLACE      STREET            TOWN       STATE ZIP
======================================================================
Ann         Collins    -          12 Highland Rd.   Jefferson  RI    02845




----------------------------------------------------------------------
Type entry or use @ commands                          @-? for Help
```

Figure 3.15: *Using "and" with negative record selection*

Tip: *Use the record-selection rules as multiple filters.*

To use multiple filtering, you must first understand that the record-selection rules are used in two different places.

The record-selection rules in the Review/Add/Change mode are separate from the record-selection rules in the report mode. If you specify selection rules in the Review/Add/Change mode and then use Apple-P to select a report format, the rules you have specified will not apply if the report format was previously saved with record-selection rules in effect.

You will normally enter record-selection rules for a report from within the report mode. You may initially see rules in effect when you select the report format, but they are from a previous report session.

The Data Base permits no more than three sets of selection rules to be applied at once. However, you can use the first selection in the Review/Add/Change mode as a filter for the second selection in the report mode. Here's how to do it:

1. From either single- or multiple-record display mode, press Apple-R and specify record-selection rules for records you do not want.

2. When the selected records appear, move them to the clipboard to get them out of the way temporarily.

3. Select a report format for printing the remaining records.

4. Specify record-selection rules within the report format.

5. Print to a printer, the clipboard, or disk.

6. Return to multiple-record layout and move the records on the clipboard back to the Data Base file.

Here the first selection in the Review/Add/Change mode filtered the records for the second selection in the report mode. If a first selection ever retrieves more than 250 records, you can move the records to another file temporarily. A tip on such temporary files appears later in this chapter.

ARRANGING RECORDS

The process of arranging records is also frequently referred to as sorting records. Although the Apple-A command is easy to use, there are some fine points to understand. AppleWorks uses a modified ASCII order for sorting, in which all letters are treated as uppercase letters. This section provides some useful insights on getting the most out of Apple-A.

Caution: *Alphabetical arranging follows a modified ASCII order.*

In the ASCII table, the digits 0–9 precede the letters A–Z, and capital letters precede lowercase letters. AppleWorks, however, treats all letters as capitals. If you arrange by last name, deRosa will appear before Zorn. Whenever you have doubts about order, consult the ASCII table in Appendix B.

Because the Data Base makes no distinction between values and labels, it left-justifies all entries. This means that you can sort a category containing numbers with either the 0–9 or the A–Z option, and commas in large values can cause incorrect sorting. If you sort a category containing both numerical and word entries using the 0–9 option, the numerical entries will appear between word entries beginning with O and P.

Tip: *When you sort by more than one category, remember to sort by the most important category last.*

In determining the most important category, you are making a judgment only within the limited context of your needs for a specific report.

For example, suppose you want to sort the Everyone list by ZIP code in numerical order and by last name in alphabetical order *within* each ZIP code. In this context the ZIP code is more important than the last name. You would therefore sort by ZIP code last, as in Figure 3.16.

What if you simply want to generate a list by last name in alphabetical order, and there are three Smiths on the list. You decide to arrange the three Smiths in numerical order according to the ZIP code. In this context the last name is more important than the ZIP code, so you sort the last name last, as in Figure 3.17.

Caution: *Arranging selected records arranges all records.*

When you select records in multiple-record layout, you may want to arrange them by one or more categories. You can do that as you would the entire database. However, the entire database will be arranged by the same criteria at the same time, which may not be what you intended.

When you need to sort selected records, create a temporary file by changing the name of the Desktop file, adding one empty record, and deleting all the other records. Load the original file from the disk to the Desktop again and begin selecting records. Copy them to the clipboard, and then move them from the clipboard to the temporary file.

Tip: *Use unique identification numbers for each record to predict the order of arrangement.*

Suppose you sort records by last name only, and two people have the same last name, such as Smith. Susan Smith may or may not precede Robert Smith. There is no way to predict the relative order unless you know the order in which they were originally entered in the database or the last criterion for which they were arranged. You also have to know which circumstance applies.

When each record has a unique identification number, it is much easier to predict order. You simply sort by the ID number first, and then by whatever criterion you choose.

```
File: Everyone            REVIEW/ADD/CHANGE            Escape: Main Menu

Selection: All records


FIRST NAME  LAST NAME   PLACE      STREET            TOWN        STATE ZIP
========================================================================
Joan        Smith       -       72 Jefferson Pike Westbrook   MA    02731
Thomas      Farmer      -       12 Field Rd.      Jefferson   RI    02845
Edward      Joiner      -       19 Mill Rd.       Jefferson   RI    02845
Robin       Jones       -       33 Field Rd.      Jefferson   RI    02845
Rob         Martin      -       22 Meadow Rd.     Jefferson   RI    02845
Joanne      Martinelli  -       25 Brook Rd.      Jefferson   RI    02845
Roberta     Miller      -       14 Brook Rd.      Jefferson   RI    02845
Susan       Smith       -       81 Main Rd.       Jefferson   RI    02845
William     Venn        -       24 East Rd.       Jefferson   RI    02845
Arnold      Wright      -       52 Field Rd.      Jefferson   RI    02845
Robert      Smith       -       28 Bayberry Rd.   Esterly     CT    06414




------------------------------------------------------------------------
Type entry or use @ commands                          @-? for Help
```

Figure 3.16: *Records sorted by last name and then ZIP code*

```
File: Everyone            REVIEW/ADD/CHANGE            Escape: Main Menu

Selection: All records


FIRST NAME  LAST NAME   PLACE      STREET            TOWN        STATE ZIP
========================================================================
Thomas      Farmer      -       12 Field Rd.      Jefferson   RI    02845
Edward      Joiner      -       19 Mill Rd.       Jefferson   RI    02845
Robin       Jones       -       33 Field Rd.      Jefferson   RI    02845
Rob         Martin      -       22 Meadow Rd.     Jefferson   RI    02845
Joanne      Martinelli  -       25 Brook Rd.      Jefferson   RI    02845
Roberta     Miller      -       14 Brook Rd.      Jefferson   RI    02845
Joan        Smith       -       72 Jefferson Pike Westbrook   MA    02731
Susan       Smith       -       81 Main Rd.       Jefferson   RI    02845
Robert      Smith       -       28 Bayberry Rd.   Esterly     CT    06414
William     Venn        -       24 East Rd.       Jefferson   RI    02845
Arnold      Wright      -       52 Field Rd.      Jefferson   RI    02845




------------------------------------------------------------------------
Type entry or use @ commands                          @-? for Help
```

Figure 3.17: *Records sorted by ZIP code and then last name*

There may be times when you will want to manage more than 30 categories of information in parallel Data Base files. In that case each file absolutely must have corresponding categories with a unique ID number for each record.

Tip: *For people-related files, social security numbers can serve two purposes.*

No two people have the same social security number, so the numbers can serve two purposes. They provide necessary information for tax purposes and unique identification numbers. In fact, social security numbers are often used by insurance companies and colleges as ID numbers.

All social security numbers have nine digits, always in the form 044-21-3368, which makes them easy to sort. The only drawback to using social security numbers is that they do not fare well in DIF file transfers, as we will see in Chapter 5.

LABELS-STYLE REPORT FORMATS

Data Base reports come in two basic formats: labels-style reports and tables-style reports. When you design a format, you must specify exactly where on the paper each category should be printed. Sometimes you will want to have all the categories print out (for example, on Rolodex cards), and sometimes you will want only pertinent categories printed (for example, on mailing labels).

In this section, there are tips on designing labels-style report formats for printing Rolodex cards and mailing labels. There are also tips on dealing with blank categories and formatting for justification. Pay special attention to the tip on printing to the screen first.

In the next section tips will be given for designing tables-style reports, and in the section on printer options you will find tips for setting printer options for printing onto Rolodex cards and mailing labels.

Tip: *Apple-P will not access the printer until you have selected a report format.*

Obviously, you cannot select a report format until you have designed one. So the first time you use the print command you may still be a long way from actually printing. This confuses people more than any other feature of the Data Base.

Caution: *Beware of report formats with lines that begin with categories that are sometimes empty.*

Earlier versions of AppleWorks had a problem adapting to blank categories. If the first of several categories on a line is blank and the next is left-justified, the line will begin with two blank spaces. You can generally design around this limitation, so think of those who never upgraded to version 1.2.

Tip: *Use left-justification for categories in mailing labels.*

The < mark means that category will be left-justified as indicated. For example, in the report format shown in Figure 3.18, the last name will be left-justified one space after the end of the first name.

Apple-J inserts or deletes left-justification when the cursor is on the first letter of the category name. Left-justification includes the number of spaces you specify. For example, if you want one category to follow the last character of the previous category by ten spaces, leave ten blank spaces. (The < mark does not count as a space.)

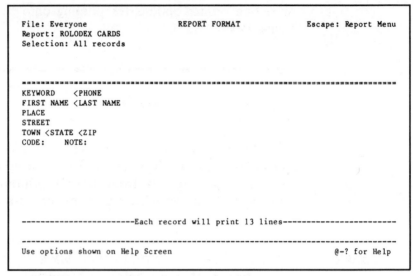

```
File: Everyone              REPORT FORMAT           Escape: Report Menu
Report: ROLODEX CARDS
Selection: All records




===========================================================================
KEYWORD     <PHONE
FIRST NAME <LAST NAME
PLACE
STREET
TOWN <STATE <ZIP
CODE:    NOTE:






------------------------Each record will print 13 lines------------------------

---------------------------------------------------------------------------
Use options shown on Help Screen                            @-? for Help
```

Figure 3.18: *Report format for Rolodex cards*

Caution: *When you delete a category from a report format line that has left-justified categories, you lose the left-justification.*

This is not a significant problem, simply because you can see the < mark disappear if you are paying attention. Once you have deleted the unwanted category, use Apple-J again to replace the left-justification where needed.

Caution: *Apple-V does not work exactly as described in the AppleWorks manuals.*

With the cursor on the first letter of a category name, Apple-V inserts or deletes that category name in the printed report. However, if a category name has been left-justified, the cursor must be on the < mark preceding the name, not on the first letter.

When the category name has been inserted, you will see a colon following the category name.

Tip: *Use the report format options to the limit.*

Category names can be designed as intended information on reports. For example, category names such as BILLED TO and SHIPPED TO can be included in a report format that produces invoices.

Reserved or empty categories can hold messages entered in new records as standard values. For example, an invoice report format might include a temporary message in an unused or reserved category. This information can be quickly changed with the Apple-' command in multiple-record layout.

You can add report titles to the top of each report page. Titles are entered using the Apple-N command from within a report format. Titles are generally more useful than page headers.

To illustrate this tip, create a labels-style report format to print Rolodex cards from the Everyone list. Follow these steps:

1. Press Apple-P and choose option 3 to create a new "labels" report.

2. Name the report ROLODEX CARDS.

3. Remembering the tips and cautions in this section, move the necessary categories into position as shown in Figure 3.18.

4. Use Apple-J where left-justification is necessary. Leave four spaces when you left-justify the PHONE category.

5. Use Apple-V to print the CODE and NOTE category names on the cards. Information in the first record appears on the screen, giving you a good idea of how things fit.

6. Delete the categories that will not be printed on the mailing label, and leave seven blank lines at the bottom of the label. The finished report format should have 13 lines. Compare it with the report format shown in Figure 3.18.

In the section of this chapter on printer options there is a tip on selecting the printer options for this report and printing it, first to the screen and then to Rolodex cards.

Tip: *You can create report formats from other formats.*

To illustrate this tip, create a labels-style report format to print mailing labels from the Everyone list. Use the ROLODEX CARDS format as a beginning, and follow these steps:

1. Press Apple-P and choose option 4 to duplicate an existing format.

2. Give the report a name, such as MAILING LABELS.

3. Remembering the tips and cautions in this section, delete the two categories in the first row, and then delete the resulting empty line.

4. Delete the two categories in the last row, and then delete all but two empty lines.

The finished report format should have six lines. Compare it with the report format shown in Figure 3.19.

In the section of this chapter on printer options, you will find tips on selecting the printer options for this report and printing it, first to the screen and then to mailing labels.

TABLES-STYLE REPORT FORMATS

The tables-style report format is sometimes the most appropriate way of presenting information. This is especially true for in-house record-keeping applications. In large management information systems, these are the reports that often come on greenbar paper more than 14 inches wide.

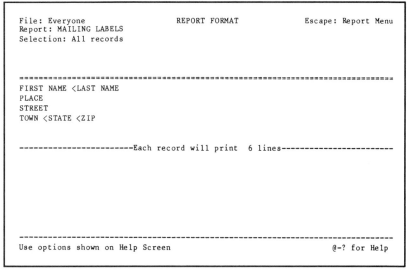

```
File: Everyone                REPORT FORMAT              Escape: Report Menu
Report: MAILING LABELS
Selection: All records




============================================================================
FIRST NAME <LAST NAME
PLACE
STREET
TOWN <STATE <ZIP


------------------------Each record will print  6 lines-------------------




----------------------------------------------------------------------------
Use options shown on Help Screen                           @-? for Help
```

Figure 3.19: *Report format for MAILING LABELS*

Tip: *Use tables-style report formats when you need to see a large array of information all at once.*

The tables-style report shown in Figure 3.20 includes only the first eight categories and one calculated category from a potentially large database of abandoned houses, many of which can be rehabilitated. The database is designed to match the right properties with the right people under the right conditions. Given those information requirements, this kind of database could logically have 10 to 30 categories. Figure 3.21 shows a single-record layout with 10 categories.

The report format name indicates that the street address (number and name) begins the table. Here the street names provide a logical basis for arranging the records in alphabetical order. In this database, you can arrange the records so that properties on the same street appear by street number in ascending order. In fact, this report could be arranged by any category column. It is important to document your choices: always circle the heading of an arranged category column or highlight it with a yellow marker.

```
File:    Housing                                                   Page  1
Report:  Street.1
  ST #  ST NAME       ZIP      FILE    UNIT  BACK TAX   SINCE    LIEN  COMBINED
  ----  ------------  -------  ----    ----  --------   -------  ----- --------
    12  Elm St.       02884     45      1      3422     1980      890    4312
    21  Elm St.       02884     51      1      1234     1979     1278    2512
    26  Elm St.       02884     54      2       287     1982     4120    4407
   127  Elm St.       02884     61      1      1435     1978     2008    3443
    14  Jackson Pl.   02883     57      1      2130     1981     3890    6020
    26  Jackson Pl.   02883     58      2       612     1983     4875    5487
    31  Kendall Rd.   02885     39      2      1882     1982              1882
   134  Kendall Rd.   02885     49      1       120     1983               120
   148  Pine St.      02884     59      1       810     1980     5461    6271
    18  Taylor Ct.    02885     46      2      4559     1978     2488    7047
                                       14*    16491*           25010*  41501*
```

Figure 3.20: Printed tables-style report

What makes the tables-style report most appropriate in this case? The database has values that should be subtotaled and totaled, it has category values that should be combined, and there are several ways to arrange the records.

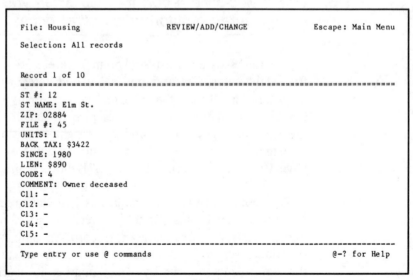

```
File: Housing                REVIEW/ADD/CHANGE              Escape: Main Menu

Selection: All records


Record 1 of 10
===============================================================================
ST #: 12
ST NAME: Elm St.
ZIP: 02884
FILE #: 45
UNITS: 1
BACK TAX: $3422
SINCE: 1980
LIEN: $890
CODE: 4
COMMENT: Owner deceased
C11: -
C12: -
C13: -
C14: -
C15: -
-------------------------------------------------------------------------------
Type entry or use @ commands                                  @-? for Help
```

Figure 3.21: Single-record layout with 10 categories

Caution: *Totaling and combining columns can produce unexpected formatting results.*

Notice that the LIEN column in Figure 3.20 has a total marked with an asterisk. To total a column in a report format, place the cursor on the column to be totaled and press Apple-T. (In this report, we chose to print the total with no decimal places.)

The COMBINED column has the sum of BACK TAX and LIEN amounts for each record. In the Report Format process you place the cursor on the column to be calculated and press Apple-K. Here the formula F + H was entered, because the columns are also lettered from left to right, as they are in the Spreadsheet. Compare Figures 3.20 and 3.21: notice that the totaled and calculated columns lose their dollar signs, and $0 becomes a blank space.

Caution: *Calculated categories exist only within tables-style reports.*

The COMBINED category in Figure 3.20 exists only in tables-style reports. You cannot use the Data Base as a worksheet in which a column C in multiple-record layout contains the formula A + B, and everything recalculates on screen. You see Data Base calculations on the screen only when you print the appropriate tables-style report to the screen.

Remember that the Data Base hardly ever functions as the Spreadsheet would, even though they share commands. They are different programs and function differently.

Tip: *You can use empty categories in multiple-record layout to denote calculated categories.*

Figure 3.21 shows a record in single-record layout. You could include a dummy COMBINED category between LIEN and

CODE. These dummy categories can then be used in multiple-record layout as a form of documentation. They can be quickly deleted from the tables-style report and replaced by calculated categories.

Tip: *Good tables-style report formats are often difficult to read.*

When you total columns, create calculated categories, or right-justify entries, the column in the tables-style report format appears with nothing but nines. Because the most readable tables-style reports use those capabilities, their report formats are often difficult to read. Figure 3.22 shows the report format used to create the report shown in Figure 3.20.

Whenever you use such a tables-style report format, print records to the screen first. When you have seen enough to be certain the report meets your needs, press Escape to return to the report format.

Tip: *For printers with an 8-inch platen width, you can design similar report formats to print just the remaining categories.*

In the case of the report format in Figure 3.20, the remaining columns can be called Street.2, to show that it is the second section of a series of tables beginning with the street address (number and street name). By carefully marking the starting point at the top of the page, you can print Street.1 on one half of a folded 11" × 17" page and Street.2 on the other half.

If this happened to be a 30-category database, there could conceivably be a Street.3 report format. Note that it is rarely necessary to print every database category in a report. However, it

```
File: Housing                  REPORT FORMAT              Escape: Report Menu
Report: Street.1
Selection: All records




============================================================================
--> or <--   Move cursor                  @-J   Right justify this category
 >   @   <   Switch category positions     @-K   Define a calculated category
--> @  <--   Change column width           @-N   Change report name and/or title
@-A  Arrange (sort) on this category       @-O   Printer options
@-D  Delete this category                  @-P   Print the report
@-G  Add/remove group totals               @-R   Change record selection rules
@-I  Insert a prev. deleted category       @-T   Add/remove category totals
----------------------------------------------------------------------------

.ST #   ST NAME       ZIP      FILE    UNIT  BACK TAX  SINCE    LIEN     COMBINED  L
-A---   -B----------  -C-----  -D--    -E--  -F------  -G-----  -H-----  -I------  e
99999   Elm St.       02884    9999    9999  99999999  9999999  9999999  99999999  n
99999   Elm St.       02884    9999    9999  99999999  9999999  9999999  99999999  7
99999   Elm St.       02884    9999    9999  99999999  9999999  9999999  99999999  7
                                       ====  ========           =======  ========
----------------------------------------------------------------------------
Use options shown above to change report format              137K Avail.
```

Figure 3.22: *Tables-style report format*

is prudent to keep a printed record of everything entered into the database.

Tip: *The "label table" is a hybrid form for report formats that include at least one relatively long narrative category.*

This type of report format begins as a labels-style report format. You can set the categories to occupy fixed widths, with no left-justification. So you're in fact setting up the report with a tabular format, just as with tables-style report formats. However, by using a labels-style report format you can give a long COMMENT category a second line all its own. The report then looks like a double-spaced table with occasional comment lines. Totals and calculations cannot be used in such a report format.

Figure 3.23 illustrates a label-table version of the Street report shown in Figure 3.20. If you need a long comment line in what

```
File:    Housing                                        Page  1
Report: Label.Table
ST #   ST NAME          ZIP     FILE #  UNITS BACK TAX  SINCE  LIEN    CODE

12     Elm St.          02884   45      1     $3422     1980   $890    4
       Owner deceased
21     Elm St.          02884   51      1     $1234     1979   $1278   0
       -
26     Elm St.          02884   54      2     $287      1982   $4120   4
       -
127    Elm St.          02884   61      1     $1435     1978   $2008   1
       -
14     Jackson Pl.      02883   57      1     $2130     1981   $3890   2
       Minor fire damage on Apr 12 84
26     Jackson Pl.      02883   58      2     $612      1983   $4875   3

31     Kendall Rd.      02885   39      2     $1882     1982   $0      4
       -
134    Kendall Rd.      02885   49      1     $120      1983   $0      3

148    Pine St.         02884   59      1     $810      1980   $5461   2
       -
18     Taylor Ct.       02885   46      2     $4559     1978   $2488   3
       Minor fire damage on Dec 28 83
```

Figure 3.23: *Printed label table*

would otherwise be a tables-style report, this is the kind of report format to use.

PRINTER OPTIONS

If you have mastered printing with the Word Processor, you are well prepared to work with the lesser number of Data Base printer options. There are a few important differences worth noting. In the Data Base you need to change platen width and paper length more often. Data Base applications use the smallest paper length (the page for a mailing label may be only one inch long), and the largest paper width (reports can be printed on very wide paper). The Data Base also takes a slightly different approach to page headers, and has some additional line adjustment options, as you will see in the tips that follow.

Tip: *Choose the paper that fits the application.*

Most Word Processor documents use standard $8^1/_2 \times 11$-inch blank white paper. Data Base applications typically use a broader range of paper stock: green-bar paper in several sizes, mailing labels, continuous index cards, and multipart forms. Determine what kind of layout would most suit your applications, and then choose paper that will meet your requirements.

This section explains how to print a labels-style report onto Rolodex cards. Rolodex makes continuous cards for tractor-feed printers. The perforated edges make the card feel slightly fuzzy at first, but over time the edges wear down. The $2^1/_6 \times 4$-inch size is large enough to include the information you need for a file of this sort.

Most stationery stores can order a range of cards, forms, and paper if they are not already in stock. In addition, many mail-order firms specialize in paper for data processing.

Caution: *The Data Base lacks some useful printer options found in the Word Processor.*

Table 3.3 lists the Word Processor printer options, noting those that are also available in the Data Base and Spreadsheet. When you design Data Base applications, think about the available printer options at the beginning. Depending on your formatting requirements, it may be necessary to copy reports to the clipboard for further editing in the Word Processor. Or it may be necessary to use the AppleWorks Mailing Program to extend reporting capabilities. For more on these subjects, see Chapter 5.

The Data Base and Spreadsheet have other specialized options, including the option to enter special codes for the printer. This option is primarily useful for changing form lengths and print densities. It can be used to begin boldfacing and underlining but cannot turn them off. This means the option cannot be used for selective underlining, as in bibliographical reports, for example.

Table 3.3: *Printer options*

Option	WP	DB	SS
Line Length, Print Density			
Platen width	X	X	X
Left margin	X	X	X
Right margin	X	X	X
Characters per inch	X	X	X
Proportional-1	X		
Proportional-2	X		
Text Positioning			
Indent	X		
Justified	X	X	X
Unjustified	X	X	X
Centered	X		X
Page Length, Line Density			
Paper length	X	X	X
Top margin	X	X	X
Bottom margin	X	X	X
Lines per inch	X	X	X
Single space	X	X	X
Double space	X	X	X
Triple space	X	X	X
Page Controls			
New page	X		
Group markers	X		
Page Calculation			
Page header	X	X	X
Page footer	X		
Skip lines	X		
Page number	X		
Place Markers			
Pause each page	X		
Pause here	X		
Set a marker	X		

Table 3.3: *Printer options (continued)*

Option	WP	DB	SS
Print Enhancements			
Boldface	X		
Superscript	X		
Subscript	X		
Underline	X		
Variable Text Entry			
Print page number	X		
Enter keyboard	X		

Tip: *Use the special codes option to control form length on your printer.*

When you installed your printer, you probably answered Yes to option 2 on the Add a Printer menu. This option asks whether the printer accepts top-of-page commands, and assumes an 11-inch page length. In the Data Base you will often use much shorter pages (as short as one inch in the case of mailing labels). The SC option to enter special codes allows you to enter your printer's codes for shorter pages. Note that pages are often called forms in printer manuals. The mechanics of entering these codes are described in Chapter 6. Special codes modify the top-of-page commands and are saved with the report format.

If you are uncertain about your printer's codes for form length, return to the Add a Printer menu. Because you have already installed the printer, it will now be called the Change a Printer menu, but the menu options are the same. Answer No to option 2. This allows the Data Base printer options to work correctly. The disadvantage of this approach is obvious: you must return to the Change a Printer menu to use the top-of-page command once again in the Word Processor.

Tip: *Take out your ruler when you select Data Base printer options.*

Take out your ruler and a hard copy of the printer options screen showing all the default settings. In most cases you will find that relatively few entries need to be changed. To set the printer options for the ROLODEX CARDS report format, change the platen width to 4.0 inches because the Rolodex card is exactly that wide. (Measure your cards, because there are several sizes available.) Set the left margin to 0.2 inches because you have no space to waste. Set the paper length to 2.2 inches—slightly longer than the 2¹/₆-inch card, but that is as close as you can get. All of the spacing has been built into the report format, so you will be printing with top and bottom margins of 0 inches. Everything should fit perfectly at six lines per inch.

All of the formatting options (SC, PD, PH, and OL) should indicate No on the screen, since there is no need to send special codes to the printer. You could print a dash when a category contains no information, but we have chosen not to do that—a Rolodex card should have blank lines, so that you can pencil additional entries in the right places later. For the same reason, do not choose to omit a line when all entries on the line are blank. KS, a fifth option to keep the same number of lines in each record, does not appear because it can only be Yes when OL is Yes. For Rolodex cards, you will not need a report header. Figure 3.24 shows the Printer Options menu, with the settings for printing Rolodex Cards.

Tip: *Print reports to the screen first, then test print several records to paper.*

The Data Base is the only AppleWorks program that lets you print to the screen. Take advantage of this option and save paper, because you may need to make a few trial runs.

```
 File: Everyone               PRINTER OPTIONS          Escape: Report Format
 Report: ROLODEX CARDS
 ===========================================================================

 -------Left and right margins--------      ------Top and bottom margins------
 PW: Platen Width          4.0 inches     PL: Paper Length          2.2 inches
 LM: Left Margin           0.2 inches     TM: Top Margin            0.0 inches
 RM: Right Margin          0.0 inches     BM: Bottom Margin         0.0 inches
 CI: Chars per Inch        10             LI: Lines per Inch        6

    Line width            3.8 inches         Printing length       2.2 inches
    Char per line (est)   38                 Lines per page        13

          --------------------Formatting options--------------------
          SC:  Send Special Codes to printer                No
          PD:  Print a Dash when an entry is blank           No
          PH:  Print report Header at top of each page       No
          OL:  Omit Line when all entries on line are blank  No




 ---------------------------------------------------------------------------
 Type a two letter option code                                37K Avail.
```

Figure 3.24: *Printer options set for Rolodex cards*

Save everything with Apple-S and print to the screen. If that works dependably, test print on plain paper. The trick is to get the left edge of the platen even with, or just inside, the left edge of the paper. Roll up the paper to exactly where the printing should begin. Remember that you are using no top margin. Then follow these steps:

1. Use the record-selection rules to select several records.

2. Press Apple-P, select your printer, and press Return.

3. Press Return again to print one copy of the report.

4. When all the card entries are printed, match the paper with the cards to see how they align.

5. Repeat the printing process with actual Rolodex cards.

6. When everything prints out correctly, as in Figure 3.25, document all the measurements and physical reference points you used.

Figure 3.25: *Two printed Rolodex cards*

Tip: *Use standard one-across mailing labels.*

AppleWorks can print only one column of mailing labels per pass. Single-column labels are commonly called one-across labels. They come in narrow, easy-to-store boxes, and they are remarkably easy to load into printers. Move the tractor or pin on the right side, and leave the left side where it is for regular paper.

If you already have labels mounted two-across on tractor-feed paper, use it in two passes. Turn the sheets around after the first pass and come back with the remaining column on the left. If the labels are three-across, use three passes, with different margin and platen settings for the middle column.

Standard one-across mailing labels are 3.5 inches wide and exactly one inch from the top of one label to the top of the next. The label itself is $^{15}/_{16}$ of an inch. Look for labels that resist smudging, especially if you use a daisywheel printer. With some attention to alignment, you can print five lines on a standard label. Most mailing label reports use only four lines.

With standard labels, the MAILING LIST report format requires only three printer option entries. Change the platen width setting to 3.5 inches, the left margin setting to 0.2 inches, and the paper length to 1 inch.

The formatting options are the same as those for the ROLO-DEX CARDS report format, except that the responses for OL and KS are Yes. You need to omit lines when they are blank, but you also need to keep the same number of lines in each label, so that the printer stays aligned with the labels. Figure 3.26 shows how the labels should look when they are printed.

Tip: *To generate more than nine copies of a record, copy records within the database.*

The print option allows up to nine copies. If you want to print 200 copies of a single return-address label, follow these steps:

1. Enter the address once in the database if you have not already done so.

2. Using Apple-C, copy the address 39 times.

3. Select the MAILING LABELS report format.

4. Select the record you want by last name.

5. Print 5 copies of the report.

You will get 200 labels because the record selected appeared 40 times in the database.

Tip: *Use continuous cards for mailing and for index cards.*

Many stationery supply stores offer continuous cards for tractor-feed printers. They come in 3 × 5-inch and 4 × 6-inch sizes, sometimes even in pale colors. They can be used as index cards, post cards, and even tags.

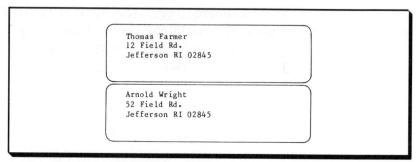

Figure 3.26: *Two printed mailing labels*

If you plan to use them for post cards, the larger ones are the more appropriate choice, simply because they can hold more information. Both take the same postage.

DESIGNING TEMPLATES

Good planning and design can save considerable time in the development and use of templates. By designing interchangeable parts you can build templates more efficiently. This section covers basic design details and offers some cautions.

Pay special attention to the difference between original category order and record layouts. As you will learn, original category order should influence many design decisions. In this section you will also find tips and cautions for record-layout options that allow you to enter records more efficiently.

Tip: *Learn the difference between original category order and record layouts.*

When you initially name categories, you name them on a category screen that determines original category order. This order generates one single-record layout and one multiple-record layout.

You will often use a single-record layout that follows original category order. If you use Apple-L to change the location of any category in single-record layout, you create a custom record layout. You will often use Apple-L to change multiple-record layout.

Adding or deleting categories causes the Data Base to lose all report formats and custom record layouts. This leaves you with the original single-record and multiple-record layouts generated by the original category order.

Remember the difference between original category order, record layouts, and custom record layouts, because this is the key to transferring records from file to file.

Tip: *When designing Data Base applications, think first about original category order.*

When the time comes to transfer information to related files, categories are transferred in their original order, defined when you first named the categories. Changes in single-record layout and multiple-record layout have no effect on transfers. For more tips on this, see the section on merging records later in this chapter.

Categories can be displayed in any order within a custom multiple-record layout, even if that order is completely different from the order of the single-record layout.

Tip: *Single-record layout often duplicates original category order, and for good reason.*

Records are almost always entered through single-record layout. Categories that require keyboard entry should be listed consecutively, in logical order, beginning with the first category. Categories with seldom-changed standard values should follow those that normally require keyboard entry. Unused or reserved categories belong at the end.

You will probably want to use the single-record layout that follows original category order. Although it is easy to change category order in a custom single-record layout, there is an important limitation. In files with more than 15 categories, you cannot create a custom single-record layout and then move the cursor from top to bottom, first down one column and then the other. You have only two choices: a left-to-right pattern moving from top to bottom, or the original order in which you defined categories. Figure 3.27 shows the menu options.

Tip: *Single-record layout is surprisingly flexible.*

The original LIST template (see Figure 3.3) had 15 categories, a tables-style report, and a labels-style report. Most applications use no more than 15 categories—an easy number to manage in single-record layout. However, with some imagination you can store additional categories in a way that has little effect on cursor movement. Figure 3.28 shows an example. Notice that the first seven categories have been individually indented, and that C15 remains usable as a CODE or DATE category.

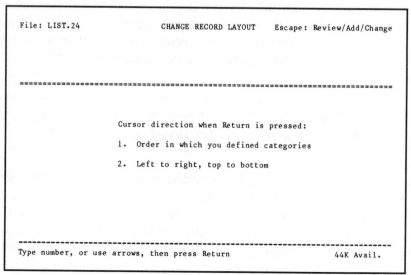

```
File: LIST.24                  CHANGE RECORD LAYOUT      Escape: Review/Add/Change


=================================================================================


                   Cursor direction when Return is pressed:

                   1.  Order in which you defined categories

                   2.  Left to right, top to bottom




-----------------------------------------------------------------------------
Type number, or use arrows, then press Return                    44K Avail.
```

Figure 3.27: *Menu options for custom single-record layout*

```
File: LIST.24              REVIEW/ADD/CHANGE              Escape: Main Menu

Selection: All records


Record 1 of 2
=============================================================================
FIRST NAME: -
 LAST NAME: -
     PLACE: -
    STREET: -
      TOWN: -
     STATE: -
       ZIP: -
C08: -
C09: -
C10: -
C11: -
C12: -
C13: -
C14: -
C15: -          C16: - C17: - C18: - C19: - C20: - C21: - C22: - C23: - C24: -
-----------------------------------------------------------------------------
Type entry or use @ commands                                  @-? for Help
```

Figure 3.28: LIST template with 24 categories

Tip: *Avoid deleting categories.*

The memory cost of carrying extra categories is minimal, and you may need the categories some day. Carrying 21 empty categories requires about 5K for 500 records. If you delete categories, you lose all the report formats in the database and must reconstruct them. If you later have to add the categories, you lose all the report formats again.

Tip: *Rename categories to avoid deleting and inserting categories.*

Apple-N offers an important option within the Data Base, that of renaming categories. A file does not lose its report formats or custom record layouts unless you insert or delete categories. Therefore, if any existing file has report formats you can use and enough categories for the data at hand, save time by modifying the existing file.

Consider this example. The Everyone list created earlier in the chapter contains eleven named categories and four that are unused. Suppose you want to put a library association membership list onto an AppleWorks database. You can develop the application quickly by modifying the Everyone list. Use Apple-N to change the Desktop file name to Members.

The association list has no need for the KEYWORD category, so change the name to YEARS, a category indicating how long a person has been a member of the association. You can continue to change names and use the categories for slightly different purposes. You can also name the three formerly unused categories and use them for records of annual donations from each member.

The MAILING LABELS report format remains in use unchanged. The ROLODEX CARDS report format undergoes minor changes to become the INDEX CARD report format.

If you have no need for the records in the Everyone list, removing them is the easiest step of all. Place the cursor on the second record, press Apple-D, Apple-9, and Return. That leaves a single record, the minimum required. You can delete that record after you enter the first association member record. Figure 3.29 shows the transformed single-record layout.

Tip: *Use generic report names.*

The Everyone list has the generic report format name MAILING LABELS. The name can serve equally well in an association's membership database. This list also has a more specific report format name—ROLODEX CARDS. If the report format was simply named CARDS, there would be no need to change the name. In this case, however, the cards differed in size and shape, so using specific names made sense.

Generic names and standard designs make component parts more readily interchangeable. That, in turn, makes AppleWorks even more useful. However, there will be times when specific names are more appropriate.

```
┌─────────────────────────────────────────────────────────────────────────┐
│  File: Members              INSERT NEW RECORDS     Escape: Review/Add/Change│
│                                                                           │
│                                                                           │
│  Record 11 of 11                                                          │
│  ======================================================================== │
│  FIRST NAME: -                                                            │
│  LAST NAME: -                                                             │
│  PLACE: -                                                                 │
│  STREET: -                                                                │
│  TOWN: -                                                                  │
│  STATE: -                                                                 │
│  ZIP: -                                                                   │
│  PHONE: -                                                                 │
│  COMMITTEE: -                                                             │
│  YEARS: -                                                                 │
│  1983: -                                                                  │
│  1984: -                                                                  │
│  1985: -                                                                  │
│  NOTES: -                                                                 │
│  RESERVED: -                                                              │
│  ------------------------------------------------------------------------ │
│  Type entry or use @ commands                               31K Avail.    │
└─────────────────────────────────────────────────────────────────────────┘
```

Figure 3.29: Single-record layout for the Members list

DEVELOPING APPLICATIONS

Design and development are closely linked. Sometimes the process of building a template will provide insights to better design. Make notes on what you found and use them to design other applications. This section covers techniques you can use in construction and revision.

AppleWorks presents some minor construction problems that you can work around. You have designed interchangeable components, and this is where you get to assemble them.

Tip: *When you must add categories, use Apple-H to minimize the time needed to reconstruct report formats.*

The ability to add categories to the Data Base is useful, even though you lose all the report formats and custom record layouts. Use Apple-H to print a hard copy of the screens showing the old report formats, custom record layouts, and printer options. It makes reconstruction much easier.

Tip: *Use short category names to make room for information in single-record layout.*

If you use a one-character category name, you still have room for another 76 characters of information on that line in single-record layout (assuming you have no more than 15 categories). Brief category names are even more important when you have more than 15 categories and available entry space in the single-record layout is limited.

Tip: *Consider category length when you use more than 15 categories.*

When a Data Base application uses only 15 categories, each category can have an entire screen line. When you use 16 to 30 categories, the default setting places them in a column on the right half of the single-record screen.

When two categories share one line, the available character space for each category decreases by more than half, to 36 characters. That may be inadequate for a long place name or a comment. When you use more than 15 categories, avoid blocking a category that needs more than 36 character spaces.

There is a way to cope with this problem. By carefully arranging the category name locations on the single-record layout screen, you can give long entries the space they need. To do this, arrange short categories side by side. For example, an Apple-Works date needs only 11 spaces (including the leading and trailing space required by all entries), so you can easily fit another category alongside it. From single-record layout, press Apple-L to change screen layouts.

Figure 3.30 illustrates one possible layout that makes maximum use of the space available. Notice that the original category order has not been changed, which means that the cursor can still move from top to bottom, first down one column and then the other.

Tip: *If you run out of entry space, you can still push the data in.*

No matter how carefully you design the single-record screen, you can still encounter an unexpectedly long entry. In that case you can fit it in with a "pushing" technique that makes the most of the insert cursor. Follow these steps:

1. Type in the right half of the long entry.

2. Go back to the first character you just entered.

3. Type in the left half of the entry, pushing the right half of the entry under the category name to the right.

You can actually store up to 79 characters this way, although the Data Base prints only 76 per category. The technique works equally well in multiple-record layout.

Caution: *The maximum record length may be less than 1,024 characters in specific applications.*

The AppleWorks Reference Manual lists the maximum record capacity as 1,024 characters. This limit does not include category names, nor does it include calculated categories.

You can actually fit up to 1,140 characters on a single-record screen. Because category names can use up to 600 character spaces, an application can easily use every character space on the screen. However, even with brief category names, you may not be able to use 1,024 characters for data.

```
File: CAT.28                    REVIEW/ADD/CHANGE              Escape: Main Menu

Selection: All records


Record 1 of 1
================================================================================
A: -                                    PHONE: (401) 888-2546
B: 123456789 123456789 123456789 123456 Q: -
C: -                                    R: -
    DATE: Sep  1 85                     S: -
E: -                                                         TIME:  5:30 PM
F: -                                    U: -
G: 123456789 123456789 123456789 123456789 123456789 V: C2
H: -                                    W: -
    I: Indented                         X: -
J: -                                    Y: -
K: -                                    ZIP: 02674
L: -                                    27: -
M: -                                    28: -
N: -
O: 123456789 123456789 123456789 123456789 123456789 123456789 123456789 123456
--------------------------------------------------------------------------------
Type entry or use @ commands                                  @-? for Help
```

Figure 3.30: Single-record layout with 28 categories

The single-record screen accepts everything you enter. If you go over the character limit, the Data Base quietly removes characters when you move to the next record. There is no warning message. When you come back, some of the most recently entered information may be missing. Unfortunately, the Data Base can begin removing information even before you reach a thousand characters.

There is a way to cope with the problem. When you design the single-record layout, enter a dummy record that uses all the available entry spaces you intend to use. If the Data Base accepts the record, you can probably count on the layout to work dependably.

Tip: *A Data Base file can have 33 categories.*

The three additional categories are calculated categories. They exist only within tables-style reports. You cannot use the Data Base like a Spreadsheet, in which column A plus column B equals column C, and everything then recalculates on screen. You can see calculated results on the screen only by printing a report to the screen.

A calculated category can reference only cells to its left, and it can calculate with only the four basic arithmetic functions.

There is another limitation. For calculation purposes, the Data Base identifies categories with column letters, as the Spreadsheet does. However, there are no columns AA through AD for the last four possible categories. That means values in categories 27 through 30 cannot be calculated. Figure 3.31 shows the far limits of a file with 33 categories.

Tip: *A Data Base file needs only one record, and that record can be empty.*

This is the minimum compliance for the Data Base's one-record requirement. It is important for one reason: it is often prudent to change the name of an existing Data Base file and delete all of its

```
File: CAT.33                 REPORT FORMAT              Escape: Report Menu
Report: Cat.33
Selection: All records



================================================================================
--> or <--  Move cursor                   @-J  Right justify this category
  >  @   <    Switch category positions    @-K  Define a calculated category
--> @   <--  Change column width           @-N  Change report name and/or title
@-A  Arrange (sort) on this category       @-O  Printer options
@-D  Delete this category                  @-P  Print the report
@-G  Add/remove group totals               @-R  Change record selection rules
@-I  Insert a prev. deleted category       @-T  Add/remove category totals
--------------------------------------------------------------------------------

22  23  24  25  26  27  28  29  30  Calculated   Calculated   Calculated   L
-V- -W- -X- -Y- -Z- --- --- --- --- ----------   ----------   ----------   e
                                    9999999999   9999999999   9999999999   n
                                    9999999999   9999999999   9999999999   2
                                    9999999999   9999999999   9999999999   3
                                                                           2
<--- More -----------------------------------------------------------------------
Use options shown above to change report format                     33K Avail.
```

Figure 3.31: Data Base report format with 33 categories

files. This process effectively copies a database structure for other data that require a similar structure.

The last record left behind from the old file should have nothing but dashes. You can create that record in the following way: go just beyond the last record in a database, and the next record will appear with nothing but dashes. Press Return in any category, and the dashes become a confirmed record.

The empty record also makes a good marker in the database. Keep it at the end of the file. Copy or move it anywhere you need visual separation in multiple-record layout. If you want to collect all the empty records, select all records in which one to three specified categories are blank.

Tip: *Apple-' can be used to make vast temporary changes in records.*

There are times when you will want to copy a file with useful information, empty all but the categories you need, and use what remains for other purposes. This approach works well, but remember to change the name of the file before doing it.

If you want to remove all the information from a category without deleting the category, follow these steps:

1. In multiple-record layout, use the record-selection rules to retrieve all the records with the information you want to replace.

2. Use Apple-Y to delete everything from the category entry in the first record.

3. Place the cursor in the same category of the next record and hold down Apple-' to quickly empty all the remaining records.

You are then free to enter your new information. For example, by copying a return address into available categories while in multiple-record layout, you can create a labels-style report format that can print both a return address and a mailing address on a post card, as shown in Figure 3.32. Or you can use a category to print AIR MAIL on the mailing labels and post cards.

As long as you remember to change the file name to prevent damage caused by accidentally saving the file, you can write over any category that has no immediate utility. There are almost no limits to what you can do.

Tip: *You can copy a Data Base file for specialized purposes.*

Databases often contain information for several different specialized purposes. For example, the Members database tells us where members of the library association live. It also provides information for annual planning and budgeting.

The Data Base multiple-record layout cannot show you all the information in every category at once. However, you can change the name of the Members file to Members.Finance and design a multiple-record layout for budgeting purposes. It can have a cal-

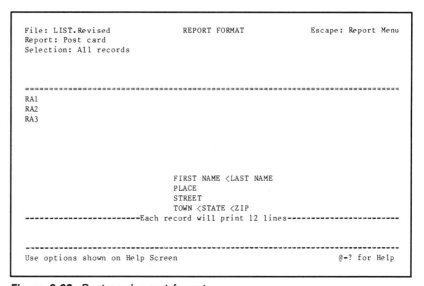

```
File: LIST.Revised              REPORT FORMAT              Escape: Report Menu
Report: Post card
Selection: All records



===============================================================================
RA1
RA2
RA3




                              FIRST NAME <LAST NAME
                              PLACE
                              STREET
                              TOWN <STATE <ZIP
------------------------Each record will print 12 lines-----------------------


-------------------------------------------------------------------------------
Use options shown on Help Screen                              @-? for Help
```

Figure 3.32: *Post card report format*

culated category to keep a record of each member's cumulative contributions over a three-year period. It can have totaled categories for total membership income in each of the three years. You can enter additional records for other sources of income. It is also possible to enter budget items, with negative numbers to represent expenditures against income. The totaled category then shows an expected net balance or deficit.

Figure 3.33 shows sample elements of a budget planning report for a library association. When you design applications, first use sample elements to test the concept. Here we have used ten of 530 members and two of 20 budget items.

It is common for associations to have many members and relatively few budget items. For such cases, the Data Base is a practical multipurpose tool. In most cases, however, the Spreadsheet is more appropriate for budgeting.

Copying a master file presents one complication. When you update records, do so on the master file only. Then copy any updated records to the clipboard, and move them to the specialized file. Before you actually make the transfer, delete the obsolete records from the specialized file.

```
File:    Members.Finance                                          Page   1
Report: Budget
FIRST NAME LAST NAME    1983    1984    1985    1983-85   PHONE
---------- ------------ -----   -----   -----   -------   --------------------
Thomas     Farmer         20      20      20        60   (401) 888-4864
Edward     Joiner                 15      30        45   (401) 888-9912
Robin      Jones          15      15      20        50   (401) 888-2276
Rob        Martin         15      15      20        50   (401) 888-3243
Joanne     Martinelli             50      50       100   (401) 888-1276
Roberta    Miller         15      15      20        50   (401) 888-1132
Susan      Smith          25      25      24        74   (401) 888-5784
Robert     Smith          15      15      20        50   (203) 358-3114
Joan       Smith          15      15      20        50   (617) 445-9082
           Smith Fund   1800    1800    2000      5600
Arnold     Wright         15      15      20        50   (401) 888-6674
                        1935    2000    2244      6179

---------- ------------                                    --------------------
           Painting     -210    -320    -580     -1110
           Repairs     -1680   -1620   -1750     -5050
                       -1890   -1940   -2330     -6160

                          45*     60*    -86*       19*
```

Figure 3.33: Budget planning report

AUDITING DATABASES

It is always a good idea to audit your own work, particularly in the design of database applications. As you learned with the record-selection rules, even the best designs fail in one way or another. This section contains several tips about designing databases to minimize problems with errors.

Caution: *The Data Base has no validation capabilities.*

Categories containing numbers often have acceptable ranges. For example, if you enter people's ages, the age values will all be between 1 and 120. There are no negative age values and no 200-year-old people. For all practical purposes you can assume that acceptable values will have only one or two digits.

Some database managers permit you to enter limits for specific categories. In this case, if someone then tried to enter an age value of 142, it would not be accepted. The AppleWorks Data Base, however, does not permit you to define limits for categories. (As you will learn in Chapter 4, it is possible to write a limiting formula for Spreadsheet cells.)

Tip: *Set column widths to detect errors in data entry.*

You can enter critical data in multiple-record layout. The columns should be just wide enough to enter the largest number in the series. If a column of age values will be no wider than two digits, make the column two spaces wide. You will then be unable to enter three digits from left to right. Never worry about the column label—you can always widen it after the data has been entered.

The same general approach works for dollar values, ZIP codes, telephone numbers, two-letter state abbreviations, social security numbers, and many other kinds of label entries. They cannot be completely entered from left to right if there is insufficient room in a cell.

In some cases a one-digit error can create serious problems. For example, suppose a town's grand list of taxable property includes homes assessed at up to $280,000. An incorrect $2,800,000 entry will increase the grand list considerably, and taxes will therefore be apportioned incorrectly. The person who receives the wrong tax bill will get the mistake corrected, to be sure, but it is then too late to reapportion taxes.

These kinds of mistakes really do occur from time to time. With large values it also helps to use appropriate commas. The Data Base will accept comma entries, but then removes them from reports.

Tip: *Scan the multiple-record display for consistent patterns.*

Category entries can be right-justified in report formats, but they are left-justified in both record layouts. Whenever title widths permit, columns in the finished multiple-record display should be just wide enough to show the largest value or text entry with one empty character space on the right.

You may be surprised how easy it is to scan individual columns and detect errors. Correct each mistake as you find it, and look for the same kinds of mistakes to recur. This process of proof-reading and correcting will make you increasingly more accurate in data entry.

Tip: *The Data Base offers convenient forms of dates and times, which can also be entered from a clock.*

AppleWorks uses no precommitted category forms, so any category can be used for any kind of information. However, if you use the word DATE in a category name, AppleWorks enters the date in the form Sep   1 85, provided you enter a reasonable approximation of the date (such as 9.1.85). Note the gap between Sep and 1 in the AppleWorks form.

If you use the word TIME in a category name, AppleWorks enters the time in the form 7:00 AM, provided that you enter a reasonable approximation such as 7. In the USA versions of AppleWorks, every time value between 7 and 11:59 is assumed to be AM unless you specify otherwise by adding the letter P. Every time value between 12:00 and 6:59 is assumed to be PM unless you specify otherwise by adding the letter A.

If you use both DATE and TIME in a category name, DATE always takes precedence.

Applied Engineering offers software that enters dates and times directly from its clock card when you press @ in the respective DATE and TIME categories. These automated functions are useful where time records are important, as in shipping and receiving operations.

Tip: *Use two or more date categories to track updates.*

Few databases are built in a day, and almost none get updated all at once. Whenever you have available space, use a DATE1 category for the date of original entry and a DATE2 category to indicate the most recent update. This is another reason to use the automatic dating described in the previous tip.

You can select date records that contain just the month, such as Sep, or any consecutive part of a date. This can sometimes save time while entering selection rules. For years since 1932, there can be no confusion in the AppleWorks form between day of the month and year.

MERGING DATABASES

In many applications you will need to merge information from several different sources. This section provides tips for merging information from two similar or markedly different Data Base files. Surprisingly few AppleWorks users even know that this can be done.

Tip: *When you merge records from two different files, their original category orders must match.*

Focus all your attention on the original category orders. From the Review mode you can press Apple-N to see the original order. Print a copy of the category names screen of the source file, then load the destination file. Compare its category names screen with the hard copy you just printed.

Suppose both files have exactly the same original category order. To merge the information, follow these steps:

1. Change the names of the Desktop files, just to be safe. Name the files Origin and Destination.

2. Using multiple-record layout, copy the records in the Origin file to the clipboard, then from the clipboard to the Destination file.

3. Check the multiple-record layout in the Destination file to make certain that the category information is consistent.

Note that when information is transferred, the categories appear in the order of the Destination file's single- and multiple-record layouts. In the multiple-record layout, the category widths are those of the Destination file.

You can ignore the single- and multiple-record layouts of the Origin and Destination files until the final check. Even if they match, the original category orders may still differ. If their orders differ beforehand, the Destination file will evaluate everything in its original category order. Focus all your attention on the original category orders.

Tip: *Two Data Base files can be merged even if they have different numbers of categories.*

Decide what categories you need to transfer from the Origin file to the Destination file. For example, Table 3.4 compares the original category orders of the Everyone list (the Origin file) and the Members list (the Destination file). The categories are identical through the eighth category, PHONE. The remaining categories have no value to the Destination file, except for NOTE, which has information that belongs in the NOTES category in the Destination file.

You can proceed with the merge almost as in the last tip. Follow these steps:

1. Change the names of the Desktop files if you have not already done so. Name the files Origin and Destination.

2. Delete all Origin file categories after PHONE, except for NOTE. Don't worry about report formats, because you will never use this file again.

3. Insert five categories between PHONE and NOTE. Name them anything, and then return to the multiple-record layout.

4. Copy the records in the Origin file to the clipboard, then from the clipboard to the Destination file.

5. Check the multiple-record layout in the Destination file to make certain that the category information is consistent.

Note that all the records from the Origin file have gained the additional categories of the Destination file. However, the Origin file records have no information in those categories.

The rules for transferring are easy to remember. If the Origin file has more categories than the Destination file, the additional categories will be lost in the merge. If the Origin file has fewer categories, it will gain the additional categories of the Destination file, but they will contain no information.

Table 3.4: *Everyone list and Members list categories compared*

Origin File	Destination File
FIRST NAME	FIRST NAME
LAST NAME	LAST NAME
PLACE	PLACE
STREET	STREET
TOWN	TOWN
STATE	STATE
ZIP	ZIP
PHONE	PHONE
NOTE	COMMITTEE
CODE	YEARS
KEYWORD	1983
R1	1984
R2	1985
R3	NOTES
R4	RESERVED

Tip: *When the original category orders of two files do not match, print the records to an ASCII file.*

Suppose the Origin file categories begin with LAST NAME and the Destination file categories begin with FIRST NAME. This presents a problem. In this case, proceed as follows:

1. Create a labels-style report format for the Origin file in the original category order of the Destination file. Count and make a note of the number of categories in the report.

2. Select the records you want to print.

3. Print the report to an ASCII file.

4. Create a new Data Base file from the ASCII file. Enter the correct number of categories for the new file.

5. Using multiple-record layout, copy the records in the Origin file to the clipboard, then from the clipboard to the Destination file.

6. Check the multiple-record layout in the Destination file to make certain that the category information is consistent.

Tip: *Merge files to find duplicate entries.*

If you have ever received two copies of a form letter or mistakenly sent two copies to the same person, you will appreciate this technique. It saves postage, paper, and embarrassment.

Suppose you have two mailing lists on separate files. By merging the records, you can find and delete duplicate entries. Create a multiple-record layout with FIRST NAME, LAST NAME, STREET, STATE, ZIP, and PLACE in that order. Arrange the records alphabetically by first name, then by last name. Scan the LAST NAME column for duplicate entries. The street address column is the next best reference point.

If the files are too large to merge, merge sections at a time. When you find obvious duplication, you may find slightly different spellings. One spelling of a name may be more plausible than the other, but such corrections are often matters of judgment.

INVENTORY AND CITATION DATABASES

Most of us store parts that we think we will need later. The Data Base can track those parts, reminding us of what we have, what we need, where to find them, and how much they cost. Inventory applications vary widely, but most require extensive arranging, record selection, and calculation. This section gives an example of an inventory that belongs in the Data Base rather than the Spreadsheet.

Like inventories, citation databases are specialized lists that depend heavily on Data Base arranging and record selection. In this section we will look at an example that uses keyword retrieval techniques.

Tip: *Plan calculated categories carefully, because the Data Base gives you only three.*

When the arithmetic is simple and the requirements for record selection are extensive, the application probably belongs on the Data Base. However, you must plan within limitations: you get only three calculated categories, and each can take information only from a column to the left.

A project parts inventory is a good example of the kind of inventory the Data Base handles well. Suppose you want to build a greenhouse addition or plant a large vegetable garden. You have to know which tools, parts, and materials the project requires. You want to know what you need, what you have, what remains to be purchased, and what it will cost. In the budget planning report (Figure 3.33) you saw the results of calculated categories, column totals, and group totals. Here you will learn how to build a structurally similar application. Figure 3.34 shows a tables-style report for a project parts inventory. You can design this kind of table on a piece of scratch paper.

Note that you need to total only one category. Calculated categories are shown with lowercase letters in the headings. Two of the three calculated categories permitted are used. The first calculated category simply subtracts the number of each part you have on hand from the total number needed for the project. The second, Total $, multiplies the number of units left to buy by the unit dollar price. It also multiplies that product by 1.06 to include sales tax.

If you wanted to know the replacement value of parts on hand, you would require the third calculated category. Then you would not be able to combine the two totals. You can see how quickly the Data Base gives way to the Spreadsheet when calculations are needed.

Tip: *Use the group totals command for category subtotals and record counting.*

The group totals command (Apple-G) serves two different purposes. First, the group-total category controls subtotal locations for every other totaled category in a tables-style report. Whenever the category entry changes, the Data Base calculates a subtotal. It is therefore important to arrange by the group-total category before getting a report format.

In the greenhouse project inventory example, you can use the GROUP category to subdivide the project logically, each with its own subtotal, as in Figure 3.34. Notice that when the category entry changed from Finish to Framing, the Data Base entered a subtotal and skipped a line. Figure 3.35 shows the tables-style report format that created the subtotals. Notice the helpful reminder:

Group totals on: GROUP

You can equally well use group totals on the SUPPLIER category to generate shopping lists and estimated costs for each supplier. Here it would be most efficient to duplicate the existing tables-style report format and revise it.

If you use values instead of text, and if you also total a group-total category, the Data Base counts and totals the values in that category for each group and for the entire report. You can therefore reserve one category for a standard counting value of 1. Then, for example, 32 records in a group will produce a subtotal count of exactly 32.

The value of 1 can be used to identify only one group. However, you can differentiate among several groups by using counting values near 1 (such as 1.0001, 1.0002). If the category displays no decimal places, the count will always show a rounded number. It will then take 5,000 records for the counting value of 1.0001 to round up to 5001. Up to that point it serves the counting purpose well. Figure 3.36 shows a report controlled by counting values matched to suppliers, creating subtotals for each

```
File:   Greenhouse                                            Page  1
Report: Group
GROUP   PART                     UNIT   NEED HAVE Buy UNIT $ Total $ SUPPLIER
------  --------------------     ------ ---- ---- --- ------ ------- -----------
Finish  4'x8' sheetrock          sheet     5    1   4   6.89   29.21 Hart Lumber
Finish  3.5"x24" fiberglass      roll      2        2  14.80   31.38 Hart Lumber
Finish  Door                     one       1        1 139.50  147.87 Hart Lumber
Finish  6"x24" fiberglass        roll      1        1  15.20   16.11 Hart Lumber
Finish  2'x8'x1" EPS foam        sheet     6    1   5   4.85   25.70 West Supply
                                                               250.28

Frame   2"x4"x8' stud            one      26   10  16   1.84   31.21 West Supply
Frame   2"x4"x10' stud           one       8        8   2.12   17.98 West Supply
                                                                49.18

Other   16d common nails         lb.       2        2    .68    1.44 RB Hardware
Other   12d common nails         lb.      10    2   8    .62    5.26 RB Hardware
                                                                 6.70

Roof    Shingles                 bundle    2        2  11.20   23.74 Hart Lumber
Roof    6" flashing              foot     50       50    .16    8.48 RB Hardware
Roof    4'x8'x5/8" plywood       sheet     2        2  14.80   31.38 West Supply
                                                                63.60

                                                               369.76*
```

Figure 3.34: *Tables-style report for a greenhouse project*

```
File: Greenhouse              REPORT FORMAT            Escape: Report Menu
Report: Group
Selection: All records


Group totals on: GROUP
================================================================================
--> or <--  Move cursor                   @-J  Right justify this category
  >  @   <   Switch category positions     @-K  Define a calculated category
--> @  <--  Change column width           @-N  Change report name and/or title
@-A  Arrange (sort) on this category      @-O  Printer options
@-D  Delete this category                 @-P  Print the report
@-G  Add/remove group totals              @-R  Change record selection rules
@-I  Insert a prev. deleted category      @-T  Add/remove category totals
-------------------------------------------------------------------------------
GROUP   PART                     UNIT   NEED HAVE Buy UNIT $ Total $ SUPPLIER    L
-A----  -B------------------     -C----  -D--  -E--  -F-  -G----  -H-----  -I--------- e
Finish  4'x8' sheetrock          sheet  9999 9999 999 999.99 9999.99 Hart Lumber n
Finish  3.5"x24" fiberglass roll  one   9999 9999 999 999.99 9999.99 Hart Lumber 7
Finish  Door                     one    9999 9999 999 999.99 9999.99 Hart Lumber 5
                                                              =======
-------------------------------------------------------------------------------
Use options shown above to change report format            227K Avail.
```

Figure 3.35: *Report format used to generate Figure 3.34*

```
File:    Greenhouse                                              Page  1
Report: Supplier
GROUP    PART                  UNIT   NEED HAVE Buy UNIT $ Total $ SUPPLIER    R1
------   -------------------- ------ ---- ---- --- ------ ------- ------------ --
Finish 4'x8' sheetrock        sheet    5   1    4   6.89   29.21 Hart Lumber   1
Finish 3.5"x24" fiberglass    roll     2        2  14.80   31.38 Hart Lumber   1
Finish Door                   one      1        1 139.50  147.87 Hart Lumber   1
Finish 6"x24" fiberglass      roll     1        1  15.20   16.11 Hart Lumber   1
Roof   Shingles               bundle   2        2  11.20   23.74 Hart Lumber   1
                                                          248.32               5

Other  16d common nails       lb.      2        2    .68    1.44 RB Hardware   1
Other  12d common nails       lb.     10   2    8    .62    5.26 RB Hardware   1
Roof   6" flashing            foot    50       50    .16    8.48 RB Hardware   1
                                                           15.18               3

Finish 2'x8'x1" EPS foam      sheet    6   1    5   4.85   25.70 West Supply   1
Frame  2"x4"x8' stud          one     26  10   16   1.84   31.21 West Supply   1
Frame  2"x4"x10' stud         one      8        8   2.12   17.98 West Supply   1
Roof   4'x8'x5/8" plywood     sheet    2        2  14.80   31.38 West Supply   1
                                                          106.26               4

                                                          369.76*             12
```

Figure 3.36: *Counting values held in a reserved category*

supplier. Here, for example, each record with West Supply uses the counting value 1.0002.

Tip: *Citation databases are becoming essential tools in an increasing number of professions.*

Many of us own reference books and periodicals, but few of us buy everything we need. People in many professional fields depend on libraries and on-line information services. Databases can help you manage information, so that you can retrieve citations efficiently to find publications or generate bibliographies. For example, the bibliography in Appendix D came from a citation database.

Citation databases have long been essential tools for research, particularly in science, technology, and medicine. These databases are now being used in a steadily increasing number of professions. In fact, control of the literature has become so important that specialized database managers have been designed to download citations and abstracts from on-line information services, reformat the information, and generate bibliographies in any of several publication formats. The AppleWorks interface to one of these programs is discussed in Chapter 5.

Tip: *Citation databases inevitably generate bibliographies.*

It is therefore important to structure and punctuate the citation entries as you would for a bibliography. For example, the author's complete name goes in one category, last name first. The entry should end with a period.

By following specific conventions, you can convert a Data Base labels-style report to a Word Processor bibliography by using a surprising technique described in Chapter 5.

Other information in the citation record helps to generate carefully defined bibliographies. Specific entries for records can vary in multipurpose notes categories: some records include catalog numbers from a university library; others may include a publisher's mailing address.

Tip: *Design bibliographical files to handle both books and periodicals.*

What kinds of categories should you include in a bibliography? The answer depends on how you plan to use the bibliography. In a multipurpose database manager you cannot handle all the forms of citation found in Kate Turabian's *A Manual for Writers* (University of Chicago Press, 1973). Nor can you include all the descriptive keywords you might want for retrieval purposes. What follows is a description of one reasonable and practical compromise that considers data entry time, memory capacity, and the limits of patience.

AUTHOR: Always try to remember a publication by the last name of the author, not the title. The author's last name comes first, because bibliographies are alphabetized that way. If a publication has two authors, both should be listed, as shown in Figure 3.37. For three or more authors, use the first author's name followed by "et al" instead of the other names. For strict bibliographical purposes, middle initials should be included if they are given on the title page. Abbreviate editor as "ed." This category serves the same purpose for both books and articles.

TITLE: This category is for book titles, where all letters are capitalized or underlined. It serves equally well for titles of articles, printed in mixed-case lettering within quotes. Titles are supposed to define what the book or article is about, but not all titles do. For example, if a title in sociology alludes to Greek mythology, it tells us little about the content. A good title includes words that are keys for logical retrieval. In fact, keywords are so useful that they will be given an additional category all their own.

OTHER: This category handles the complications that often come after a book title. These complications are well documented in the Turabian book mentioned earlier. This is where you put such things as "2nd edition."

```
File:   Citations                                    Page  1
Report: File Cards
Selection: KEYWORDS contains /FINANCE
   or      KEYWORDS contains /GRAPHICS

Dooley, Thomas, and David Spiller.
FINANCIAL PLANNING IN TRANSIT.
Washington: U.S. Dept. of Transportation, 1983.

Flast, Robert.
54 VISICALC MODELS.
New York: Osborne/McGraw-Hill, 1983.

Tufte, Edward R.
THE VISUAL DISPLAY OF QUANTITATIVE INFORMATION.
Cheshire, CT: Graphics Press, 1983.




Press Space Bar to continue                    184K Avail.
```

Figure 3.37: *Bibliographical listing by author*

PUBLISHER: In the case of books, this is for the home city and name of the publisher. In the case of articles, it is for the name of the periodical (all letters capitalized or underlined). The NOTES category can be used for the address of book or magazine publishers, because they may be difficult to track down later. Always take information when you can get it.

YEAR: This is for the publication date. For books enter just the year. For articles enter the volume (in Roman numerals) and number, followed by the month and year of publication. The month and year alone will do in a pinch.

Never name this category DATE, nor anything with that sequence of letters in it. If a category contains the word *date*, you cannot enter just the month and year in the preferred form, because AppleWorks converts anything in a DATE category to its own date form. That means Jun 83 instead of (June 1983).

PAGES: This category is for articles only. Use the fewest numbers that clarify the information (for example, "pp. 123–6" rather than "pp. 123–126"). Consider the paging to be consecutive if the article is broken only by advertisements (for example, "pp. 123–4, 126" is unnecessary if page 125 is just an ad.) This is a made-up rule, but you will appreciate it if you enter articles from journals such as *Byte*.

KEYWORDS: This category can be used to include selected keywords in a series separated by slash marks. When the citation records include keywords, you can retrieve information more accurately. If the literature in your field has standard keywords, use them. Some journals include suggested keywords with the articles. Figure 3.38 shows a record with several keywords. You can use "good" as a short keyword substitute for excellent, and thereby search for the best entries associated with any keyword.

NOTES: As already mentioned, this category serves many purposes, and it deserves a full entry line of 76 characters.

CODE: Codes can store much information in a small space. For example, a code in the form A2 can serve two purposes. The letter can represent a subject time period, and the number can indicate a library where the title can be found. For example, the code D2 might indicate a book about 19th-century botany in a specific university library.

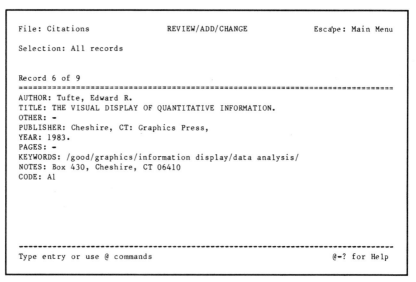

```
File: Citations              REVIEW/ADD/CHANGE          Esca'pe: Main Menu

Selection: All records


Record 6 of 9
================================================================================
AUTHOR: Tufte, Edward R.
TITLE: THE VISUAL DISPLAY OF QUANTITATIVE INFORMATION.
OTHER: -
PUBLISHER: Cheshire, CT: Graphics Press,
YEAR: 1983.
PAGES: -
KEYWORDS: /good/graphics/information display/data analysis/
NOTES: Box 430, Cheshire, CT 06410
CODE: A1




---------------------------------------------------------------------------
Type entry or use @ commands                              @-? for Help
```

Figure 3.38: *Citation record with keywords*

Caution: *You cannot underline selectively in Data Base reports, so think ahead about how to handle titles.*

AppleWorks has specific limitations. Underlining (Control-L in the Word Processor) is not available in the Data Base, so you may want to capitalize book and periodical titles in your bibliography. For thesis writing it would be better to enter titles in mixed-case lettering, then insert underlining marks in the Word Processor.

Tip: *Use keywords for information retrieval.*

Keyword searching depends on the descriptive value of the title and additional information in a KEYWORDS category. The fastest way to search is with the find command (Apple-F), but that checks all categories. As with any other Data Base application, record-selection rules are more specific.

For example, suppose you want to find information on spreadsheet templates in a file of citations. Finding all entries containing *spreadsheet* would also retrieve spreadsheet review articles. Using the "contains" record-selection rule for KEYWORDS can better define the search. Here you would request all records in which the KEYWORDS category contains *spreadsheet* and *template*.

Sometimes a keyword such as *ship* can also be contained in longer words, as in *apprenticeship* and *shipping*. You can specify the keyword as */ship/* with the preceding and trailing slash marks included. If you use this technique, the last entry in the KEY-WORD category must always be followed by a slash.

Tip: *Use consecutive categories for abstracts.*

An abstract is a precise summary of a publication. Sometimes the table of contents in a periodical will describe the contents of an article in one or two lines. Some journals specifically summarize dozens of publications in 200-to-500-word abstracts. This saves time for researchers tracking specific information.

You can write your own abstracts in citation records by reserving a number of 76-character lines. Name them A1, A2, and so on until you have enough room. There is no need to use every line for every record. For example, you may have a very limited and specific interest in an article. The abstract is for your own purposes and should reflect that fact.

SUMMARY

This chapter has reviewed a broad range of options and problems in the Data Base. You will find that you can use many of the tips and techniques repeatedly. As you understand more about the Data Base, you will be able to develop advanced applications more efficiently.

The next chapter will draw upon what you have learned in this chapter about printer options and the arranging command. You will continue to change file names, copy to the clipboard, and use AppleWorks commands for unexpected purposes. You will find more tips and techniques for building component parts that can be used again and again in many useful applications. In Chapter 5, some of those parts will be transferred back to the Word Processor and elsewhere.

4

The Spreadsheet

T he VisiCalc spreadsheet was the first program to make people understand that the Apple II could be used effectively in a broad range of professional applications. VisiCalc quickly became a standard Apple program. It is fitting that the AppleWorks Spreadsheet uses similar notation and reads most VisiCalc files. However, as you will see, the AppleWorks Spreadsheet encourages some unique approaches to applications design.

AppleWorks has fewer functions than standard VisiCalc: no trigonometric or logarithmic functions, no graphing capability, and fewer logic functions. Both allow you to set individual column widths (now that VisiCalc has been improved). The Spreadsheet has a useful sorting function that VisiCalc lacks, as well as 999 rows and 127 columns for larger worksheets. The AppleWorks Spreadsheet is much faster than VisiCalc when loading data, recalculating, and accepting data entries.

The AppleWorks Spreadsheet has several unusual features, including some difficult sequences for setting manual recalculation and changing column widths. The Spreadsheet does not have a function to convert formula results to pure value entries, and it cannot read all VisiCalc files. The Spreadsheet creates binary files that VisiCalc cannot read. Thus only Spreadsheet DIF files can be loaded into VisiCalc.

One of the Spreadsheet's greatest strengths is its file transfer capability. Experienced users can quickly copy formulas from other sources. This capability makes it possible to overlook how difficult it can sometimes be to construct formulas from such a limited number of functions.

You can build self-contained components in a PARTS file, copy them to the clipboard, move them into another worksheet, and fit them into a larger system. No other spreadsheet for the Apple can match this building-block facility. This program has been vastly underestimated, by Apple as much as by anyone.

This chapter provides tips in thirteen sections. It begins with the most generally useful tips for anyone using the Spreadsheet. A section on creating budgets includes useful information on designing worksheets for multiple purposes. The next two sections include tips that review worksheet recalculation and the available math functions. You should particularly note the functions that work in two different ways. The section on available printer options includes important information on managing worksheet width.

Spreadsheet applications require much attention to design. This chapter includes sections on designing and developing Spreadsheet templates. The tips in the following sections cover logical, financial, and other Spreadsheet functions. In each of these sections, small templates are provided to illustrate some of the special capabilities of AppleWorks. The next section outlines graphics options, including an important relationship to SuperCalc 3a. The following section examines the rules for transferring VisiCalc and DIF files to the Spreadsheet. Finally, the last section reviews techniques for using the Spreadsheet as a specialized database manager. All this taken together should make the Spreadsheet easier to use for large applications.

GENERAL SPREADSHEET TIPS

The tips that follow apply throughout the Spreadsheet. The Spreadsheet requires attention to detail, and you should pay special attention to the tip on documenting everything you do.

Tip: *Print and annotate hard copies of the Spreadsheet menus.*

You will need a hard copy of the Spreadsheet menu and the Spreadsheet Printer Options menu, as well as menus for the Apple-L, Apple-P, and Apple-V commands. If you have not yet done so, print copies of all these screens using Apple-H, and post the copies on a note board near your Apple. Pencil in notes about when you use each option. A hard copy of the Spreadsheet menu appears in Figure 4.1.

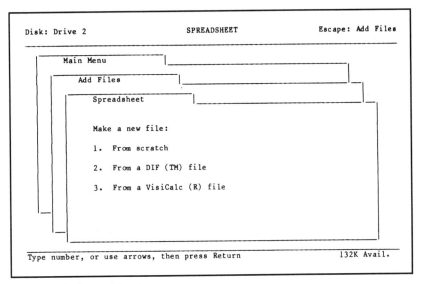

Figure 4.1: *Spreadsheet menu*

Tip: *No matter how you save a Spreadsheet file, it loads in a predictable way.*

No matter how you save a Spreadsheet file, the cursor always reappears where you left it, and in the normal display mode (rather than formula display mode). On the Desktop, the cursor also remains where you left it, and the display mode remains unchanged.

Note that the cursor location in the Spreadsheet differs from the convention used in the Word Processor and Data Base. In those programs the cursor returns to the beginning of the file when you reload the file.

Tip: *Use lowercase letters in worksheet titles and formula entries.*

When VisiCalc was first developed, the Apple II had only uppercase letters. Many of the printed templates for worksheets were therefore written entirely in capitals, but using both cases makes titles easier to read. The titles can always be set off with row borders made of repeated dashes or equal signs.

Formula entries accept lowercase letters. When the formula has been completed and entered, lowercase letters automatically convert to uppercase. However, if you have experience with VisiCalc, you may prefer to depress the Caps Lock key when writing formulas.

Tip: *Once you change the name of a Spreadsheet file that has been saved, you can do almost anything with it.*

This is an important tip, and the concept will be adapted for specific purposes throughout this chapter. Once a file is saved to primary and backup disks, you can change the name on the Desktop and make as many changes as you want without the risk of damaging the previously saved files. You can copy, delete, replace, and rearrange data for any purpose. If you make a serious mistake, simply remove the file from the Desktop, load the original file again, and change its name on the Desktop once more.

Tip: *Microprocessor cards can make the Spreadsheet recalculate faster on the Apple IIe.*

Several firms offer accelerator cards that use high-speed versions of the 65CO2 microprocessor used in the Apple IIc and Enhanced Apple IIe. The processor on the card takes over from the motherboard processor, recalculating the Spreadsheet in less than half the normal time. If you use very large models with a high percentage of formula cells (as opposed to data cells), consider using such a card. It can also arrange Data Base records in less than half the normal time.

The AppleWorks programs were developed with limited functions so that they consume minimal memory and maximize their operating speed within the limits of an Apple II. As newer and faster microprocessors appear for the Apple II series, Apple will have to consider expanding AppleWorks to take advantage of the capabilities of the new microprocessors.

Tip: *Spreadsheet design can be done with pencil and paper.*

When two or more people use the same Apple, there will be times when one person wants to use AppleWorks and cannot. That is a good time to start working with pencil and paper. For example, you can design worksheets using a grid form printed by the Spreadsheet itself. You can often design formulas on paper more efficiently than on screen. You can do preliminary calculations on the back of an envelope with an inexpensive scientific calculator. Use hard copies of related worksheets. Use a hard copy of the Printer Options menu that shows all the default values, as shown in Figure 4.2. Pencil in proposed changes for a specific report.

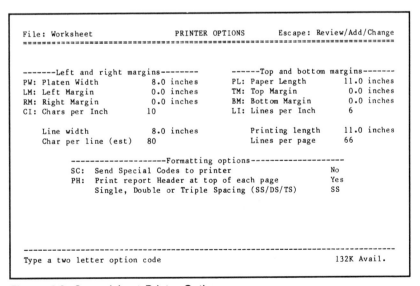

```
File: Worksheet              PRINTER OPTIONS      Escape: Review/Add/Change
==============================================================================


-------Left and right margins-------      ------Top and bottom margins------
PW: Platen Width            8.0 inches     PL: Paper Length          11.0 inches
LM: Left Margin             0.0 inches     TM: Top Margin             0.0 inches
RM: Right Margin            0.0 inches     BM: Bottom Margin          0.0 inches
CI: Chars per Inch          10             LI: Lines per Inch         6

    Line width              8.0 inches         Printing length       11.0 inches
    Char per line (est)     80                 Lines per page         66

            ------------------Formatting options------------------
        SC:  Send Special Codes to printer                    No
        PH:  Print report Header at top of each page          Yes
             Single, Double or Triple Spacing (SS/DS/TS)      SS




-------------------------------------------------------------------------
Type a two letter option code                                132K Avail.
```

Figure 4.2: Spreadsheet Printer Options menu

Tip: *Document all your work.*

When you write a report on the Word Processor, you rarely need directions when you load it again several weeks later. When you develop a Spreadsheet template, you may get lost later unless you have written yourself some directions.

The documentation you write should explain why you developed the application. It should include step-by-step instructions on how to load and use the Spreadsheet file. It should note any problems encountered with the data. It should include hard copies of important screens: key formulas, input values, and report formats along with their respective printer option settings.

Every application should have its own manila file folder or something functionally equivalent. Print a report with key formulas and all data used in the template.

Tip: *Save your work to disk at least every 20 minutes.*

Press Apple-S at least every 20 minutes to save what you have entered. Save it to a backup disk as well on every second or third save. You may want to save a file even more often if you happen to be writing difficult formulas.

PLANNING BUDGETS

If letters are the most common Word Processor files, budgets are probably the most common Spreadsheet files. The tips in this section will help you to construct a budget template. From this starting point, you can use copying techniques to create more complex budget applications. The budget example in Figure 4.3 will provide a reference point for many tips in this chapter. Turn to this figure whenever necessary.

```
File: Apple.Budget          REVIEW/ADD/CHANGE              Escape: Main Menu
=========A=========B========C========D========E=======F========G========H====
 1|Apple IIe System                                      6%
 2|                                         Base        Sales
 3|Item                        Code    Cost Shipping     Tax    Total
 4|  -------------------------------------------------------------------
 5|80-column 64K card            1    149.95    3.00    0.00    152.95
 6|Two disk drives               2    359.90    8.00    0.00    367.90
 7|Control card                  3     49.00    2.00    0.00     51.00
 8|Dot matrix printer            4    359.95   20.00    0.00    359.95
 9|Buffered printer card         5    159.95    0.00    9.60    169.55
10|Monochrome monitor            6     90.00    8.00    0.00     98.00
11|  -------------------------------------------------------------------
12|Totals                            1168.75   41.00    9.60   1199.35
13|
14|                                                            1219.35
15|
16|
17|
18|
  --------------------------------------------------------------------------
G8: (Value, Layout-F2) +D8+F8

Type entry or use @ commands                              @-? for Help
```

Figure 4.3: *Budget worksheet template*

Tip: *When you teach others about the Spreadsheet, teach them first about structure.*

Worksheet rows are horizontal and numbered; columns are vertical and lettered. A cell is described by its column letter and row number, such as B4. Cells can contain values (12, −1.23, 3.14159) or labels (Cost, 1984 Losses, ------, Totals). Note that numerals can be used in labels or as labels by themselves. Just start the entry with a quotation mark (") so the Spreadsheet will recognize it as a label. (The quotation mark does not appear in the cell.) You must also use the quotation mark to enter a border of dashes (------) that would otherwise be interpreted as minus signs.

Tip: *Think about how your budget would look on paper, because it will look about the same on the Spreadsheet.*

You can transfer many useful applications from paper to worksheets almost directly. That goes for most budgets, like the sample budget worksheet shown in Figure 4.3. This budget supposes that a library association has received a classic 1983 Apple IIe, the kind with white key lettering. We need a budget for completing the system to use with AppleWorks. We have six lines of information to enter, and the number we ultimately care about will be on the bottom line in cell G12. (Notice that items shipped from out of state are not subject to sales tax.)

The budget would look the same on paper, with the exception of the Code heading for column C. This column is for arranging the rows in the worksheet back into their original order once they have been sorted according to another criterion. Arranging is a process that is difficult to do on paper but simple on a computer.

Tip: *Follow common practice in using dividing borders.*

Type in a dividing border of dashes (remember to begin by typing a quotation mark). The common practice is to enter a border in the row just below the column heading and another in the row just above the totals row. Some people use the equal sign to make borders in other places. For example, if two or more different templates appear in the same file, an equal-sign border is commonly used to separate them.

Tip: *Make just one border, then copy it to other rows.*

When you enter row borders across an entire screen, you have to do it in two sections because a repeating label accepts only 69 characters. The most efficient way to copy label rows is to and from the clipboard.

Tip: *Use code numbers to arrange rows back to their original order.*

The column of code numbers in Figure 4.3 can be used to arrange the rows back to their original order after they have been rearranged for some other purpose. You will sometimes list items in a logical order that AppleWorks cannot appreciate; in such cases you should also enter an original-order code. In Figure 4.3, related peripherals are grouped together. AppleWorks cannot appreciate this order, but it understands the ascending values used in the Code column.

A unique code or identification number for each record can make that record unique. As you may remember from Chapter 3, this is also a key to predicting arranged order in records.

RECALCULATING WORKSHEETS

Like most spreadsheets, the AppleWorks Spreadsheet offers the option for manual recalculation. After you choose this option, use Apple-K to recalculate (not the exclamation mark used in other spreadsheets). This section includes several tips and a caution for using Apple-K more efficiently.

Tip: *Use manual recalculation most of the time.*

Whenever you enter new values, the Spreadsheet automatically recalculates your worksheet. This may be helpful when you first start work on a template, but it eventually takes more time than it is worth. When you get impatient, set manual recalculation.

Tip: *Know when to use row calculation order.*

Most worksheets can be calculated in either column or row order. Column order is the default; you must specify row order when you want it. Look first at the calculation process. If any cell formula depends on a calculated cell above and to the right, use row order. If any cell formula depends on a calculated cell below and to the left, use column order. You cannot normally have both dependency cases in the same worksheet.

When order makes no difference in the calculation process, look at the shape of the template. If it has many calculated columns and few rows, use the row order of calculation, because it is slightly faster with that shape. If the template is long and narrow, use column order.

Tip: *The manual recalculation setting stays with the file.*

Once you select manual recalculation, that selection (or "standard value") stays with the file, just as it does in VisiCalc. Therefore, when you save the worksheet as a Spreadsheet file, it will return with the manual recalculation selection when you load it again. This is not true of all spreadsheet programs. In Multiplan, for example, the manual recalculation selection remains independent of a file and must be chosen each time you use the file.

Caution: *If the Spreadsheet has been set for manual recalculation, it will not automatically recalculate when saved.*

VisiCalc and Multiplan both automatically recalculate worksheets when they are saved, even under the manual recalculation setting. The AppleWorks Spreadsheet is consistent: it does not recalculate. This provides more flexibility and requires greater responsibility on your part.

Tip: *It is almost always a good idea to recalculate a worksheet before saving it as a Spreadsheet file.*

There are several good and bad consequences of having a Spreadsheet that does not automatically recalculate when you save it. For example, you might want to save a worksheet quickly just before going to lunch, knowing that you will soon get back to it. You can save it faster without recalculating. On the other hand, if something comes up and you cannot get back to it for another week, there is some chance that you will print out an incorrect report. It is therefore generally prudent to recalculate before saving.

MATH FUNCTIONS AND FORMULAS

If you can write formulas correctly, you can design and build a broad range of useful applications templates. This is where you have the most control over AppleWorks. Many people find spreadsheet design challenging and satisfying.

You will no doubt be surprised by some of the math functions available. Pay special attention to the tips for series calculations.

Tip: *Although a formula is limited to 69 characters as originally entered, you can add up to nine more by editing.*

AppleWorks is considerably more restrictive than other spreadsheets in formula length limitations. You will probably reach the 69-character limit from time to time. By going back to edit with Apple-U, you can add up to nine more characters to a formula. This may save you from having to continue the formula to another cell. Continued formulas can sometimes be difficult to interpret.

Tip: *Use @SUM to add continuing series, and mark the series with the cursor.*

In the budget example (Figure 4.3) the total cost for a given component is base cost plus the shipping plus the sales tax. For row 5, this can be written as

+ D5 + E5 + F5

meaning "the contents of cell D5 plus cell E5 plus cell F5." This kind of formula can be tedious, and if you begin a formula with a cell name and forget the + before the cell, you get an unwanted label.

And how do you total column G for a result in G12? You could write the formula +G5+G6 . . . , but that would be even more tedious. The Spreadsheet has a summation function that allows you to write

@SUM(G5. . .G10)

This means "sum (or add up) the series beginning with G5 and ending with G10." Named functions in the Spreadsheet all begin with the at symbol (@).

With the @SUM function, you can use the cursor to mark the beginning and ending cells of a series. To do so, follow these steps:

1. Move the cursor to the cell that will contain the formula.

2. Enter @SUM(in the cell.

3. Move the cursor to G5, the beginning cell in the series.

4. Enter . . . (three periods) in the cell. The cursor moves back to the formula cell.

5. Move the cursor to G10, the ending cell in the series.

6. Press) and the formula is complete.

By convention, the beginning cell is the left-most cell in a series, or the cell nearest row 1.

Tip: *Include border rows in summation formulas.*

In the budget example (Figure 4.3) you can write @SUM(G4 . . .G11) to avoid a pitfall. You include border rows that have no effect on the calculation, because someone else may later want to arrange (sort) rows 5 through 10 in ascending order of total cost. The value $152.95 and the rest of row 5 would end up in row 7. The value $98.00 and the rest of row 10 would end up in row 6. The formula @SUM(G5. . .G10) would then become @SUM(G7. . .G6). With the border rows included in the formula that cannot happen, because those rows are not being rearranged.

The border rows provide similar protection when you insert, delete, or move rows.

Tip: *Use empty columns one character wide to provide protection for row totals and related operations.*

In template design it is common to move certain columns several times while trying to decide how a report should look. By setting a border column one character wide, you can prevent unwanted changes to formulas for row totals.

Relatively few people have learned to do this, because until recently the standard VisiCalc program lacked the option to specify the width of an individual column. All columns had to have the same number of character spaces. With the ability to create one narrow column, the protection is easy to include and does not clutter the worksheet.

Caution: *The @AVG function works two different ways, depending on the formula structure used.*

Although @AVG(E1. . .E3) will ignore an empty cell at E3, the formula @AVG(E1+E2+E3) will count the empty cell. The two formulas will therefore produce two different averages. The same discrepancy holds for formulas using @COUNT, @MIN, and @MAX. For example, in the formula @MAX-(E1,E2,E3) an empty cell is the maximum value if the other two cells contain negative values.

Tip: *Use the exponentiation function to its limits.*

Exponentiation uses the caret (^) mark. The Reference Manual makes little reference to this function, but it has great range. To begin with the simplest form, 3^2 is 3 squared, or 9. The power can be represented as a value in another cell, as with 23^{B5}. If B5 contains no value, the power 0 is assumed, and the resulting value is 1.

The exponent can also be a decimal fraction, as in $3^{.5}$, an alternative to @SQRT(3) that saves four character spaces. For calculation, however, using the @SQRT function is several times faster than using the exponentiation formula.

Caution: *The Spreadsheet uses left-to-right order of operations, not the algebraic order of operations used in BASIC.*

Consider the difference between the two orders of operation. Suppose you want to evaluate $(4+A1)*(6+3)$. If $A1 = 3$, the formula is the same as 7*9. In the Spreadsheet and VisiCalc you can get the correct result, 63, by writing $4+A1*(6+3)$. In an algebraic calculator, such a formula would be interpreted as $4+27$, or 31.

Multiplan uses the algebraic order of operations. SuperCalc 3a uses left-to-right order. You can use enough parentheses in the Spreadsheet so everyone can understand the formulas. Many serious users always write formulas with parentheses throughout. Extra parentheses require more memory and take more time for recalculation, but in this case the differences are less than five percent, barely a matter of principle.

Tip: *Use parentheses consistently for documentation purposes.*

Whether you use extra parentheses or the minimum required, do it consistently. Someone else may have to review your work.

Although most people can interpret minimal left-to-right notation, formulas with extra parentheses are easier to follow. It is very difficult to review formulas that use inconsistent notation.

Tip: *Relative formula references are more common than "no change" references.*

Return again to Figure 4.3 and note cell G5. Recall that the formula for that cell was + D5 + E5 + F5. Suppose you want to copy the formula in G5 to cells G6 through G10. When you copy formulas, you will see a message asking whether there is "no change" in D5 or whether it is "relative." Press Return three times to indicate that all three cells are relative references.

You are saying, in effect, "Make the formula relate to the row it will be in. Use a D6 in the copy of the formula meant for row 6, not a D5." Most references in spreadsheets are relative. (A "no change" example appears later in this section.)

Tip: *Use RN notation to document formula design.*

Sometimes formulas must make absolute references to a value in one cell. For example, an interest rate used throughout a worksheet may be located in cell B6. Every formula that includes the interest rate must reference B6.

Because formulas can contain both relative and absolute references, it's helpful to use some kind of notation to keep track of which references are relative and which are absolute. When you copy formulas down columns, use a notation somewhere in the column to denote whether the cell references in the formula are relative (R) or absolute (N for no change). You can make the notation when you write the first formula. The notation belongs in a cell that will not be printed in reports. Figure 4.4 shows the notation below cell G12 in the budget template. When you copy formulas across rows, use a notation somewhere in the row, again in a cell that will not be printed.

```
File: Apple.Budget          REVIEW/ADD/CHANGE              Escape: Main Menu
==========A==========B========C========D========E========F========G=======H====
  1|Apple IIe System                                    6%
  2|                                          Base     Sales
  3|Item                             Code     Cost Shipping    Tax    Total
  4| -------------------------------------------------------------------
  5|80-column 64K card                 1    149.95     3.00    0.00   152.95
  6|Two disk drives                    2    359.90     8.00    0.00   367.90
  7|Control card                       3     49.00     2.00    0.00    51.00
  8|Dot matrix printer                 4    359.95    20.00    0.00   379.95
  9|Buffered printer card              5    159.95     0.00    9.60   169.55
 10|Monochrome monitor                 6     90.00     8.00    0.00    98.00
 11| -------------------------------------------------------------------
 12|Totals                                                           1219.35
 13|
 14|                                                                  RRR
 15|
 16|
 17|
 18|
------------------------------------------------------------------------------
G14: (Label, Layout-R) RRR

Type entry or use @ commands                                    @-? for Help
```

Figure 4.4: *RN notation in the budget template*

Tip: *You can copy formulas in any direction.*

In Figure 4.3, the appropriate formula for cell G12 is

@SUM(G4. . .G11)

Try copying the formula in G12 to cells F12 through D12. That sounds backwards, but it works. There will be many times when you can save time by copying from right to left, or bottom to top.

Caution: *Spreadsheet rows have undocumented capacity limits for formulas.*

Although 127 values can fit in one row, 127 summation formulas cannot. For example, if you attempt to copy a formula from cell A1 through cell CZ1, you will probably get an unexpected warning that some cells were lost. Figure 4.5 shows the error message. It means the requested copying could not go as far as you specified.

Whenever this happens, follow the row until you find the last column to which the formula was copied. Blank the last copied cell, move the cursor down one row, and continue with an appropriate revision of the original formula. If you save the worksheet shown in Figure 4.5 without blanking the last copied cell, AppleWorks cannot load the file again. Instead, you will see the error message in Figure 4.6.

Table 4.1 lists simple formulas, along with the last cell to which they can be copied from column A.

Tip: *The arithmetic operations in AppleWorks are generally accurate to at least 14 places.*

This accuracy means that trigonometric functions generated with Taylor series calculations can actually be more accurate on the AppleWorks Spreadsheet than on other spreadsheets. There are more tips on series calculations later in this chapter.

Although the Spreadsheet lacks scientific notation, precise values can be stored as multiples of ten to a specified power.

```
File: ROW.LIMITS                    COPY            Escape: Review/Add/Change
========A========B========C========D========E========F========G========H====
  1|     256
  2|
  3|
  4|      16
  5|
  6|
  7|
  8|         When you press the Space Bar, AppleWorks will insert the
  9|         copied formulas as far as they go, in this case to cell CH4.
 10|
 11|
 12|
 13|
 14|
 15|
 16|
 17|
 18|
---------------------- Some cells were lost from row 4 ----------------------
A4: (Value) @SQRT(A1)
@SQRT(A1)
Press Space Bar to continue                                    84K Avail.
```

Figure 4.5: *Error message for formula copying*

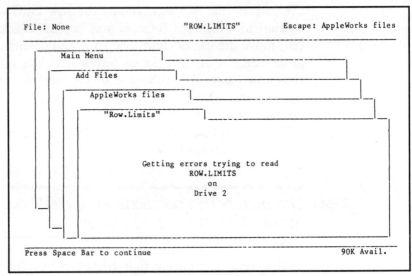

```
File: None                    "ROW.LIMITS"        Escape: AppleWorks files

    Main Menu           |_____
      Add Files         |_____|_|
        AppleWorks files |_____|_|
          "Row.Limits"         |_____|_|



                    Getting errors trying to read
                              ROW.LIMITS
                                 on
                              Drive 2




Press  Space  Bar  to  continue                      90K  Avail.
```

Figure 4.6: Error message for inaccessible file

Table 4.1: Sample formulas with copying limits

Formula	Last Column through Which Formula Can Be Copied
1 + A1	BI
+ A1 + 1	BG
@SQRT(A1)	CH
+ A1 ^.5	BG
@IF(A1 > 0,324,0)	AF
@NPV(.12,A1. . .C1)	AT
@SUM(A1. . .A11)	BO

PRINTER OPTIONS

If you have mastered Word Processor printing, you are well prepared to work with the lesser number of Spreadsheet printer options. There are a few important differences worth noting. In the Spreadsheet you are generally most concerned with fitting all the needed columns onto the paper. The Spreadsheet also takes a slightly different approach to page headers, more like that in the Data Base program.

Caution: *The Spreadsheet lacks some useful printer options found in the Word Processor.*

Table 4.2 shows which Word Processor printer options are also found in the Data Base and Spreadsheet. Each has other specialized options. The Data Base and Spreadsheet have the option to enter special codes for the printer. This option is primarily useful for changing form lengths and print densities. It can be used to

---

Table 4.2: *Printer options*

Option	WP	DB	SS
Line Length, Print Density			
Platen width	X	X	X
Left margin	X	X	X
Right margin	X	X	X
Characters per inch	X	X	X
Proportional-1	X		
Proportional-2	X		
Text Positioning			
Indent	X		
Justified	X	X	X
Unjustified	X	X	X
Centered	X		X
Page Length, Line Density			
Paper length	X	X	X
Top margin	X	X	X

Table 4.2: *Printer options (continued)*

Option	WP	DB	SS
Page Length, Line Density			
Bottom margin	X	X	X
Lines per inch	X	X	X
Single space	X	X	X
Double space	X	X	X
Triple space	X	X	X
Page Controls			
New page	X		
Group markers	X		
Page Calculation			
Page header	X	X	X
Page footer	X		
Skip lines	X		
Page number	X		
Place Markers			
Pause each page	X		
Pause here	X		
Set a marker	X		
Print Enhancements			
Boldface	X		
Superscript	X		
Subscript	X		
Underline	X		
Variable Text Entry			
Print page number	X		
Enter keyboard	X		

begin boldfacing or underlining but cannot turn them off. Thus, you cannot boldface or underline selectively in the Spreadsheet.

When you design Spreadsheet applications, think about these limitations at the beginning. It may be necessary to print reports to the clipboard for further editing in the Word Processor. For more on this subject, see Chapter 5.

Tip: *Use small margins in standard template files.*

Provide just enough space for a small margin, something like 0.5 inches as a standard setting. Use no margin on the right. If the printer has an eight-inch platen width, you will often be faced with a tight fit. You may even need to set a 0-inch left margin and shift the paper to the left to use all of the available platen.

Tip: *Pay special attention to the estimate of characters per line.*

This estimate is almost always the critical measurement in printing worksheets. If the number of characters you want to print is greater than the number of characters the printer can physically fit between the margins, the printer will wrap the line onto a second line, and you have another sheet of paper for the recycling bin.

After setting the printer options, press Escape to return to the document. Press Apple-P to print. Note the options. "All" means the block bounded by cell A1, the last row with something in it, and the right-most column with anything in it. Use the "block" option whenever you are uncertain about dimensions, and outline the block by moving the cursor. Note how quickly Apple-9 highlights vertical space.

Press Return, then select the printer. This is the moment of truth when you find out if the number of characters you want to print is more than the printer can physically fit on its line. If you ever need to bail out at this point, simply press Escape and go back to widen the platen width, specify more characters per inch, or define a block with fewer columns.

Figure 4.7 shows the message you will get before you print a worksheet block that is too wide for the printer. In this case you should bail out.

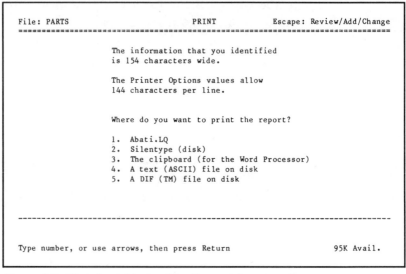

```
File: PARTS                      PRINT           Escape: Review/Add/Change
===========================================================================

                    The information that you identified
                    is 154 characters wide.

                    The Printer Options values allow
                    144 characters per line.


                    Where do you want to print the report?

                    1.  Abati.LQ
                    2.  Silentype (disk)
                    3.  The clipboard (for the Word Processor)
                    4.  A text (ASCII) file on disk
                    5.  A DIF (TM) file on disk



         ------------------------------------------------------------------


Type number, or use arrows, then press Return                95K Avail.
```

Figure 4.7: *Worksheet block wider than printer capacity*

Caution: *When you print a header, check the platen width first.*

This caution applies to printers with platen widths of more than eight inches. After printer selection, note that you have the option to enter a date. It is normally printed in the upper-right corner of the page, under the page number. However, both the date and page number will be at the far right of the platen setting, which may be beyond the right edge of the paper.

If you are using 8½-inch paper in a wide carriage, the print head can move beyond the paper, print on the roller, and rip into the paper on the return pass. Be certain to check the platen width setting first.

DESIGNING TEMPLATES

Good planning and design can save considerable time in the building and use of templates. By designing interchangeable parts you can build Spreadsheet templates efficiently. It is also always a good idea to audit your own work, particularly in the design of spreadsheet applications. This section covers many design details and several cautions about designing templates to minimize problems with errors.

Tip: *Learn to design and build templates yourself.*

You can buy ready-made templates on disk, and they have a place, but it is much easier to modify and maintain a template when you have assembled the component parts yourself. It takes relatively little time to learn efficient worksheet design, and AppleWorks makes it easy to use a building-block development strategy.

Experienced spreadsheet users do purchase templates on disk when those templates include significant amounts of entered data that they need. They may also purchase templates to see how a competent specialist approaches a difficult problem in some substantive field. Such templates tend to have complicated formulas and structures.

Tip: *For the most appropriate applications templates, consult sources in your own field.*

Journals and other reference sources in your own field can provide information on preferred calculation methods and reporting formats for specific applications. In some professional journals you can now find printouts of Lotus and VisiCalc spreadsheet templates. More often, you will find a manual calculation method that can be converted as it appears on paper. Most applications developers simply need to see one common example of the way things are done. They can then write the appropriate spreadsheet formulas for almost any example.

Tip: *Write templates based on common examples you understand.*

The most useful kind of template is really just a worked example, preferably a common example that you thoroughly understand. To reuse this kind of template, you replace the existing information with new information.

Tip: *Read VisiCalc and Lotus template examples.*

Many good template articles have been written for VisiCalc. VisiCalc notation remains widely used because so many other spreadsheets have followed its conventions. Many user groups offer templates at minimal cost, and you can develop a good utility collection this way.

Many good template articles have been written for Lotus software. Symphony and 1-2-3 use notation similar to that of the AppleWorks Spreadsheet. Following are a few hints on how to make sense of the differences.

Ignore the macro instructions, because AppleWorks has no macro facility. If a function looks completely different, there probably is no equivalent in AppleWorks. For example, @ROUND is a Lotus function that takes the place of a rounding formula described in this chapter. On the other hand, @V,LOOKUP,1 looks something like @LOOKUP in AppleWorks. In Lotus notation you must specify whether the lookup table is vertical or horizontal. The 1 means that the second row in the table is one column farther away than it would be in AppleWorks. If the offset is 0, as in AppleWorks, you would simply see @V,LOOKUP.

You can often understand the gist of an application without reading the details of every formula. Look for the key formulas and highlight them with a yellow marker.

Tip: *Give yourself plenty of time in the design stage.*

Most spreadsheet applications require considerable thought in the design stage. What data do you really need? Where are you going to find the data? Remember that collecting information is usually the most time-consuming part of any application. Time spent in the design stage saves far more time later.

Tip: *Spreadsheet reports should include all assumptions.*

An assumption is a variable that is taken for granted. For example, you can assume that interest rates will remain at 10 percent throughout the life of a construction project. The Spreadsheet model may just include .10 in every relevant formula, with no provision to enter another variable except by editing each formula. Interest rates are almost never built in as assumptions.

Whenever there is a potential for disagreement about an assumption, make a provision to enter it as a variable along with other input data. When you do build in assumptions, make it easy for others to find the assumptions on which the calculations were based. It is surprising how many people either forget or neglect to do this.

If you read spreadsheet reports from other people, consider all of the assumptions carefully: they are probably wrong more often than the actual calculations.

Tip: *Move the work area around to make concise reports.*

Sometimes a necessary work area will separate the input data from the results. It is generally not a good idea to clutter a report with unnecessary information and intermediate results.

What do you do with an intrusive work area? In models calculated by columns, you can drop the working formulas and intermediate results far down into lower rows by inserting rows. The formula references will be automatically adjusted.

If you make the work-area columns one or two characters wide, they will virtually disappear. The distance between input data and results in the report will then be minimal. You can find the formula cells by looking for the pound sign (#), which simply indicates that the columns are too narrow to display the values.

Figures 4.8 and 4.9 provide a simple example of how the technique works. In many cases the work area will be more than 10 columns wide.

In models calculated by rows, you can move the working formulas and intermediate results to the right into other columns.

Caution: *Value entries can only be right-justified, and some formats have no buffer space to the right.*

In the Spreadsheet most right-justified values really are right-justified, without the one-character buffer space found in VisiCalc and Multiplan. Therefore, there is no space between those values and flush-left labels in the next column to the right. To make the worksheet readable, you should begin each label entry with a space or insert a buffer column one space wide.

Caution: *Value entries in the dollar and comma formats do include the buffer space to the right.*

Financial reports generally use comma or dollar formats. These formats are identical except for the dollar sign. The buffer space is needed for closed parentheses that designate negative values (other formats simply use the minus sign). If you use dollar or comma formats in the same column with other value formats, the column will appear ragged on the right. Pay special attention to choices when you format value cells by blocks: use comma formats consistently within columns. Figure 4.10 shows differences in value formats.

Tip: *There are three kinds of dates appropriate to Apple-Works, and each has a particular advantage.*

The form 10/23/84 is used to set dates for ProDOS files. In the Data Base, this form is automatically converted to the form

```
File: TRIG.A                    REVIEW/ADD/CHANGE              Escape: Main Menu
========A=======B=========C=========D========E========F========G========H====
 1|
 2|        Enter             Sine
 3|        Degrees           Result
 4|        in B8             in D8
 5|
 6|        Degrees           Sine
 7|        ---------------------------
 8|           72              .9510565
 9|                   1.2566371
10|                    .9510568
11|                   -.0000003
12|        ---------------------------
13|
14|
15|
16|
17|
18|
--------------------------------------------------------------------------------
C9: (Value, Layout-A0) +B8/57.29578

Type entry or use @ commands                              @-? for Help
```

Figure 4.8: Exposed work area

```
File: TRIG.A                         LAYOUT           Escape: Review/Add/Change
========A=======B===C=====D=========E========F========G========H========I====
 1|
 2|        Enter    Sine
 3|        Degrees  Result
 4|        in B8    in D8
 5|
 6|        Degrees  Sine
 7|        -------------------
 8|           72    .9510565
 9|
10|
11|
12|
13|
14|
15|
16|             ##
17|             ##
18|             ##
--------------------------------------------------------------------------------
C16: (Value, Layout-F2) +B8/57.29578

Press @ and arrows to change column widths                142K Avail.
```

Figure 4.9: Hidden work area

```
File: Formats                   REVIEW/ADD/CHANGE              Escape: Main Menu
========A=========B======C=====D=========E========F=========G========H====
 1|
 2|                  Value  Layout
 3|              ------------------------------------------------------------
 4|                -1840.1  Appropriate, Negative
 5|
 6|                   1840  Fixed: 0 decimal places
 7|
 8|               1,840.10  Commas, Fixed: 2 decimal places
 9|
10|             $1,840.10  Dollars, Fixed: 2 decimal places
11|
12|           ($1,840.10)  Dollars, Negative, Fixed: 2 decimal places
13|
14|                  .254  Appropriate
15|
16|                 25.4%  Percent, Fixed: 1 decimal place
17|              ------------------------------------------------------------
18|
--------------------------------------------------------------------------------
B12: (Value, Layout-D2) -1840.1

Type entry or use @ commands                               @-? for Help
```

Figure 4.10: *Differences in value formats*

Oct 23 84 in categories that have "date" in their name. These dates can then be arranged by chronology or reverse chronology. In the Spreadsheet, however, such dates are recognized simply as labels.

Spreadsheet dates in the form 9.04 can be arranged by ascending or descending values within a year. Years in the form 1985 can also be arranged as values. First arrange the month.day column, and then the year column.

Spreadsheet dates in the form 85.09.04 can be entered as labels and arranged in either A–Z or 0–9 order. However, the form is unwieldy, and you are more likely to make mistakes this way.

Tip: *Use whole numbers for percentage entries.*

The Spreadsheet allows you to enter .12 into a cell that uses the percent format. The entry then appears as 12%. When someone else enters a replacement value, they might enter it in a form such as 12.4, which then appears as 1240%.

It is generally prudent to avoid the percent format. Use a whole number and % or percent in an adjacent label cell, and divide the value by 100 in formulas where .12 or .124 are needed.

Tip: *You can use tests to validate data entered in worksheets.*

Categories containing numbers often have acceptable ranges. For example, if you enter people's ages, all of the age values will be between 1 and 120. There are no negative age values and no 200-year-old people. For all practical purposes we can assume that acceptable values will have either one or two digits.

You can test entries for specific categories by writing a limiting formula. For example, suppose you designate B4 as a cell for entering age values. You can then have cell C4 test whether to accept or reject the value. This requires the following conditional formula:

@IF(B4<100,B4,@ERROR)

If someone enters 142 or 100 in cell B4, cell C4 will display the word ERROR. This may not be very friendly, but NA is the only other message you can use. The formula above does not allow for the possibility of someone entering a 0 or negative number. To catch such an entry, you would have to include another condition in the formula.

When you use this kind of validation, all subsequent operation on the input data must reference the validation cell, in this case C4. Remember that cell B4 will accept anything. Figure 4.11 shows two examples of the application. The formulas in cells C5. . .C8 are copied from C4, with all references relative.

The second example accepts only those age values from 21 through 99, and the formula is more complicated. The section on logic functions later in this chapter explains how formulas with two conditions are written.

```
File: Input.Tests                 REVIEW/ADD/CHANGE               Escape: Main Menu
========A========B========C========D========E========F========G========H=====
   1
   2    Enter Ages Below
   3    ----------------
   4               ·12       12      @IF(B4<100,B4,@ERROR)
   5               99        99
   6                8         8
   7              142      ERROR
   8               23        23
   9
  10
  11    Enter Ages Below
  12    ----------------
  13               12      ERROR     @IF(B13<100,@IF(B13>20,B13,@ERROR),@ERROR)
  14               99        99
  15                8      ERROR
  16              142      ERROR
  17               23        23
  18
--------------------------------------------------------------------------
C4: (Value) @IF(B4<100,B4,@ERROR)

Type entry or use @ commands                               @-? for Help
```

Figure 4.11: Testing input values

Tip: *Set column widths to detect errors in data entry.*

This is an alternate way of detecting errors in entered values. In most cases, columns should be just wide enough to show the largest number. If a column of age values will be no wider than two digits, make the column two spaces wide. Any mistaken entry of three digits will appear as ##. Never worry about a column label: you can always accommodate it with an empty column to the left or right.

If the dollar total of a column will be no more than 99,999, use commas format and make the column seven character spaces wide. (Remember that comma formats have a buffer space on the right.) Any mistaken entry above 99,999 will be easy to recognize as you scan the column, because it will appear as #######. If you plan to total the column, widen it to accommodate the total after you make all the entries.

A slightly different approach works for ZIP codes, telephone numbers, two-letter state abbreviations, social security numbers, and many other kinds of label entries of fixed length. They will spill over if there is insufficient room in a cell and thereby become conspicuous. By carefully setting column widths, you can scan patterns in columns and correct errors. Figure 4.12 shows some examples.

Tip: *Use a cross-checking formula to validate column totals.*

In practice, people often total columns and forget about whether the row total gives the same result. If one of the summation formulas uses an incomplete cell series, there could be a significant discrepancy. Figure 4.13 illustrates a case in which it is prudent to check the row total against the column total. The formula in G14 is

@SUM(D12. . .F12)

The discrepancy is caused by an incorrect formula in G8.

```
 File: Width.Controls              REVIEW/ADD/CHANGE            Escape: Main Menu
 ========A=======B===C=D==E===F===G======H=========I========J========K====
  1|
  2|       Amount  Age   ZIP     SS #
  3|       -------------------------------------------
  4|        8,345   12   02987   048-38-2124
  5|       99,000   99   11234    023-12-234
  6|       ######    8   947102  023-67-4587
  7|        3,412   ##   22341   039-43-5498
  8|          986   23
  9|
 10|
 11|
 12|
 13|
 14|
 15|
 16|
 17|
 18|
 -----------------------------------------------------------------
 H5: (Label, Layout-R) 023-12-234

 Type entry or use @ commands                        @-? for Help
```

Figure 4.12: *Using column widths and formatting to find errors*

Some people prefer a longer formula that does the checking and totaling entirely within one cell, in which case this would be the formula in G12:

@IF(@SUM(C13. . .E13) = @SUM(F9. . .F12),
@SUM(F9. . .F12),@ERROR)

If the sums do not match, you can expect to find ERROR in cell G12. Unfortunately, AppleWorks sometimes generates ERROR when none exists. The problem appears to be caused by the underlying binary representation of decimal values. We will discuss a similar problem in the section on financial analysis and rounding.

Tip: *Use cell protection to keep from writing over formulas.*

Appleworks permits cell protection when you use Apple-V to select the protection option. Thereafter, you can set conditions about what can be entered in a given cell: values only, labels only, nothing, or anything. In day-to-day use, it is easy to destroy a formula by entering a value into a formual cell, so allow nothing in completed formula cells. In cells where input values are entered, allow values only. AppleWorks will not permit you to make illegal entries in protected cells until you remove the protection. When you use Apple-U to edit a protected cell, however, AppleWorks will not warn you that the cell is protected, so always check the protection status displayed in the layout prefix.

Tip: *Use unique identification numbers for each record to predict the order of arrangement.*

Suppose you sort records by last name only, and two people have the same last name, such as Smith. Susan Smith may or may not precede Robert Smith. There is no way to predict the relative order

```
File: Apple.Budget          REVIEW/ADD/CHANGE          Escape: Main Menu
=========A=========B========C=======D========E=======F========G=======H====
   1│Apple IIe System                                        6%
   2│                                         Base        Sales
   3│Item                            Code     Cost Shipping  Tax      Total
   4│ ---------------------------------------------------------------------
   5│80-column 64K card                1    149.95    3.00  0.00     152.95
   6│Two disk drives                   2    359.90    8.00  0.00     367.90
   7│Control card                      3     49.00    2.00  0.00      51.00
   8│Dot matrix printer                4    359.95   20.00  0.00     379.95
   9│Buffered printer card             5    159.95    0.00  9.60     169.55
  10│Monochrome monitor                6     90.00    8.00  0.00      98.00
  11│ ---------------------------------------------------------------------
  12│Totals                                                          1219.35
  13│
  14│
  15│
  16│
  17│
  18│
-------------------------------------------------------------------------
G12: (Value, Layout-F2) @SUM(G4...G11)

Type entry or use @ commands                            @-? for Help
```

Figure 4.13: *Column total summation error*

unless you know the order in which they were originally entered in the worksheet or the last criterion for which they were arranged. You also have to know which circumstance applies.

When each record has a unique identification number, it is much easier to predict order. You simply sort by the ID number first, and then by whatever criterion you choose.

Tip: *Use Apple-H to print out key formulas.*

Zoom to the formula display mode. Widen the columns enough to show the complete formulas. The Apple-H command can then print a group of formulas with row and column borders. Values are left-justified in the formula display mode, but that is a minor inconvenience.

If you need to document just one formula, use the normal display mode. When the cursor is on the key cell, the formula, format, and location for that cell will appear at the bottom of the screen that Apple-H prints. This method is particularly useful for long formulas, where it would otherwise be necessary to increase greatly the width of a column. It is the only way to document formulas longer than 69 characters.

DEVELOPING TEMPLATES

Efficient template development depends on many small time-saving techniques. It is important to know significant limitations and options that were not documented in the AppleWorks Reference Manual.

Tip: *Make a PARTS file for formulas and template components.*

A utility file can be used as a warehouse for component parts. The idea is to group together the modules you use regularly in worksheet design. One obvious example is storage space for the letter and number borders. The Spreadsheet uses letters to designate columns and numbers to designate rows, and these references enable users to identify cell locations. Unfortunately, you have to add the borders into the worksheet if you want to see them in a printout. Hence B2 is the first cell you can use for labels, values, or formulas in an artificially bordered worksheet.

Copying the border row from the utility file is simple enough, because the copy function handles rows very well. The row number border is a different matter, because you can copy only entire rows to the clipboard, not isolated columns. You can generate the numbers by copying a relative reference formula $(1 + A2)$, where cell A2 contains the entered value 2. However, when you zoom in (Apple-Z) to the formula display mode, the generated border numbers appear as their formulas.

You can alternatively store actual values (2 through at least 100) below everything else in the utility file, where the rows are clear. Copy them into clear rows on other Spreadsheet documents, and then into exact locations within the document when the template is complete. These borders are often essential for documentation of applications that are both large and complex.

The sample file in Figure 4.14 includes border letters and numbers and a small template for the area of a circle. The formula for D17 is C17^2*B17. A file might hold dozens of formulas, each self-contained within one or more rows. These formulas and sample data are the most basic building blocks.

Caution: *It is difficult to edit labels that cross cell boundaries.*

Although labels that are wider than a cell's width will automatically continue into other cells, subsequent editing is done cell by cell. If you must add or delete letters, it is usually easier to start the original entry over again. Repeated border labels will also continue into other cells, but they cannot be edited.

Tip: *To reach cell A1, use Apple-F and the "last selection" option.*

There are no direct commands for moving to the beginning (upper-left) and end (lower-right) cells. Apple-1 through Apple-9

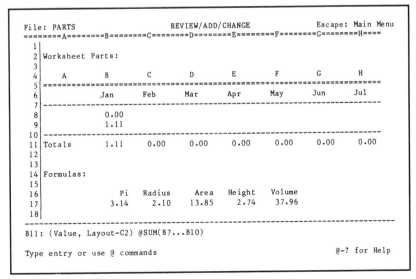

```
File: PARTS                    REVIEW/ADD/CHANGE              Escape: Main Menu
========A========B========C========D========E========F========G========H====
  1
  2 Worksheet Parts:
  3
  4     A        B        C        D        E        F        G        H
  5 =============================================================================
  6          Jan      Feb      Mar      Apr      May      Jun      Jul
  7 ---------------------------------------------------------------------
  8          0.00
  9          1.11
 10 ---------------------------------------------------------------------
 11 Totals   1.11     0.00     0.00     0.00     0.00     0.00     0.00
 12
 13
 14 Formulas:
 15
 16          Pi      Radius    Area    Height   Volume
 17         3.14     2.10     13.85     2.74    37.96
 18
--------------------------------------------------------------------------
B11: (Value, Layout-C2) @SUM(B7...B10)

Type entry or use @ commands                              @-? for Help
```

Figure 4.14: PARTS file

move the cursor to the beginning and end of the column in which it is located. Apple-← or Apple-→ will move the cursor through a row one screen at a time.

Apple-F will propose the last selection as a default, and if that happens to be cell coordinate A1, it gets you back there quickly. Apple-Q will erase the last selection, however, so you would have to specify cell A1 again.

Tip: *Insert a column whenever that is faster than changing a column's width.*

When you insert a column, it will be the same width as the column to the right of it. It is sometimes easier to insert and move columns of a desired width than to use the layout command sequence.

Tip: *When constructing template sections, use catercorner layout.*

Suppose you want to make another budget template similar to the Apple IIe System budget in Figure 4.4, and you want to store it in the same file. The existing template ends in cell G14 if you include the RN notation. The next template should begin in cell H15, or any other cell below it and farther to the right.

Using this kind of catercorner layout allows you to change column widths without affecting the worksheet section above. It also allows you to copy rows to the clipboard without affecting the worksheet section to the left.

To make a quick catercorner copy of the budget template, follow these steps:

1. Insert seven columns to the left of column A.

2. Copy rows 1 through 14 to the clipboard.

3. Delete the seven empty columns you just inserted.

4. Move the cursor to row 15 and move from the clipboard.

The process varies from case to case only in the number of columns inserted and the number of rows copied. From the cater-corner layout a template section can be quickly and neatly transferred almost anywhere.

Caution: *When you set value and label formats, the row and column options have no effect on subsequent entries.*

The row and column options format only those values and labels that have already been entered in the worksheet. They have no effect on future entries into cells that are currently empty.

The AppleWorks Reference Manual explains this limitation as it applies to cell protection, but not to cell formats. It was a wise design choice, because there is no need to allocate memory to a complete row or column when you need only a defined area. The following tip shows a simple way around the problem created by this design choice.

Tip: *You can use the block option to set value and label formats in blank areas.*

The block option formats values and labels that have already been entered in the worksheet, as well as future entries into cells that are currently empty. The block option works dependably even if you define one row or column as a block.

Incidentally, the block option works the same way for cell protection, although the AppleWorks Reference Manual does not point that out.

Tip: *Use Apple-W and Apple-T together to partition areas on the screen.*

Apple-W creates windows that are either side by side or on the top and bottom of the screen. Apple-W always adds a row or column border. Apple-J will jump across the border.

Apple-T fixes the location of rows above the cursor, columns to the left of the cursor, or both. Apple-T is called the title command because it is commonly used for title rows and columns, but this does not have to be the case. Apple-T can simply set off any fixed area. It never adds a row or column border, and Apple-J will not jump to the fixed part of the screen.

The two commands can complement each other. If you want to show four different areas, for example, use Apple-W to set windows side by side. Then use Apple-T to set titles first in the left window, then in the right to create a horizontal separation in addition to the vertical partition created by Apple-W. To move from the lower-right area to the lower-left area, use Apple-J to jump across the column border. To move the cursor to the upper-left or upper-right area, you must remove one of the titles. Figure 4.15 shows an example of a screen divided into four areas.

When you press Apple-T to remove one of the titles, the lone menu option says None. This means that if you choose that option, you will have no fixed title areas within that window. The other title partition will remain in effect until you use Apple-T with the cursor in the other window.

```
File: Apple.Budget                REVIEW/ADD/CHANGE              Escape: Main Menu
==========A==========B=========D=========E=======F=======G=======H=====
   1│Apple IIe System    1│                        6%
   2│                    2│        Base          Sales
   3│Item                3│        Cost Shipping   Tax     Total
   4│------------------- 4│ -------------------------------------
   5│80-column 64K card  5│      149.95    3.00   0.00    152.95
   6│Two disk drives     6│      359.90   ₋8.00   0.00    367.90
   7│Control card        7│       49.00    2.00   0.00     51.00
   8│Dot matrix printer  8│      359.95   20.00   0.00    379.95
   9│Buffered printer card 9│    159.95    0.00   9.60    169.55
  10│Monochrome monitor 10│       90.00    8.00   0.00     98.00
  11│------------------- 11│ -------------------------------------
  12│Totals             12│     1168.75   41.00   9.60   1219.35
  94│-------------------994│ -------------------------------------
  95│                   995│
  96│  Row 96           996│ Row 996
  97│                   997│
  98│                   998│
  99│                   999│
------------------------------------------------------------------------
H999

Type entry or use @ commands                               @-? for Help
```

Figure 4.15: Four display areas in one worksheet

Caution: *Some Spreadsheet blocks are limited.*

The copy command allows you to copy whole rows, whole columns, or blocks within the document. Unlike the blocks used for printing, these blocks can include part of only one row or column. The move command within the document moves only whole rows and columns. Given these limitations, these are the guidelines to follow when you need to move a block between files:

1. Copy the block into open rows, below the last row currently being used.

2. Move or copy the rows containing the isolated block to the clipboard.

3. Move or copy from the clipboard into open rows in the new document.

4. Copy within the document to maneuver the block to where you want it.

All moving and copying must be completed without recalculating. Moving or copying a row from the clipboard will push subsequent rows down. Moving a column will push subsequent columns to the right. Copying a block within a worksheet will overwrite any existing unprotected cells in its way.

LOGIC FUNCTIONS

Mathematical formulas tell the Spreadsheet what operations to perform on cell values. Logic statements define the conditions under which those operations should be performed. Logic statements add another dimension to templates. Most AppleWorks users would benefit from using logic functions more often. We have reviewed logical statements in the Data Base record-selection rules, but in the Spreadsheet they work almost perfectly. This section decribes some interesting and useful approaches. You will learn how to use flags to control formulas, how to use @COUNT in logical statements, and several other techniques that may well surprise you.

Caution: *The Spreadsheet does not let data "pop through" as VisiCalc does.*

Many spreadsheet applications involve large amounts of data and relatively simple processing. When you run out of space or memory, how do you transfer subtotals from one sheet to another? In VisiCalc DIF files the data from other worksheets can "pop through" into blank cells. The AppleWorks Spreadsheet does not let that happen. Nor does the Spreadsheet have the Visi-Calc pound function (#) to turn the results of a formula into a pure value entry, which would make it easy to transfer formula results through the clipboard.

Tip: *Use logic functions to transfer data efficiently.*

There is a way to transfer data between worksheets. Suppose you are looking at the bottom line of large financial report. The bottom line values are to be input to another worksheet. The idea is to turn values generated by formulas into pure value entries, something that the Data Interchange Format does very well. Figure 4.16 provides an example.

```
      ==A===================B=============C==========D====E===F==
181   Item 162           23,128.09     18,128.87
182   Item 164           12,568.64     34,886.02
183   -----------------------------------------------------------
184   Total          2,128,290.32  2,346,980.87           99 Flag
185
```

Figure 4.16: *Flagging a worksheet for data transfer*

The formula for cell B184 might be @SUM(B8. . .B183). If you copy row 184 to row 9 of another Spreadsheet document, the formula will simply not work and the cell will display an error message. You could print the cells in row 184 to a DIF file, begin a new Spreadsheet document, and move the resulting row of values to row 9 of the intended destination document. However, this is a tedious way to transfer just a few formula results.

Suppose you simply avoid the problem with a different summation formula:

@IF(E184 = 99,@SUM(B8. . .B183),B184)

If E184 has anything other than the value 99 in it, the formula is disabled and the value itself is returned. The formula says, in effect, "If cell E184 has a value of 99 in it, sum the column indicated. Otherwise, enter the value already in B184." This technique is called *flagging,* and 99 is the flag. Those who believe in Murphy's Law use more improbable flags, such as -1.618, while the fearless use 1.

Note that if you put the flag in row 185 of our example, the transfer can effectively remove the flag. Such a formula would read as follows:

@IF(E185 = 99,@SUM(B8. . .B183),B184)

Tip: *Use logic functions to post accounts.*

Posting is a basic task in accounting. The task here is to enter amounts in the correct column, indicated by a code number at the top of the column. (These numbers are sometimes called object codes.) Posting is easy if you learn how to use conditional statements. Figure 4.17 shows an example. The formula for cell G4 is

@IF(E4 = 1,D4,0)

That part is easy enough. If you need more than one condition in a logic statement, read further.

The Spreadsheet lacks the VisiCalc @AND and @OR functions, which are very useful for stating multiple conditions.

```
File: Posting.Accts                REVIEW/ADD/CHANGE              Escape: Main Menu
======A=======B========C=========D=======E=======F========G=======H====
  1|   Entry   Order                                      Date
  2|  Number   Date      Item   Amount   Code     Paid        1        2
  3|--------------------------------------------------------------------
  4|      14   3.12      Paper    51.12     1      4.11    51.12     0.00
  5|      15   3.18    Pencils    18.96     2      4.18     0.00    18.96
  6|                      Pens    24.84     2               0.00     0.00
  7|                               0.00                     0.00     0.00
  8|                               0.00                     0.00     0.00
  9|                               0.00                     0.00     0.00
 10|--------------------------------------------------------------------
 11|                              94.92                    51.12    18.96
 12|
 13|
 14|
 15|
 16|
 17|
 18|
----------------------------------------------------------------------
G7: (Value, Layout-F2) @IF(E7=1,@IF(F7>0,D7,0),0)

Type entry or use @ commands                              @-? for Help
```

Figure 4.17: Posting to numbered account columns

However, you can create "and" conditions by nesting @IF functions properly. There are three parts to the above formula within the parentheses:

1. The "if" condition

2. The "then" result

3. The "otherwise" result

If you wanted to post only the items paid, this is the formula you would use:

@IF(E4 = 1,@IF(F4>0,D4,0),0)

This means, "If E4 equals 1 and F4 is greater than 0, take the value in D4." As you can see, there are two ways to get a 0 in this formula, but only one way to get D4. The second part of the original formula has been expanded. The "or" condition is nested differently:

@IF(E4 = 1,D4,@IF(F4>0,D4,0))

This formula has two ways to get D4 and one way to get 0. The third part of the original formula has been expanded. It would be pointless to use an "or" condition in this particular application, but there are times when it can be useful. The point to remember is this: in multiple-condition statements you must define the branching very carefully.

Tip: *Use the @LOOKUP function in place of complex logical tests.*

Suppose you use many specific object codes. You might post accounts to groups of those codes. Consider a group that includes object codes 18, 34, and 56. Figure 4.18 shows an example. Here you need a conditional formula that will mean, "If the object code is 18, 34, or 56, enter it in column G." This can be done with the @LOOKUP function. Enter the values − 1, 18, 34, and 56 in cells K4. . .N4, and then again in cells K5. . .N5. We could use this formula in cell G4:

@IF(@LOOKUP(E4,K4. . .N4) = E4,D4,0)

It means, "If you look up the value of E4 in cells K4 through N4, and the value selected equals E4, enter the value of D4 in cell G4." The value 56 would retrieve a perfect match, but a value of 42 or 72 would not. The − 1 value handles possible object code values of less than 18 that would otherwise generate the NA result. The formula in the lower-left corner in Figure 4.18 is used to post only the items paid.

Tip: *Keep at least two rows with zeroed entries at the bottom of an accounts sheet.*

The process described in the next paragraph will spare you the tedium of entering formulas from scratch or copying them column by column each time you need additional rows for new entries.

```
File: More.Posting                REVIEW/ADD/CHANGE              Escape: Main Menu
======A=======B=======C=======D=======E=======F=======G=========H=====
  1|  Entry   Order                                Date
  2| Number   Date    Item    Amount   Code       Paid    18,34,56         72
  3| -----------------------------------------------------------------------
  4|    14     3.12    Paper    51.12    18        4.11      51.12        0.00
  5|    15     3.18   Pencils   18.96    72        4.18       0.00       18.96
  6|                  Pens      24.84    72                   0.00        0.00
  7|                            0.00                          0.00        0.00
  8|                            0.00                          0.00        0.00
  9|                            0.00                          0.00        0.00
 10| -----------------------------------------------------------------------
 11|                           94.92                         51.12       18.96
 12|
======I=====J=====K=====L=====M=====N==================O=================
  1|
  2| Lookup tables
  3| ---------------------    ----------
  4|  -1    18    34    56    -1    72
  5|  -1    18    34    56    -1    72
    -----------------------------------------------------------------------
H7: (Value, Layout-F2) @IF(@LOOKUP(E7,M4...N4)=E7,@IF(F7>0,D7,0),0)

Type entry or use @ commands                                  @-? for Help
```

Figure 4.18: *Posting to account columns with several numbers*

Keep at least two extra rows containing formulas used for cells in columns G and H and any following columns to which you must post. If the entries for cells in columns A–F are blank, the related formulas in columns G and H will generate 0.00. When you need more rows, copy the two zeroed rows to the clipboard, and then repeatedly copy from the clipboard until you have more than enough rows for the new entries. Figures 4.17 and 4.18 show extra rows with 0.00 entries for Amount (column D) and calculated values of 0.00 in columns G and H. In both figures, the formulas shown in the lower-left corner are from those extra rows.

Tip: *Use logic functions to keep running totals.*

The time record template in Figure 4.19 demonstrates another use of flagging. In this case, it matters whether the flag 99 has been removed from cell F4. It is removed only at the end of each week and reentered at the beginning of each week.

```
      ====B=========C===D===E===F===G===H====I=======J=======K=========
   3  Hours Allocated
   4  Project B                      99 Flag
   5                                            Week     Last    New
   6  Person     Mon Tue Wed Thu Fri Sat      Total    Total   Total
   7  ---------------------------------------------------------------
   8  Smith        4   3   5   2   7   0        21      141     162
   9  Brown        2   2   2   4   5   2        17      129     146
  10  Wright       3   4   1   2   0   2        12      114     126
  11  ---------------------------------------------------------------
  12               9   9   8   8  12   4        50      384     434
```

Figure 4.19: *Template using running totals*

The formula for the weekly total in I8 is

@SUM(C8. . .H8)

To find the cumulative hours for the entire year ending this week, you add the week total to the cumulated total (Last Total). The formula for the cumulated new total in K8 is

@IF(F4 = 99,K8,I8 + J8)

This means, "If cell F4 equals 99, take the value already in this cell (K8); otherwise add together the values of I8 and J8." Only at the end of the week will a new total appear in column K.

Once you have the new total, how do you get it into the Last Total column? Next week is, after all, another week. The formula for the last cumulated total in J8 is

@IF(F4 = 99,K8,J8)

This means, "If cell F4 equals 99, take the value in cell K8; otherwise take the value already in this cell (J8)." When you remove 99, the value in this cell will not change. When you restore 99, the value in New Total will come in to take its place during the next recalculation.

So all week long 99 stays in cell F4, keeping columns J and K under control. Just before going home on Saturday, you blank out F4 and recalculate (with Apple-K). On Monday morning, you put 99 back in F4, recalculate, and start another week.

Spend some time with this example, because the concept is useful in many different circumstances. Many things are counted with daily, weekly, and year-to-date totals. In this sense, there is little structural difference between tracking hardware sales and wildlife migrations.

Tip: *Use logic functions and iteration to generate and store results for a range of "what-if" cases.*

Here logical flagging is used to control iteration. Some spreadsheet programs have automated iteration functions. With the AppleWorks Spreadsheet, you can create a practical, manually controlled model. This is a difficult model to describe, because it has several moving parts. You may want to read about the model once, and then enter the formulas to see it work.

Suppose you want to generate a series of annual mortgage payment calculations based on a change in one variable, the interest rate (see Figure 4.20). You start at .11 (or 11 percent), and add one percentage point with each recalculation. You also keep a record of the results at the bottom of the worksheet.

```
File: Iteration                 REVIEW/ADD/CHANGE              Escape: Main Menu
======A=====B=====C=======D========E========F========G========H========I====
  1|    Iteration
  2| --------------------------------------------------------------------------
  3|    99 Flag
  4|             0 Counter Seed
  5|             4 Counter
  6|           .01 Variable Increment
  7|           .11 Variable Seed
  8|                              .15 Interest Rate
  9|                              10 Years
 10|                         1178.00 Amount (1000s)
 11|                       4.0455577 (1+I)^N
 12|                          234.72 Annual Payment (1000s)
 13|
 14|
 15|                              .12    208.49 (1000s)
 16|                              .13    217.09
 17|                              .14    225.84
 18|                              .15    234.72
   --------------------------------------------------------------------------
F18: (Value, Layout-F2) @IF(C5=4,F8,F18)

Type entry or use @ commands                                @-? for Help
```

Figure 4.20: Iteration model

Cells F10 and F11 contain the mortgage formula in two parts (convenient for later calculation of interest and principal). The first part is contained in cell F11:

1 + F8 ^ F9

The second part is in cell F10:

+ F10 * F8 * F11/(F11 − 1)

If you use mortgage formulas, you now have one for future reference. (The two cells can equally well be considered a black box, appropriate for processing many kinds of formulas.)

The formula for cell C5 is

@IF(A3 = 0,C4,C5 + 1)

This means, "If cell A3 equals 0, take the value in C4 (here a 0); otherwise add 1 to the value already in this cell (C5)." The formulas in cells F15 through G18 reference the counter in cell C4 to determine where the results of the calculations will be recorded. Looking at the most recent iteration first, the formula for cell F18 is

@IF(C5 = 4,F8,F18)

This means, "If C5 equals 4, take the value of F8; otherwise leave the value already here (in cell F18)." Cell F17 directly above has a similar formula:

@IF(C5 = 3,F8,F17)

Cell F17 was calculated on the previous iteration; from now on it will remain the same.

While the effective interest rate for each iteration goes into column F, the annual mortgage payment result goes into column G. The formula for G18 is

@IF(C5 = 4,F12,G18)

This means, "If C5 equals 4, send down the result of the calculation; otherwise leave what is already here."

The formula for cell F8 is

@IF(A3 = 0,C7,F8 + C6)

This formula determines the interest rate. When A3 equals 0, the interest rate is the seed number in C7; otherwise the number in F8 is incremented by .01 (one percentage point). You can see that this series began at .11 and has reached .15 on this iteration.

When 99 (or anything other than 0) is in A3, the iteration mechanism works each time you recalculate the worksheet. When A3 contains 0, it is time to load in the values for the next series.

Tip: *Pressing Apple-K twice initiates two recalculations.*

This is a useful option for iterative applications. For example, with a large model that uses the structural approach of the example in Figure 4.19, you can press Apple-K twice and take a longer lunch.

This technique is probably most useful for worksheets containing recursive formulas. For example, an invoice form may require a total in the upper-left corner. But if cell A4 depends on the results of a summation formula in cell E42, the total can only be known to cell A4 on the second recalculation.

Caution: *The Spreadsheet lacks some of VisiCalc's logic functions.*

VisiCalc includes the logic functions @AND, @OR, @ISNA, @ISERROR, @TRUE, and @FALSE. These serve a number of purposes. The @AND and @OR functions allow you to clearly specify multiple conditions in logic statements. In the AppleWorks Spreadsheet it is difficult to use multiple conditions.

The @ISNA function allows you to check for the value NA in a cell and act on the finding. The @ISERROR function allows the same options with ERROR. The AppleWorks Spreadsheet can enter NA and ERROR but cannot check for the values. Hence it cannot act on a finding.

The @TRUE and @FALSE functions are probably the least-used VisiCalc logic functions. They provide an alternate path for managing multiple conditions in logic statements.

Tip: *The @COUNT function can be used in place of the @ISNA function.*

The @NA function enters NA in an AppleWorks or VisiCalc cell, designating the cell as a value cell with no available value. The @ISNA function allows VisiCalc users to check for NA in a cell and act upon that finding. For example, if the @ISNA formula finds NA, that cell has a special status and will not be considered to have a value of 0. AppleWorks lacks the @ISNA function, so NA in a cell simply produces the result NA in any formula that references that cell.

There is a way to make @COUNT replace the @ISNA (and @NA) function in AppleWorks. You may recall from a previous tip that the @AVG function works in two different ways, depending on the formula structure used. Although @AVG(E1. . .E3) will ignore a cell with no value entered at E3, the formula @AVG(E1 + E2 + E3) will count the cell. The two formulas therefore produce two different averages.

@COUNT also works in two different ways. Although @COUNT(E1. . .E3) will ignore a cell with no value entered at E3, the formula @COUNT(E1 + E2 + E3) will count the cell. This rule holds even for one cell: @COUNT(E1. . .E1) will likewise ignore an empty value cell or any label cell. You can therefore use @COUNT to replace VisiCalc's @ISNA function.

Suppose you use @NA in VisiCalc to enter NA (not available) in cell B6 to designate no entry. You would like to use a conditional statement in cell B8 that says, "if the value NA appears in cell B6, enter 0 in B8, otherwise enter 1." In VisiCalc the formula would be written as follows:

@IF(@ISNA(B6),0,1)

This formula allows you to make a distinction between no entry and an entered value of zero.

In the AppleWorks Spreadsheet you can substitute a structurally similar formula that uses @COUNT. First enter the label

na

in B6. Use lowercase letters to remind yourself that this entry must be a label, not the result of a formula containing @NA. The formula for B8 would then be

@IF(@COUNT(B6. . .B6) = 0,0,1)

Figure 4.21 shows the application of the formula to four entries (the formula has been copied with relative references for each entry). Note that letters other than na will also serve our purposes. For example, xx is often used to denote cells reserved for input values. Figure 4.21 shows both xx and na serving the same purpose.

FINANCIAL ANALYSIS AND ROUNDING FORMULAS

Spreadsheets are probably most often used for financial analysis. The only financial function the AppleWorks Spreadsheet includes is @NPV, which means you have to write your own formulas for financial functions found in other spreadsheets, most notably a formula for internal rate of return. In this section you should pay special attention to the caution on using the @NPV function. If you are an accountant, note the problem with a commonly used rounding formula.

Caution: *The @NPV function is slightly different from the @NPV function in VisiCalc.*

Financial statements must consider the present value of earnings in future years. Money earns interest, hence an amount

Figure 4.21: *Using @COUNT as a logic function*

placed in the bank today will become a much larger sum in five years. The Spreadsheet has a net present value function; it is used in the worksheet shown in Figure 4.22.

The formula for cell F7 in this example is

@NPV(C7,B4. . .F4)

This means, "find the net present value for the series from year 1 to year 5, assuming .10 is the discount rate." The amount of $236.48 would be divided by 1.10 (1 plus the discount rate). The amount of $456.36 would be divided by 1.10^2 (equal to 1.21),

```
     ===A==============B=======C======D=======E=======F=====G========
 1
 2   Project Year:   1       2       3       4       5
 3   -----------------------------------------------------------------
 4   Earnings:     236.48  456.36  781.54  654.91  218.56
 5   -----------------------------------------------------------------
 6
 7         Discount Rate:    .10            NPV: 1762.34
```

Figure 4.22: *Calculating net present value*

and so on. Add the adjusted amounts and you have the net present value. This is what the @NPV function does automatically.

The Spreadsheet's @NPV function always considers the cell nearest to cell A1 in a series to be year 1. In the formula

@NPV(C7,F4. . .C4)

C4 is considered year 1. In VisiCalc, however, F4 is considered year 1 in this formula. If you use such a formula in a VisiCalc application, then create a Spreadsheet directly from the Visi-Calc file, the Spreadsheet gives a completely different result, according to its own rules.

The VisiCalc approach is preferable, because it allows you to quickly understand the structure of a cash flow. Some projects are back-loaded, paying relatively larger amounts in the later years. In such cases, the NPV calculated from right to left is much higher than the NPV calculated from left to right. The extent of difference can be measured as a ratio of one NPV to the other.

Tip: *Although the Spreadsheet has no @IRR function, you can use an efficient template model for calculating internal rates of return.*

The Spreadsheet has no internal rate of return (@IRR) function, but you can construct a multiple-pass IRR template. The multiple-pass method demonstrates an interesting use of the @LOOKUP function.

Begin with ten years of net cash flow. There are generally at least half a dozen rows of revenue, depreciation, taxes, and so on above this line, but in this example the bottom line will be a given. (See Figure 4.23.)

First, you should know that this template is being calculated by rows. Most financial analysis models enter years (or months or quarters) in a row, and the row-order mode of calculation is usually the more efficient for this kind of application.

```
      ==C====D====E====F====G====H====I====J====K====L====M====N
  5   Year   0    1    2    3    4    5    6    7    8    9    10
  6   ----------------------------------------------------------
  7   Flow -696  142  180  196  222  246  174  210  245  290  322
  8   ----------------------------------------------------------
  9          1.1   1   .9   .8   .7   .6   .5   .4   .3   .2   .1
 10   P1    -545 -528 -507 -481 -447 -401 -337 -243  -97  149  601
 11          1.1   1   .9   .8   .7   .6   .5   .4   .3   .2   .1
 12
 13           .3  .29  .28  .27  .26  .25  .24  .23  .22  .21   .2
 14   P2     -97  -78  -58  -37  -15    9   34   60   88  117  149
 15           .3  .29  .28  .27  .26  .25  .24  .23  .22  .21   .2
 16   ----------------------------------------------------------
 17   IRR   25%
```

Figure 4.23: *Internal rate of return template*

The net cash flow is given in thousands of dollars. In this case, there is a net $696,000 investment in year 0. Years 1 through 10 have positive cash flows, although negative flows in any given years can be evaluated as well. This is a reasonably good project, with an IRR of 25%. But how do you find that out? An interesting multiple-pass approach is used. Row 9 lists possible internal rates of return from 110% to 10%, in decimal form. The value in D9 is 1.1. The formula for E9 is +D9−.1 (easily copied across the row, with +D9 being relative).

Row 10 is a sequence of net present value formulas, because at some point you will cross over from a negative to positive NPV. The formula in D10 is

> @NPV(D9,E7. . .N7)+D7

D7 gets added on at the end because the @NPV function never evaluates year 0. When copying this formula across the row, D9 is the only relative reference, while the other cells are absolute references requiring no change.

Row 11 is identical to row 9. We need to repeat the possible internal rates of return for the @LOOKUP formula in cell D13:

> @LOOKUP(0,D10. . .N10)

In this case the formula takes the value in the cell just below L10, the last cell with a value less than or equal to 0. That means the value .3 will begin the next list of possible internal rates of return in row 13, and the series will end with .2 in column N.

The possibilities have narrowed: the IRR will certainly fall between .3 and .2 (30% and 20%). The formula for E13 is +D13−.01 (easily copied across the row, with +D13 being relative). Note that each cell is now reduced by .01 (rather than .1).

Row 14 is similar to row 10. In this case, you cross over from a negative to a positive NPV between .26 and .25, hence the IRR will be more than 25% and less than 26%. Row 15 is identical to row 13, to allow for the @LOOKUP formula in cell D17:

> @LOOKUP(0,D14. . .N14) − .01

In this case the formula finds the value in the cell below H14, the last cell with a value less than or equal to 0. You can therefore safely say that the IRR is at least .26 − .01 (equal to .25). The D17 cell is in percent format, hence the resulting 25%.

For greater accuracy, you can use another pass to find another significant digit, or you can interpolate, but for most purposes the solution given is adequate.

Experienced spreadsheet users might wonder why row 9 ends with the value .1 rather than 0. Remember that the model is looking for an upper limit to begin row 13, not a lower limit. If the IRR had been negative, D17 would have shown an ERROR message. If the IRR had been greater than 110%, D17 would have shown the NA (not available) message. You can experiment with several different cash flows to test the limits of the template.

You have a few design options with this model. The NPV can run for any number of years (20 is common). The cash flow for a 20-year model would run to column X, but the multiple-pass work area would still end in column N. The only formula change would be to the NPV formula:

> @NPV (D9,E7. . .N7) + D7

would become

> @NPV(D9,E7. . .X7) + D7

You can also use a 20-year model for less than 20 years. Just remember to fill the unused years with zeros.

Caution: *There is a problem with the @INT function, and it affects a rounding formula used by accountants.*

Accountants need to worry about small discrepancies. If you write a sales tax formula that generates such values as 18.246 and 24.784, the column total might eventually differ from conventional rounding practice by a few pennies. Whenever a value in the third decimal place is 5 or more, round up to the next penny. Figure 4.24 shows sales tax values to three decimal places in column C, manual rounding of those values in column F, and rounding with an equivalent accounting formula in column G. Notice the discrepancy between cells E12 and F12. What you see in cell E7 has been rounded to 2 digits for diplay purposes only, and the display is not the reality. The reality is 18.246.

Accountants need to round the reality as well. The essential formula for cell E7 would therefore be

$$@INT(B7*.05*100+.5)/100$$

Think about how this works. The value is processed through the following sequence: 18.246, 1824.6, 1825.1, 1825 (the integer),

```
File: Rounding                   REVIEW/ADD/CHANGE              Escape: Main Menu
=====A========B=========C=====D==========E==========F=========G==========H====
  1|
  2|
  3|
  4|                             Fixed with 2    Manual       Formula
  5|           Amount   5% Tax   Decimal Places  Rounding     Rounding
  6|           ------------------  ------------------------------------
  7|           364.92   18.246            18.25     18.25        18.25
  8|           153.90    7.695             7.70      7.70         7.70
  9|           495.68   24.784            24.78     24.78        24.78
 10|           223.92   11.196            11.20     11.20        11.20
 11|           ------------------  ------------------------------------
 12|          1238.42   61.921            61.92     61.93        61.93
 13|
 14|
 15|
 16|
 17|
 18|
     ---------------------------------------------------------------------
     G7: (Value, Layout-F2) @INT(B7*.05*100+.5)/100

     Type entry or use @ commands                          @-? for Help
```

Figure 4.24: Example for the rounding formula

and 18.25. The sequence for cell E9 has a different outcome: 24.784, 2478.4, 2478.9, 2478 (the integer), and 24.78.

The underlying numerical evaluation routine used in Apple-Works has a problem that shows up when the @INT function is used in the rounding formula. Unfortunately, it handles the .5 decimal fraction inconsistently. Consider the following formula:

@INT(3.99 * .5 * 100 + .5)/100

The result is a correct 2.00, because half of 3.99 is 1.995, which should be rounded upward. Substitute 1.99 for 3.99 in the formula and the result should be 1.00, because half of 1.99 is .995, which should also be rounded upward. However, the Spreadsheet gives an incorrect result of .99. If you use such a formula in a VisiCalc application, it gives the correct 1.00 answer. If you then create a Spreadsheet directly from the VisiCalc file, the Spreadsheet still gives an incorrect .99 result.

Tip: *There are ways to cope with the rounding problem.*

The rounding problem is a problem with binary representation of decimal values. You can handle a case of 1.99 with an unorthodox variation of the essential formula:

@INT(1.99 * .5 * 100 + .5000001)/100

The modified formula then produces the correct result of 1.00. This formula correctly handles the many cases of .5, leaving you vulnerable only to the decidedly remote case of .4999999 (which almost no one cares about anyway). In fact, for all practical purposes, you can use .501 in the formula.

Once understood, inconsistent rounding may not even be a problem for most operations that use AppleWorks alone. The rounding formula exists so that totals can be reconciled. You want to eliminate discrepancies caused by accumulations of undisplayed tenths of a cent. The standard formula still meets that requirement, despite its inconsistency.

OTHER FUNCTIONS

Tip: *Use series calculations for trigonometric functions.*

The Spreadsheet lacks trigonometric functions, but you can use a Taylor series calculation for the sine calculation. (Many applied math and engineering textbooks explain Taylor series in detail, listing many related series calculations as well.)

Suppose you need to find the sine of 72 degrees. You must first convert the degrees to radians. There are 180/pi radians in a circle. Each radian equals 57.29578 degrees. Therefore, divide 72 by 57.29578 to convert degrees to radians.

The standard sine formula uses factorials, indicated by exclamation marks. The formula follows the algebraic order of operations:

$$X - X^3/3! + X^5/5! - X^7/7! + \ldots$$

The cosine formula follows an equally obvious pattern:

$$1 - X^2/2! + X^4/4! - X^6/6! \ldots$$

Figure 4.25 shows a template for trigonometric functions. The Spreadsheet adaptation of the sine formula begins in cell B6:

$$+ B5 - (B5^3/6) + (B5^5/120) - (B5^7/5040) + (B5^9/362880)$$

The formula for B7 adds a little more accuracy:

$$- (B5^{11}/39916800) + (B5^{13}/6227020800)$$

The formula in C4 adds B5 and B6 together. The summation could have been handled just as well in B6. Because the Spreadsheet accepts only 69 characters in a formula entry, this series requires two cells. Note, however, that the second cell adds little to accuracy, so you can generally use a one-cell version of the formula.

```
File: TRIG.Functions            REVIEW/ADD/CHANGE            Escape: Main Menu
=======A=======B=======C=======D=======E=======F=======G=======H====
   1|
   2| Degrees              Sine
   3| ----------------------------
   4|     72              .9510565
   5|           1.26                    Enter degrees in A4.
   6|       .9510568                    Press Apple-K to calculate
   7|      -.0000003                    sine, cosine, and tangent.
   8| ----------------------------
   9| Degrees              Cosine
  10| ----------------------------
  11|     72              .309017
  12|           1.26
  13|       .3090197
  14|      -.0000027
  15| ----------------------------
  16| Degrees              Tangent
  17| ----------------------------
  18|     72             3.0776834
------------------------------------------------------------------------
B6: (Value) +B5-(B5^3/6)+(B5^5/120)-(B5^7/5040)+(B5^9/362880)

Type entry or use @ commands                              @-? for Help
```

Figure 4.25: *Template for generating trigonometric functions*

The cosine formula is similar. The formula for B13 is

$$1 - (B12 \wedge 2/2) + (B12 \wedge 4/24) - (B12 \wedge 6/720)$$
$$+ (B12 \wedge 8/40320)$$

The formula for B14 adds a little more accuracy:

$$- (B12 \wedge 10/3628800) + (B12 \wedge 12/479001600)$$

The tangent is equal to the sine divided by the cosine.

Tip: *Logarithms and inverse trigonometric functions use similar kinds of formulas.*

In applied math and engineering textbooks you can find additional series calculations used to generate other functions. Some series converge very slowly, or not at all beyond specified boundaries. In the case of logarithms, for example, efficient convergence requires a combination of lookup tables and formulas.

Tip: *For statistical functions and data analysis techniques, read VisiCalc template articles.*

The A.P.P.L.E. Co-op has published a remarkable data analysis series by Jeffrey Jacques. It appeared in 11 parts from December 1983 through May 1985. Table 4.3 lists the topics and dates.

The templates in this series were actually written for THE Spreadsheet, which is similar to VisiCalc. Many of the templates use @ROUND, which is missing from both VisiCalc and Apple-Works. @ROUND is functionally equivalent to the rounding formula for accounting described in a previous tip. Many of the templates also use @ISNA to good advantage, but in its place you can use the @COUNT technique described in a previous tip.

Deane Arganbright has chapters on statistics and probability in *Mathematical Applications of Electronic Spreadsheets* (McGraw-Hill, 1985). The book uses VisiCalc notation, and introduces many other mathematical functions and operations.

Table 4.3: Data analysis series in CALL-A.P.P.L.E. *journal*

Issue Date	Pages	Part #	Subject
Dec 83	21–26	1	Introduction
Jan 84	37–39, 42	2	Frequency distributions
Feb 84	28–31	3	Contingency tables
Mar 84	37–39, 42–43	4	Measures of association
Apr 84	21–24	5	Linear regression
May 84	56–59	6	Chi-square
Jun 84	38–39, 42–46	7	Chi-square
Aug 84	34–38	8	F-test
Feb 85	32–38	9	Analysis of variance
Mar 85	25–29	10	Analysis of variance
May 85	21–23, 26, 28–29	11	Multiple regression

GRAPHICS

Business graphics are generally used to make quantitative information easy to understand. If you already understand, don't bother with the graphics. If you want to present information to others, data tables may serve your purpose. In this section we will look at several options.

SuperCalc 3a, an advanced spreadsheet, has business graphics capabilities that should meet the needs of most AppleWorks users, and it can translate files from the Spreadsheet.

Caution: *The Spreadsheet has no graphing capabilities.*

AppleWorks has no component data graphing program. The Spreadsheet does not have the VisiCalc graph format that uses asterisks. It also lacks the ability to leave a cell blank as one result of a conditional statement (a surprisingly important graphics option).

Tip: *VisiCalc has some limited graphics capabilities.*

You can use the graph format in VisiCalc, save the horizontal bar graph as a text file, and use that in the AppleWorks Word Processor. Advanced VisiCalc offers additional graphics options through its @LABEL function. If this option meets your needs, and you aleady have VisiCalc, use it. Figure 4.26 shows an example of such a transfer.

Tip: *Use data tables to do the work of conventional business graphics.*

The Spreadsheet's arrange function can generate effective data tables. Edward Tufte's *The Visual Display of Quantitative*

```
File: Graph.Transfer            REVIEW/ADD/CHANGE            Escape: Main Menu
=====|====|====|====|====|====|====|====|====|====|====|====|====|====|====|===


     Value                 Graph format
     ------------------------------------------------------------------
     664 *************************************************
     661 *************************************************
     459 **********************************
     221 ****************
      99 *******
      73 *****
      62 ****
      57 ****
      55 ****
      52 ***
      43 ***

     ------------------------------------------------------------------



     ------------------------------------------------------------------
Type entry or use @ commands            Line 2  Column 1         @-? for Help
```

Figure 4.26: Graph format transferred from VisiCalc

Information (Graphics Press, 1983) includes a section on the utility of such tables. The most instructive example in Tufte's book presents voting preferences in the 1980 presidential election using a supertable containing 410 percentage values neatly grouped in an ordered series of smaller data tables.

Sometimes the range and distribution of numbers make tables particularly effective. Consider the data in Figure 4.27 on the

	=====A=========B=======C======D==		===F========G=======H====		
		Arable Acreage	Yield in			
2		in Thousands	Metric Tons	Percent	Units	Degrees
3	Crop	of Hectares	per Hectare	100	50	360
4	-------------	---------	---------	------	----	-------
5						
6	Hay	664	4.3	27.1	50.0	97.7
7	Barley	661	3.4	27.0	49.8	97.3
8	Oats	459	3.4	18.8	34.6	67.6
9	Autumn wheat	221	4.5	9.0	16.6	32.5
10	Spring rape	99	1.7	4.0	7.5	14.6
11	Rye	73	3.4	3.0	5.5	10.7
12	Spring wheat	62	3.9	2.5	4.7	9.1
13	Mixed grain	57	2.9	2.3	4.3	8.4
14	Autumn rape	55	2.4	2.2	4.1	8.1
15	Sugar beet	52	44.0	2.1	3.9	7.7
16	Potatoes	43	28.7	1.8	3.2	6.3
17	-------------	---------	---------	------		-------
18	Total	2446		100.0		360.0

Figure 4.27: Spreadsheet data table

main agricultural crops in Sweden from 1977–81 (columns A–D), adapted from a Swedish Institute publication. The changes included arranging the crops in descending order of acreage, and adding a total.

The table works well because there are only 22 data points, and the three-digit numbers stand out. A hectare equals about 2.47 acres, so the visual pattern would change if acres were the units of measurement. If yield were the significant variable under discussion, you would arrange the rows by yield, again altering the visual pattern.

Tip: *Data-table formulas can help you design graphics.*

If you need graphics only once in a great while, consider drawing them, particularly if you need large graphics. Hand-drawn graphics generally look friendlier than printed or plotted graphics.

The work area in columns F through H can provide insights to other ways of presenting the acreage information. For example, the percentage column may tell us all we additionally need to know about distribution of acreage. You can include the percentages in the data table, to the right of column B, and that may well eliminate the need for a graphic. The formula for cell F5 is

+B6/B18*F4

You can calculate bar lengths and draw a chart, but note that it will have some short bars. If the vertical axis has 50 units, the highest bar has 50, and the other bars are proportionately shorter. The formula in cell G6 does the necessary calculations:

+B6/@MAX(B5. . .B17)*G4

Caution: *Think twice before using pie charts.*

There are many understandable reasons for misgivings about pie charts. In perspective view, partly rotated, with irrelevant surfaces in the third dimension, they distort the basic perception of comparative surface area that you need in order to make judgments. With the crop data some of the slices would be too thin.

However, if you want to create a pie chart, the method for calculating degrees is similar to that for finding percentages. The formula for H6 is

B6/B18*H4

Flat pie charts sometimes make sense for metaphorical reasons, such as illustrating how a budget pie is being sliced. You can buy a circular (360-degree) protractor, mark off the slice angles, and draw the pie to any size you want.

When rectangular pixels on the screen make curved or angled lines, the choppy effect is called aliasing. Because printers faithfully reproduce that aliasing, hand-drawn circles always look better.

Tip: *Consider using good DOS 3.3 graphing and mapping programs that accept DIF and ASCII files.*

Several DOS 3.3 graphics programs accept either DIF or ASCII files or both. For example, if you have a specialized thematic mapping application, it may be worth the effort to convert the file from ProDOS to DOS 3.3. Having a ProDOS graphics program means nothing if it cannot do the specialized work you need. We will discuss the mechanics of conversion to DOS 3.3 in Chapter 5.

Tip: *Use SuperCalc 3a if you need graphics and more spreadsheet functions.*

SuperCalc 3a includes good business graphics options, and it can translate AppleWorks files. To use SuperCalc 3a, you need an Apple IIc, Enhanced IIe, or a standard Apple IIe upgraded with the Enhancement Kit (a set of four new chips that includes a 65C02 processor).

SuperCalc 3a comes on three disks. The Tools disk contains a program to convert AppleWorks Spreadsheet files to SuperCalc files. Once the AppleWorks file is converted, you can create business graphics in several forms: bar chart, stacked bar chart, pie chart, line chart, and so on.

Caution: *SuperCalc 3a has some transfer limitations.*

The remarkably thorough SuperCalc 3a manual explicitly notes the limitations. The most important limitations include the following items that cannot be converted correctly:

- Data in cells beyond column BK or row 254
- Some formulas containing @NPV
- Some formulas containing @CHOOSE

You should also know that SuperCalc 3a uses Super Data Interchange, a superset of the Data Interchange Format (DIF). We will look at this in some detail in Chapter 5.

CONVERTING VISICALC AND DIF FILES

There is nothing more satisfying than watching AppleWorks convert a classic VisiCalc template. Conversion saves considerable time in applications development, and you can find almost any kind of template imaginable. However, there are potential problems with conversion, and you should learn to work around them. The tips and cautions in this section will help you do that.

Tip: *If you plan to use VisiCalc and Advanced VisiCalc often, get the ProDOS versions.*

If you have a DOS 3.3 version of VisiCalc, review the procedures in Chapter 5 for converting to ProDOS. If you have the new

ProDOS version of VisiCalc, your files are already in the right format. In either case, you must cope with limitations to formula transfers that were not documented in the Reference Manual.

Caution: *If a VisiCalc formula contains more than 74 characters, you lose the formula during the attempted transfer.*

The formula disappears without a trace. You may not even realize that it is missing. However, if other cells depend on the results of that formula, they will have the expected reference problems.

Caution: *The Spreadsheet lacks some of VisiCalc's functions.*

The Spreadsheet does not include trigonometric functions, logarithmic functions, and some important logic functions. Table 4.4 compares key functions in several spreadsheets. If a VisiCalc formula contains any of the functions missing from the AppleWorks Spreadsheet, you lose the entire formula. The affected cell typically contains a zero, and the cell formula will be @ERROR. If other cells depend on the results of that formula they will have the expected reference problems. Figure 4.28 shows some examples of attempted transfers.

Tip: *Rewrite VisiCalc formulas that cannot be transferred.*

You can cope with the 74-character limit by using additional cells to rewrite long VisiCalc formulas before transfer. You can sometimes rewrite VisiCalc formulas using only the functions available to the Spreadsheet, but that is considerably more difficult. The VisiCalc pound function (#) can change the results of "unacceptable" formulas into pure value entries. This capability allows the ProDOS version of advanced VisiCalc to complement the Spreadsheet by accepting data in DIF files, processing it with advanced functions, and returning intact worksheets. The column

Table 4.4: *Key functions affecting file translations*

Function	SuperCalc 3a	VisiCalc	MAGICALC	AppleWorks
AND	X	X	X	
ACOS	X	X		
ASIN	X	X		
ATAN	X	X		
CHOOSE		X	X	X
COL			X	
COS	X	X		
COUNT	X	X	X	
EXP	X	X	X	
FALSE	X	X	X	
ISERROR	X	X	X	
ISNA	X	X	X	
LN	X	X	X	
LOG	X	X	X	
NOT	X	X	X	
NPV	X	X	X	
OR	X	X	X	
PI	X	X	X	
ROUND			X	
ROW			X	
SIN	X	X		
TAN	X	X		
TRUE	X	X	X	

showing VisiCalc results in Figure 4.28 was created by copying each formula from column B and then using the pound function on the results.

Tip: *You can edit in up to four more characters to complete a VisiCalc formula after transfer to the Spreadsheet.*

With the Apple-U edit feature, you can add up to four more characters to a 74-character formula after transfer to the Spreadsheet. If you find a VisiCalc formula that is a close fit, abridge

```
File: VC.Transfer              REVIEW/ADD/CHANGE           Escape: Main Menu
===============A================B==========C=====D=====E========F========G====
    3                          Result in    Result in
    4 VisiCalc Formula        AppleWorks     VisiCalc
    5 ---------------------------------------------------
    6 A1+B1+C1                         6             6  Note: The following values
    7 @IF(@OR(A1=1,B1=3,2,4)          0             2  are used: A1=1, B1=2, C1=3,
    8 @IF(@ISNA(D1),2,0)             0             2  D1=NA.
    9
   10 @SIN(.4)                        0         .3894  VisiCalc values shown were
   11 @PI*A1                          0        3.1416  preserved with the pound
   12 @LN(3.1)                        0        1.1314  (#) function in VisiCalc
   13 @EXP(1.131402)                  0        3.1000  before transfer.
   14
   15 @INT(1.99/2*100+.5)/100      .99             1
   16 @NPV(.12,A1...C1)          4.6226        4.6226
   17 @NPV(.12,C1...A1)          4.6226        4.9847
   18
   19 79-character formula                     120016
   20
   ---------------------------------------------------------------------------
   B8: (Value, Layout-A0) @ERROR

   Type entry or use @ commands                              @-? for Help
```

Figure 4.28: *Examples of VisiCalc file transfer limitations*

the formula before transfer, then add the missing section after transfer.

Tip: *Adjust the column widths in AppleWorks after transferring a VisiCalc file.*

VisiCalc has always offered the option to change column widths. Recent versions of standard VisiCalc offer the option to change one column width individually. Advanced VisiCalc has always offered this option.

Suppose you have a VisiCalc file with column A 9 characters wide, column B 24 characters wide, and column C 4 characters wide. When you create an AppleWorks Spreadsheet file from a VisiCalc file, the default column-width settings for the Spreadsheet will prevail. Column A will be just the right width, column B will be too wide for the data, and column C will show only part of the data. Use Apple-L to widen column C until all the data shows. Then make column B narrower.

Tip: *AppleWorks can convert files from spreadsheets that are similar to VisiCalc.*

MAGICALC creates files that are largely interchangeable with VisiCalc. IACcalc and THE Spreadsheet are generic versions of MAGICALC. These spreadsheets include @ROUND, which is functionally equivalent to the rounding formula for accounting described in a previous tip. AppleWorks cannot convert formulas containing @ROUND. These spreadsheets use DOS 3.3, so read Chapter 5 for the mechanics of converting these files to ProDOS.

Caution: *VisiCalc cannot translate Spreadsheet files.*

The Spreadsheet creates binary files that VisiCalc cannot translate, but you can generate DIF files to send data to VisiCalc or other programs that use the Data Interchange Format. This presents an interesting dilemma: would you rather send DIF files out to VisiCalc for processing and receive VisiCalc files back, or would you rather send AppleWorks files to SuperCalc 3a for processing and receive DIF files back from that spreadsheet program? There is no right or wrong answer to that question, but it is a point to consider in the development of any advanced application that requires supplemental processing outside Appleworks.

USING THE SPREADSHEET
FOR DATABASE MANAGEMENT

A surprising number of people use the Spreadsheet for database management. If you use the Spreadsheet often, it can be a matter of convenience.

Consider the significant differences between the Data Base and the Spreadsheet. The Data Base dimensions are 1,350 records by

30 categories of up to 75 characters each, expandable to more than 5,000 records. The Spreadsheet dimensions are effectively 999 records by 127 categories of up to 70 characters each. The additional categories make all the difference. With these complementing capabilities you can, in theory, manage more than 5,000 records with 127 categories. See Chapter 5 for additional information on the subject.

Tip: *Some database applications work better on the Spreadsheet.*

A database application is not necessarily a Data Base application. You may realize that after you develop the application. There are ways to evaluate your options before you develop the application, however.

If data-related calculations are important, use the Spreadsheet. Calculations in the Data Base are limited to column totals, three row calculations, four math functions, and 30 characters per formula. You may sometimes know that there is a good chance you will exceed the calculation limits and no chance that you will exceed 999 records.

If you need to see a large array all at once, use the Spreadsheet. You can scroll across the entire worksheet to view all the categories. If you know that there is a good chance you will need more than 30 categories, use the Spreadsheet.

Tip: *Some database applications work equally well on the Spreadsheet and Data Base.*

If it makes no difference where a database goes, use the program you personally prefer. Many AppleWorks users seem to prefer the Spreadsheet to the Data Base.

Figure 4.29 shows part of a list of 109 records that includes telephone area codes, the major city within the area code, the first three ZIP code digits for the city, state names, and two-letter state abbreviations. It can be arranged by any category, with each arrangement printed as a report. It requires no calculation, no record selections, and no labels-style report format. All five categories can be displayed at once in the Data Base multiple-record layout. This application is a good example of one that works equally well on the Data Base and Spreadsheet.

The most important limiting factors in the Spreadsheet are its lack of record-selection rules and labels-style report formats. If you print only tables-style reports of all records, use the Spreadsheet.

Tip: *Some database applications require both the Spreadsheet and the Data Base.*

The obvious candidates in this class have one or more of these characteristics:

- More than 999 records and 30 categories

- Many calculation and record-selection requirements

- Many calculation and labels-style reporting requirements

In Chapter 5 we will examine such options as downloading selected Data Base categories and records for extensive calculations on the Spreadsheet. As extended memory becomes more common, this may become the most important complement in AppleWorks.

Tip: *Sometimes numbers should be entered as labels rather than as values.*

There are many reasons to enter numbers as labels. ZIP codes must be entered as labels because Spreadsheet values do not display leading zeros, and ZIP codes begin with zero in several states. Social security numbers must be entered as labels because they contain two dashes. Apple-F will not find numbers in

```
File: Area.Code                 REVIEW/ADD/CHANGE            Escape: Main Menu
======A=========B=========C===D===E=========F==========G========H========I====
  7|                   Postal Area   Key              ZIP
  8|         State  Abbreviation Code   City           Digits
  9|         -----------------------------------------------------
 84|         North Dakota    ND    701   Bismarck        585
 85|         Ohio            OH    216   Cleveland       441
 86|         Ohio            OH    419   Toledo          436
 87|         Ohio            OH    513   Cincinnati      452
 88|         Ohio            OH    614   Columbus        432
 89|         Oklahoma        OK    405   Oklahoma City   731
 90|         Oklahoma        OK    918   Tulsa           741
 91|         Oregon          OR    503   Salem           973
 92|         Pennsylvania    PA    215   Philadelphia    191
 93|         Pennsylvania    PA    412   Pittsburgh      152
 94|         Pennsylvania    PA    717   Harrisburg      171
 95|         Pennsylvania    PA    814   Altoona         166
 96|         Rhode Island    RI    401   Providence      029
 97|         South Carolina  SC    803   Columbia        292
 98|         South Dakota    SD    605   Pierre          575

   --------------------------------------------------------------------------
   G84: (Label) 585

   Type entry or use @ commands                              @-? for Help
```

Figure 4.29: *Database on the Spreadsheet*

Spreadsheet values, but Apple-F can find these numbers, and that makes database management possible.

In some cases there is an option. For example, let's say you want to store the names of people and their respective ages in a worksheet you are designing. The ages can be entered either as values or as labels. As labels they cannot be summed, but they can be found with Apple-F. As Spreadsheet values they can be summed but not found. The preferred form of entry depends on what you intend to do with the information. Table 4.5 compares the find command in each program.

Caution: *Alphabetical arranging follows the order of characters in the ASCII table.*

In the ASCII table, the digits 0–9 precede the letters A–Z. When you arrange rows, empty cells come first, then digits, then letters. (AppleWorks treats all letters as capitals.) Figure 4.30 shows an ASCII arrangement with selected examples. If you ever

Table 4.5: *Options available for find and replace functions*

Option	Word Processor	Data Base	Spreadsheet
Finds text	X	X	X
Finds case-sensitive text	X		
Finds numbers	X	X	as labels only
Finds page numbers	X		
Also finds	markers		coordinates
Searches from	cursor	beginning	cursor
Replaces one instance	X		
Replaces all instances	X		
Maximum number of characters	30	30	25

have specific questions about order, consult the ASCII table in Appendix C.

Tip: *You can arrange labels alphabetically even if they include nothing but numbers.*

ZIP codes and telephone numbers must be labels rather than values in the Spreadsheet, but you can still arrange them in ascending or descending ASCII order by arranging from A to Z.

There are some cautions that go with this. Keep the same format and numbers of digits for each entry in a given column, otherwise you can have serious problems. For example, consider the case of .618 and 0 in the same column. The decimal point comes before 0 on the ASCII table, so a label with .618 will precede 0 when AppleWorks arranges from A to Z. Likewise, 1,200 with a comma will precede 1000 because the comma precedes 0 in the ASCII table. Figure 4.30 shows some selected examples.

Although it is generally not a good idea, you can arrange worksheet rows from A to Z even if they include both labels and values. The values come first, then the labels beginning with numbers, and finally the labels beginning with letters. When you

```
File: ASCII.Sort             REVIEW/ADD/CHANGE           Escape: Main Menu
========A========B========C========D========E========F========G========H====
  1|
  2|
  3|              ***      42      Column C shows ASCII decimal
  4|         ---------     45      values for the beginning
  5|             .618      46      character of each label in
  6|                0      48      column B.
  7|            1,200      49
  8|             1000      49      AppleWorks treats lowercase
  9|         286-1234      50      letters as uppercase for all
 10|         323-3112      51      arranging.  The d in B12 is
 11|         =========     61      ASCII character 100, here
 12|           deRosa     100      treated as character 68.
 13|            Eaton      69
 14|             Zorn      90
 15|        [bracket]      91
 16|
 17|
 18|
-----------------------------------------------------------------------------
B7: (Label, Layout-R) 1,200

Type entry or use @ commands                             @-? for Help
```

Figure 4.30: *ASCII order in arranging labels*

arrange from 0 to 9, the labels beginning with numbers come first, then the labels beginning with letters, and finally the values.

SUMMARY

This chapter has reviewed a broad range of options and problems in the Spreadsheet, and provided many tips and techniques that you can use repeatedly.

As you understand more about the Spreadsheet, you can develop advanced applications more efficiently. This is where most people do their best and most interesting work.

In the next chapter we will be drawing upon what we have learned in the first four chapters. We will continue to change file names, copy to the clipboard, and use AppleWorks commands for unexpected purposes. You will learn to use the clipboard, ASCII files, and DIF files to move component parts between AppleWorks programs, as well as to and from AppleWorks. In Chapter 5 some of the parts assembled here will be transferred back to the Word Processor and elsewhere.

5
Transferring Information

*A*ppleWorks is an integrated package. The term *integration* generally means that the component programs use the same command logic, that you can transfer data easily from one program in the package to another, and that the data in one program's file can interact with the data in another program's file. AppleWorks offers reasonably complete integration in a practical and easy-to-learn form.

First, AppleWorks offers a good example of unified command logic. Most of the Apple commands have the same or similar functions in all three programs.

Second, the process of transferring information between files of the different programs is almost as easy as transferring information between files of the same program. Transfers from the Spreadsheet and Data Base to the Word Processor use the clipboard, though in a slightly different way than we have used it previously. Data transfers between the Spreadsheet and the Data Base, however, depend on the use of ASCII and DIF files.

Finally, although AppleWorks lacks automated data interaction capabilities (for example, it cannot merge a Data Base file with a Word Processor document to produce form letters), the AppleWorks Mailing Program can work with your AppleWorks files to provide most of the functions you will need. Each time you enter an AppleWorks command sequence you must enter it from the keyboard, but AppleWorks' fast highlighting capabilities make this process easier. Highlighting is used extensively in this chapter.

This chapter provides tips and techniques for transferring information between AppleWorks programs and between AppleWorks and other programs. The chapter is divided into nine sections, beginning with the most general tips. A section on transfer methods introduces techniques used throughout the chapter. The third section provides tips for transferring information between the Word Processor and the Spreadsheet. The next two sections cover transfers between the Word Processor and the Data Base, including use of the AppleWorks Mailing Program. Following that, tips are provided for transferring data between the Data Base and the Spreadsheet.

In the seventh section, tips are provided on file conversions between ProDOS and DOS 3.3 formats. Pay special attention to the limitations of the Convert program. The following section presents some case studies in transferring information to and from AppleWorks for special purposes. The final section provides tips for using the Word Processor to write Applesoft BASIC programs, and it presents some programs you can use to complement the capabilities AppleWorks provides.

GENERAL TRANSFER TIPS

This section contains general insights about managing information transfers. The general tips below apply throughout the chapter, and they include minor cautions. Transferring information requires attention to detail; you should pay special attention to the need for documenting everything you do here.

Tip: *Learn each program thoroughly before working with two at once.*

You will usually begin with information in files from two different programs. It is important that you understand the operation of the two programs you are using, especially when you work with the Spreadsheet and Data Base. Pay attention to details about line length and data formats within a program, especially when using ASCII and DIF files.

Tip: *Print and annotate hard copies of all transfer menus.*

You will need copies of the Desktop menus for making new files from ASCII files and DIF files, along with the Spreadsheet and Data Base menus for printing to the clipboard. If you have not yet done so, print copies of all these screens using Apple-H, and hang the copies on a note board near your Apple. Pencil in notes about when you use each option.

Tip: *Document all your work.*

Write a Word Processor template that lists the steps you generally use when transferring data. When an application requires you to transfer information, write specific documentation for that transfer from this template.

The documentation should explain why you need to transfer the information. It should note any problems encountered with various forms of the data, particularly in DIF transfers. It should include hard copies of important data screens. File the transfer documentation in the same manila folder that you use for the other documentation pertaining to that application.

Tip: *Plan your information transfers with pencil and paper.*

When two or more people use the same Apple, there will be times when one person wants to use AppleWorks and cannot. This is a good time to start working with pencil and paper. For example, you can sketch out information transfers on graph paper. Once you decide where information should be transferred, read your documentation for the generic steps in the transfers. The idea is to master the mechanics of transfer for the sake of your objectives.

TRANSFER METHODS

This section introduces the three basic transfer methods in AppleWorks—using the clipboard, using DIF files, and using ASCII files. Most transfers within AppleWorks are performed by copying, moving, or printing to the clipboard. Transfers between the Data Base and Spreadsheet normally use Data Interchange Format (DIF) files. For these transfers, it is important that you understand the implementation of DIF in AppleWorks. Transfers from the Word Processor to the Data Base normally use ASCII files. Some specialized transfers from the Spreadsheet to the Data Base and from the Data Base to the Word Processor also use ASCII files. Two kinds of ASCII files are discussed: unformatted and formatted. Formatted text files can be generated by a dummy Silentype printer, which works simply and effectively. See Chapter 6 for information on selecting the Silentype as one of your available printers. Since the Silentype only simulates an actual printer, you don't have to own one.

Tip: *Use the clipboard whenever possible, because it is the simplest route.*

Most data transfers will use the clipboard. To transfer information between files of the same program, you move or copy lines to the clipboard. To move information from the Data Base or Spreadsheet to the Word Processor, you print to the clipboard. When you press Apple-P, the print menu will ask where you want to print the report. Choose "The clipboard (for the Word Processor)". Printing to the clipboard is functionally equivalent to copying, because the lines also remain in the source file. You can then either move or copy the information from the clipboard.

When you print to the clipboard, make certain that you have turned off the Spreadsheet or Data Base option to print a report header at the top of each page. (A header would be just one more thing to edit from your Word Processor file.)

Table 5.1 shows the most common routes for data transfer within AppleWorks. The clipboard is used for five of the eight direct transfers. The route from the Word Processor to the Spreadsheet is indirect, requiring an intermediate stop at the Data Base.

Tip: *The Data Interchange Format has been well documented.*

AppleWorks uses standard tools for data transfers, including DIF files. There are two outstanding books on the subject of DIF

Table 5.1: *Common routes for transferring data within AppleWorks*

From	To Word Processor	To Data Base	To Spreadsheet
Word Processor	Copy to clipboard	Print to ASCII file	Through Data Base
Data Base	Print to clipboard	Copy to clipboard	Print to DIF file
Spreadsheet	Print to clipboard	Print to DIF file	Copy to clipboard

---

files: Donald Beil has written *The DIF File* (Reston, 1983), a book with good graphic illustrations and many useful case studies. Douglas Hergert has written *Mastering VisiCalc* (SYBEX, 1983), a book containing practical BASIC programs for creating and processing DIF files.

The Data Interchange Format was created by Software Arts in 1979 to transfer VisiCalc spreadsheet information to and from other programs. DIF has since become an industry standard. AppleWorks is one of many programs that can send and receive DIF files.

DIF files are text files with a defined structure. VisiCalc information can normally be defined in two dimensions—the worksheets are so many columns wide by so many rows long. The DIF technique places a header on the file to define the dimensions of the rectangle. When the file is saved it will be cataloged by ProDOS as a text file.

Tip: *Understand the AppleWorks implementation of DIF.*

The AppleWorks implementation of DIF can produce some unexpected surprises. The Spreadsheet can generate DIF files in row order or in column order, but it always receives files in column order. Row order converts existing columns into rows, in effect rotating them 90 degrees, but maintaining correct relative positions. Figure 5.1 shows the same data in column order (cells C4 to D9) and row order (cells B12 to G13). Notice how DIF transfers the repeated label in C5 to cell C12. The Data Base sends and receives DIF files in column order only.

The Spreadsheet explicitly defines values and labels, so labels in the Spreadsheet will always be treated as labels by the DIF file. The DIF file does not contain formulas, however—only the cell values generated by the formulas. The DIF file contains neither layout nor protection attributes. Values are right justified; labels are left-justified. Figure 5.2 shows a column of entries originally made in the Spreadsheet (column B), along with the transformations those entries underwent through various transfers (columns D, F, and H). Column D contains the results of the original Spreadsheet file, copied to a DIF file and then back to a Spreadsheet file. Notice how the labels are now left-justified because of the DIF file transfer.

The Data Base does not explicitly define values and labels, so you must know the AppleWorks rules for deciding which entries become values. Column F in Figure 5.2 shows the end result of the original Spreadsheet file printed in column order to a DIF file, made into a Data Base file, printed again to a DIF file, and finally converted back into a Spreadsheet file. As expected, the labels and values lost their layout attributes. The label entry #234

Figure 5.1: *Spreadsheet file in column order and row order*

```
File: DIF.Changes              REVIEW/ADD/CHANGE            Escape: Main Menu
========A==========B=======C========D=======E========F=======G=======H======
  1│DIF.Changes
  2│
  3│SS Layout        SS Entry          SS-SS          SS-DB-SS          DB-SS
  4│ --------------------------------------------------------------------------
  5│Value            $97.40            97.4              97.4             97.4
  6│
  7│Value            1,234.56          1234.56           1234.56          1234.56
  8│
  9│Label              #234  #234                          234              234
 10│
 11│Label             02678  02678                        2678             2678
 12│
 13│Label              -  -                                  0
 14│
 15│Label         042-67-4581  042-67-4581              42674581          42674581
 16│
 17│Label      (401) 888-2345  (401) 888-2345  (401) 888-2345  (401) 888-2345
 18│
     --------------------------------------------------------------------------
   B5: (Value, Layout-D2) 97.4

   Type entry or use @ commands                               @-? for Help
```

Figure 5.2: *Data transferred through DIF files*

became a value on the DIF trip from the Data Base, as did the 02678 ZIP code, the single dash (–), and the 042-67-4581 social security number. Only one Spreadsheet label in this group remained a label: the telephone number was protected by the parentheses around the area code. If it had been written in the form 401-888-2345, the telephone number would have suffered the same fate as the social security number. On the other hand, a social security number in the form SS 042-67-4581 would have remained a label.

In summary, whenever you plan to transfer data back and forth between the Data Base and Spreadsheet, you should enter data in a form that will survive DIF transfers intact. If you have any doubts about whether data in a specific form will survive, make some test transfers with just a few records.

Caution: *Empty Data Base records are omitted from DIF files.*

In Figure 5.2, the empty cells in column B (even-numbered rows 6–16) became empty records when transferred to the Data Base file. On the return trip, these empty records were omitted from the DIF file: the empty cells you see in column F had to be reinserted before the final move into position within the worksheet.

There is one more twist. Figure 5.2 also shows the results of a third test case. The original column B entries were entered directly into a Data Base file and printed to a DIF file. Column H contains the actual results copied from a Spreadsheet file that was made from that DIF file. Here the single dash disappeared instead of becoming a zero. Because the record contained only a single dash in the Data Base, the record was considered empty and was therefore removed on the DIF trip to the Spreadsheet. The empty cells you see in column H, including H13, were reinserted before the final move into position within the worksheet.

In summary, whenever you plan to transfer data back and forth between the Data Base and Spreadsheet, insert the characters xx or something similar in at least one category of otherwise empty records.

Tip: *ASCII files come in two basic forms.*

Chapters 6 and 8 of Apple's *BASIC Programming with ProDOS* (Addison Wesley, 1985) cover ASCII files in some detail. This tip concerns the first thing you need to know about using ASCII files with AppleWorks.

AppleWorks includes the built-in capability to create unformatted ASCII files. The information in unformatted files occupies the entire 80-character screen, with no word wrapping. Unformatted ASCII files have carriage returns only at the end of each paragraph and in blank lines (which can be considered paragraphs without characters). When you make a Word Processor file from an ASCII file, the Word Processor default margins give the text a defined shape, complete with word wrapping.

Formatted ASCII files preserve the Word Processor line length and word wrapping by entering carriage returns at the end of each line. In AppleWorks, the only way you can create formatted ASCII files is by adding a special printer (the Silentype) to print files to disk. In the Data Base, formatted ASCII files place carriage returns at the end of each report format line. In the

Spreadsheet, formatted ASCII files enter carriage returns at the end of each row within a specified block of cells.

As you will see, both kinds of ASCII files have advantages for specific applications.

Tip: *Use a dummy Silentype printer to print formatted ASCII files to disk.*

Chapter 6 describes the mechanics of adding the Silentype printer as one of your three printers, but you don't need an actual Silentype printer to print formatted ASCII files to disk. You use the Silentype simply because it is the only listed printer that recognizes none of the character controls for print enhancement. This means that no matter what character controls you use, the Silentype will print a formatted ASCII file to disk, placing carriage return markers at the end of each printed line.

The actual Silentype always prints at ten characters per inch (10 CI), but the dummy can also print to disk at 12 CI and 17 CI. The actual Silentype has a 7.3-inch platen width, but the dummy can print to disk with much wider platen widths.

With carriage return markers at the end of each line, you can easily send files from the Word Processor to the Spreadsheet and to on-line information services, such as CompuServe. The carriage return markers also permit other interesting transfers that will be described later in this chapter.

You can test the Silentype printing process. Change the setting for the Silentype platen width from the default 7.3 inches to a standard 8 inches, and then follow these steps:

1. Enter text in the Word Processor with the default margin settings. Figure 5.3 shows an example.

2. Print the file to disk as a formatted ASCII file using the Silentype printer.

3. Make a Word Processor file from the ASCII file created by the Silentype.

4. Reset the left margin to 0 inches.

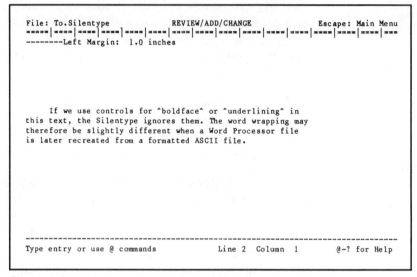

```
File: To.Silentype              REVIEW/ADD/CHANGE           Escape: Main Menu
====|====|====|====]====|====|====|====|====|====|====|====|====|====|===
--------Left Margin:  1.0 inches




       If we use controls for ^boldface^ or ^underlining^ in
this text, the Silentype ignores them. The word wrapping may
therefore be slightly different when a Word Processor file
is later recreated from a formatted ASCII file.







-------------------------------------------------------------------------
Type entry or use @ commands           Line 2  Column  1      @-? for Help
```

Figure 5.3: *Word Processor file to be printed to disk with Silentype*

Figure 5.4 shows the resulting text format (without showing the carriage return markers).

Notice that the Silentype prints the spaces required for the left margin, just as if the disk were paper. You can avoid this and still maintain the same line length by setting the left margin to 0 inches and the right margin to 2 inches *before* you enter any text in the original Word Processor file. Figure 5.5 shows the format created by this revision (without showing carriage return markers).

Tip: *It takes much longer to print an ASCII file to disk than to save an AppleWorks file, but the process is very dependable.*

It takes less than 40 seconds to save a 40K Word Processor file, but it may take two minutes to print the file to disk as an ASCII file. Be patient, because the process works dependably. In fact, if you should ever experience difficulty saving a Word Processor file to disk, you may still be able to print it to disk as an ASCII file.

```
File: From.Silentype          REVIEW/ADD/CHANGE              Escape: Main Menu
=====|====|====|====|====|====|====|====|====|====|====|====|====|====|====|===
--------Left Margin:  0.0 inches




              If we use controls for boldface or underlining in this
          text, the Silentype ignores them. The word wrapping may
          therefore be slightly different when a Word Processor file
          is later recreated from a formatted ASCII file.






    ----------------------------------------------------------------------
    Type entry or use @ commands          Line 2  Column 1      @-? for Help
```

Figure 5.4: *Word Processor file from formatted ASCII file*

```
File: From.Revised            REVIEW/ADD/CHANGE              Escape: Main Menu
=====|====|====|====|====|====|====|====|====|====|====|====|====|====|====|===
--------Left Margin:  1.0 inches




      If we use controls for boldface or underlining in this
  text, the Silentype ignores them. The word wrapping may
  therefore be slightly different when a Word Processor file
  is later recreated from a formatted ASCII file.







    ----------------------------------------------------------------------
    Type entry or use @ commands          Line 2  Column 1      @-? for Help
```

Figure 5.5: *Word Processor file from revised formatted ASCII file*

WORD PROCESSOR AND SPREADSHEET

This is one of several sections on transfers for specific purposes. In AppleWorks, you will often transfer financial reports and data tables from the Spreadsheet to the Word Processor. This section provides information on "build-and-transfer" techniques for doing that. Occasionally, you will need to transfer text from the Word Processor to the Spreadsheet. Although the AppleWorks Reference Manual does not address the subject, the method is surprisingly easy.

Tip: *You can print single Spreadsheet cells to the clipboard.*

In the Spreadsheet you can move and copy complete rows to the clipboard, but not single cells. However, you can print single cells (and large blocks) to the clipboard for the Word Processor. The Word Processor is then the only place it can go, and the block can be no more than 75 characters wide. Anything beyond the 75th character is truncated.

Incidentally, try copying from the clipboard back to the Spreadsheet and read the error message. Is there a better choice of words?

Tip: *Use the Spreadsheet for lists and outlines.*

Because the Spreadsheet can print to the clipboard quickly, you can construct lists and outlines on worksheets for later transfer to the Word Processor. Lists grow unevenly: entries are added here and there. The Spreadsheet allows you to insert up to nine rows at a time. When it comes time to number the list, use the formula for generating row numbers. If cell A1 is 1, the formula for A2 will be

1 + A1. Copy this formula down the worksheet list as far as Apple-9 will take you. Remember that A1 is a relative reference.

Outlines are more complicated, but here again you often need to insert rows. There is really no reason to use Roman-numeral headings, capital-letter subheadings, and so forth, because indents alone will serve the same structural purpose. Make columns A, B, and C two or three character spaces wide. Begin main headings in column B, second-level headings in C, and third-level headings in D. Reserve column A as empty space between the outline and the row numbers. Figure 5.6 shows the basic outline for the beginning of this chapter.

When you finish the outline, print a block to the clipboard. The block should not include column A unless you want everything indented in the Word Processor. If you do want everything indented, include column A and change its width to the number of character spaces you need. Incidentally, this is the only way to indent: printing to the clipboard ignores any margin settings.

```
File: C5.Outline               REVIEW/ADD/CHANGE            Escape: Main Menu
=====A==B==C=============D=====================E=================F======
   1 =A==B==C============D================::=========E============
   2
   3    Chapter 5: Integration
   4       Overview
   5       General Transfer Tips
   6          Print and annotate hard copies
   7          Document all work
   8          Plan information transfers on paper
   9       Transfer Methods
  10          Use clipboard whenever possible
  11          DIF has been well documented
  12
  13
  14
  15
  16
  17
  18
-------------------------------------------------------------------------
C6

Type entry or use @ commands                              @-? for Help
```

Figure 5.6: *Outline in the Spreadsheet*

Tip: *Use the Spreadsheet to construct and store large tables for the Word Processor.*

Use the overstrike cursor in the Word Processor to construct small tables. With simple data tables up to four columns wide and a dozen rows long, you generally get it right on the first layout. With larger, more complicated tables, you rarely get it right the first time. Your initial design attempt often provides a better understanding of the problem, leading to new insights and significant revisions. When you have to copy long vertical borders, calculate results, and align many columns, nothing matches the versatility of the Spreadsheet.

When you construct a table, use the PARTS template shown in Figure 4.14 for borders and other small parts. When you finish the table, print it to the clipboard. Make certain it is no longer than the Word Processor line or 75 characters. If the table is longer than the Word Processor line, the table lines will wrap. If the table is longer than 75 characters, the extra characters will be truncated when you print to the clipboard.

If you send a narrow table to the Word Processor, you can use column A to include a left margin. You can then use the overstrike cursor to enter a label from the Word Processor. Figure 5.7 shows an example.

Tip: *Expand the Spreadsheet PARTS file to serve as a note pad and calculator for the Word Processor.*

This is most useful when you have enough memory to load the AppleWorks program into a RAM drive, which allows AppleWorks to change instantly from one program to another.

The expanded PARTS file can be divided into five sections: calculations, notes, template parts, commonly used formulas, and reference data (see Figure 5.8). The first ten rows are for calculations, the next ten for notes, the next twenty for parts, and so on. If you enter the label Last Cell in row 81, you can move the cursor to the beginning of each section by using Apple-1 through

```
File: Data.Table            REVIEW/ADD/CHANGE           Escape: Main Menu
=====|====|====|====|====|====|====|====|====|====|====|====|====|====|====|===

Exhibit 28a:            Arable Acreage  Yield in
                        in Thousands   Metric Tons
              Crop       of Hectares   per Hectare
              ------------------------------------
              Hay            664        4.3
              Barley         661        3.4
              Oats           459        3.4
              Autumn wheat   221        4.5
              Spring rape     99        1.7
              Rye             73        3.4
              Spring wheat    62        3.9
              Mixed grain     57        2.9
              Autumn rape     55        2.4
              Sugar beet      52       44.0
              Potatoes        43       28.7
              ------------------------------------
              Total         2446

--------------------------------------------------------------------------
Type entry or use @ commands           Line 2  Column  1      @-? for Help
```

Figure 5.7: *Spreadsheet table edited on the Word Processor*

Apple-6. Using row 81 simply controls the dividing points, so change the location according to your space needs.

You can leave calculations on the worksheet for future reference. The PARTS file should be locked, so that you cannot save

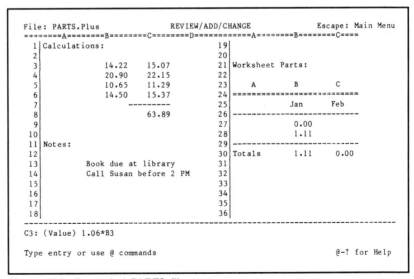

```
File: PARTS.Plus            REVIEW/ADD/CHANGE           Escape: Main Menu
========A========B========C========D============A========B========C====
   1|Calculations:              19|
   2|                           20|
   3|        14.22   15.07      21|Worksheet Parts:
   4|        20.90   22.15      22|
   5|        10.65   11.29      23|    A        B        C
   6|        14.50   15.37      24|========================
   7|              ---------    25|            Jan      Feb
   8|                63.89      26|------------------------
   9|                           27|            0.00
  10|                           28|            1.11
  11|Notes:                     29|------------------------
  12|                           30|Totals      1.11     0.00
  13|        Book due at library 31|
  14|        Call Susan before 2 PM 32|
  15|                           33|
  16|                           34|
  17|                           35|
  18|                           36|
--------------------------------------------------------------------------
C3: (Value) 1.06*B3

Type entry or use @ commands                             @-? for Help
```

Figure 5.8: *Expanded PARTS file*

it by that name. However, you can save the file as Calculator or some other appropriate name. If the calculations support a Word Processor file named Farm.Report, you can name the Spreadsheet file C.Farm.Report, using just a prefix.

Tip: *You can convert addresses in Spreadsheet rows to mailing labels in the Word Processor.*

The Spreadsheet is often used as a database manager, but it has no facility for creating labels-style report formats. Nevertheless, you can produce mailing labels by printing an unformatted ASCII file to disk and then making a Word Processor file from the ASCII file. The worksheet cells will be transferred in stacked form, with each cell ending in a carriage return marker.

If you plan to create mailing labels this way, use one worksheet cell for each complete address line. Figure 5.9 shows the Spreadsheet format, and Figure 5.10 shows the Word Processor result. Notice that the transfer included empty worksheet column E to place empty lines between addresses in the Word Processor. The

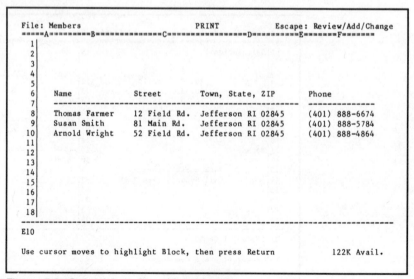

```
File: Members                          PRINT            Escape: Review/Add/Change
=====A=========B================C=================D=========E=======F=======
  1|
  2|
  3|
  4|
  5|
  6|   Name            Street          Town, State, ZIP      Phone
  7|   ------------     -----------     ----------------      --------------
  8|   Thomas Farmer    12 Field Rd.    Jefferson RI 02845    (401) 888-6674
  9|   Susan Smith      81 Main Rd.     Jefferson RI 02845    (401) 888-5784
 10|   Arnold Wright    52 Field Rd.    Jefferson RI 02845    (401) 888-4864
 11|
 12|
 13|
 14|
 15|
 16|
 17|
 18|
    -----------------------------------------------------------------------
E10

Use cursor moves to highlight Block, then press Return            122K Avail.
```

Figure 5.9: *Spreadsheet file with addresses*

```
File: Members.Stack          REVIEW/ADD/CHANGE          Escape: Main Menu
====|====|====|====|====|====|====|====|====|====|====|====|====|====|====|===
Thomas Farmer
12 Field Rd.
Jefferson RI 02845

Susan Smith
81 Main Rd.
Jefferson RI 02845

Arnold Wright
52 Field Rd.
Jefferson RI 02845




---------------------------------------------------------------------------
Type entry or use @ commands          Line 1   Column  1      @-? for Help
```

Figure 5.10: *Word Processor file from unformatted ASCII file*

same general approach works with other kinds of lists in Spread-sheet rows.

Note that printing to the clipboard does not accomplish the same thing: it prints the formatted block as it appears on the worksheet. Printing to the disk with Silentype also prints the whole formatted block, and it includes any margins specified in the printer options.

Tip: *Use the Spreadsheet to print multicolumn text.*

Many newsletters and manuals use a multicolumn layout. There are advantages to printing master copies in multicolumn layout rather than cutting and pasting. You can print in two columns by loading text from the Word Processor into the Spreadsheet. This also allows you to move columns around to change the layout. Start by opening a Word Processor file and proceed as follows:

1. Write the text. You may prefer to do this within the default margins.

2. Set the left margin to 0 inches. Use the right margin setting to create the line length you need for one column of a multicolumn layout.

3. Insert the characters xx into each of any blank lines in your file to preserve those lines in a DIF file. Figure 5.11 shows the file just before printing.

4. Using the Silentype, print the file to disk.

Because a Spreadsheet cannot be created from an ASCII file, the formatted ASCII file must first be converted to a Data Base file. To do this, follow these steps:

5. Return to the Main Menu, and make a new Data Base file from an ASCII file. The Data Base should have only one category, and you will see only the beginning of each line. Figure 5.12 shows the Data Base file in multiple-record layout.

6. Create a tables-style report format. Accept what is shown, even though you still see only the beginning of each line.

7. Print the report to a DIF file on the disk.

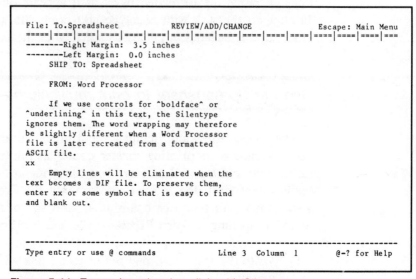

Figure 5.11: *Text to be printed to disk with Silentype*

```
File: Temp                    REVIEW/ADD/CHANGE              Escape: Main Menu

Selection: All records


Category 01
================================================================================
        SHIP TO: S
-
        FROM: Word
-
        If we use
underlining in
ignores them. T
be slightly dif
file is later r
ASCII file.
xx
        Empty line
text becomes a
enter xx or som
and blank out.
--------------------------------------------------------------------------------
Type entry or use @ commands                                  @-? for Help
```

Figure 5.12: *Text in a one-category Data Base file*

Finally, the DIF file must be converted to a Spreadsheet file, as follows:

8. Return to the Main Menu and make a new Spreadsheet file from the DIF file.

9. Widen the column you will be using.

Figure 5.13 shows the completed transfer. This is the starting point for using the Spreadsheet as a layout surface for multi-column text.

Tip: *Use the worksheet as a layout surface for a newsletter.*

Think of the worksheet as a large layout surface, something like a drafting table. Suppose you have transferred a column of text that is 90 rows long. Once that single column of text is on the worksheet, you can quickly copy sections of it to any place on the layout surface (leaving column space wherever any illustrations will

```
 File: Shipped                 REVIEW/ADD/CHANGE              Escape: Main Menu
 ========================A=========================B========C========D====
   1|      SHIP TO: Spreadsheet
   2|      FROM: Word Processor
   3|      If we use controls for boldface or
   4|underlining in this text, the Silentype
   5|ignores them. The word wrapping may therefore
   6|be slightly different when a Word Processor
   7|file is later recreated from a formatted
   8|ASCII file.
   9|xx
  10|      Empty lines will be eliminated when the
  11|text becomes a DIF file. To preserve them,
  12|enter xx or some symbol that is easy to find
  13|and blank out.
  14|
  15|
  16|
  17|
  18|
 -------------------------------------------------------------------------
 A9: (Label) xx

 Type entry or use @ commands                              @-? for Help
```

Figure 5.13: *Text in the Spreadsheet*

be inserted). You can then blank the original text location whenever you want.

Given enough memory, a worksheet can hold up to 999 rows in a column and up to about 30 columns of 45-character lines (fewer columns if the lines are longer). Remember from Chapter 4 that rows have capacity limits, and they apply to text as well.

There is a basic technique for using the worksheet as a layout surface. Recall that the copy command allows you to copy whole rows, whole columns, or blocks within the document. Unlike the blocks used for printing, these blocks can include part of only one row or column. The move command within the document moves only whole rows and columns.

To move text from rows 80–90 in column A to rows 10–20 in column B, copy within the worksheet. Follow these steps:

1. Press Apple-C to begin the sequence.

2. Press W for within.

3. Use the arrow keys to highlight the source block.

4. Press Return.

5. Move the cursor to cell B10, the first cell of the destination block.

6. Press Return again.

7. Blank cells B80 to B90 if they are no longer needed.

Notice that you did not have to specifically indicate the beginning and end of the destination block: there is only one way for a self-contained block to fall into place. A block of text has no references to any cells beyond its boundaries.

Caution: *In the Spreadsheet, proportional printing works with one column only.*

You can use proportional printing by entering the appropriate printer control codes under SC in the printer options. It will work as long as you have only one column of text in block paragraph form, within the limits described in Chapter 2.

Proportional printing will not work for multicolumn printing. If one column line fills only part of the available line space, characters in the next column to the right will shift over to fill some of that space.

Tip: *Use the Word Processor to document Spreadsheet templates, then copy the documentation to another Spreadsheet file.*

This is useful when you are not using the AppleWorks program in a RAM drive. The reason for putting Spreadsheet template documentation on another worksheet is simple: AppleWorks can change between Spreadsheet files faster than between files of two different programs.

When a Spreadsheet template requires considerable documentation, write the documentation on the Word Processor. Using the same procedures described in the tip on printing multicolumn text, send the text to a Spreadsheet file. Make column A narrow, and place the text in a wide column B. If the application is named BUDGET, the documentation file should be named BUDGET.DOC.

WORD PROCESSOR AND DATA BASE

The Word Processor and the Data Base can complement one another well, but few people use this capability to advantage. The AppleWorks Mailing Program provides the most useful techniques— tips on using this program are provided in the next section.

In AppleWorks, you will often transfer mailing lists from the Data Base to the Word Processor. This section provides some efficient techniques for doing this. You will sometimes need to transfer mailing lists from the Word Processor to the Data Base. After a few transfers you should feel confident about using ASCII files. Then you can use the same techniques with information other than mailing lists.

Tip: *Use the Word Processor to complete the editing of Data Base reports.*

You may find that you need to underline book and periodical titles in a Data Base report used for citations. In a financial report, you may want to add dollar signs or boldface print. You may want to replace selected words or numbers with new information. In short, you can use the Word Processor for what it does best.

In this kind of transfer, you print to the clipboard from a report format. Note that the report can also include category names with this method.

Tip: *You can convert Word Processor mailing lists to Data Base files.*

A list of mailing addresses in the Word Processor will normally appear as shown in Figure 5.14. By entering carriage returns after first name, town, and State, you can create the format shown in Figure 5.15, which the Data Base can then easily interpret when you make a new Data Base file from an ASCII file.

Notice the slash mark (/) in Figure 5.15. It indicates the end of a record, so you will know that it was an intentional entry, not a blank line entered by mistake. Another mark will do, provided you use it for this purpose only. The pound sign (#) would not be a good choice, because it is commonly used in addresses with rural routes, box numbers, apartment numbers, and so on. It helps to see a consistent pattern of six lines and a standard mark. You can remove the marks quickly with Apple-' once everything has been transferred to the Data Base.

```
File: Members.List            REVIEW/ADD/CHANGE            Escape: Main Menu
=====|====|====|====|====|====|====|====|====|====|====|====|====|====|====|===
Thomas Farmer
12 Field Rd.
Jefferson RI 02845

Susan Smith
81 Main Rd.
Jefferson RI 02845

Arnold Wright
52 Field Rd.
Jefferson RI 02845




---------------------------------------------------------------------------
Type entry or use @ commands        Line 1  Column  1       @-? for Help
```

Figure 5.14: Address list in the Word Processor

```
File: Members.List.2          REVIEW/ADD/CHANGE          Escape: Main Menu
=====|====|====|====|====|====|====|====|====|====|====|====|====|====|===
Thomas
Farmer
12 Field Rd.
Jefferson
RI
02845
/
Susan
Smith
81 Main Rd.
Jefferson
RI
02845
 /
Arnold
Wright
52 Field Rd.
Jefferson
RI
02845
---------------------------------------------------------------------------
Type entry or use @ commands          Line 1  Column  1          @-? for Help
```

Figure 5.15: Revised format of Figure 5.14 for transfer to the Data Base

Caution: *Several things can go wrong during ASCII file conversions.*

First, count the number of categories in your mailing list. In Figure 5.15 there are seven, including the / category. Make a note of the number. If you enter the wrong number, the categories will be filled incorrectly.

Second, remember to calculate pages (with Apple-K) before printing from the cursor. If you print from the cursor without calculating pages first, AppleWorks may print text from the previous page. You must use Apple-K first to ensure accurate printing.

Enter a pause here marker (PH) right after the mailing list, and print from the cursor. In this case you are printing to an unformatted ASCII file. Begin printing, and when the flashing cursor reappears on the print menu, press Escape—you want to stop at the end of the mailing list rather than print to the end of the file.

Tip: *You can add mailing lists created in the Word Processor to existing Data Base files.*

This is a useful extension of the tip for converting a Word Processor mailing list to the Data Base. Once you create a new Data Base file from an ASCII file, the records can be copied to another Data Base file. As we learned in Chapter 3, the original category order of the Data Base source file must match the original category order of the destination file, at least for the categories in question. Consult Chapter 3 for the necessary details.

Tip: *The Word Processor can be used to separate combined Data Base categories.*

Suppose you have entered the town name, state postal abbreviation, and ZIP code in the same Data Base category, as in Jefferson RI 02881. In some cases that may be a wise allocation of categories and data entry time; in other cases it can be a design error, especially if you need to sort by ZIP code to take advantage of lower mailing rates.

How do you separate combined categories? You create a new database by following these steps:

1. Print copies of the single- and multiple-record layout screens and any other screens you will need to reconstruct the Data Base file.

2. Create a tables-style report format with all the categories in the order you want them.

3. Print the report to an unformatted text (ASCII) file on disk.

4. Create a Word Processor file from the ASCII file.

5. Separate the combined records by pressing the Return key each time you want a new category.

6.   Print the edited text to an ASCII file.

7.   Make a new Data Base from the ASCII file.

8.   Reconstruct the report formats and custom record layouts.

Notice that this procedure is similar to the one that was used in Figures 5.14 and 5.15. After you have separated combined categories once, you will learn to design record layouts with a sharp eye to future needs.

Tip: *Use the Word Processor to document Data Base templates, then copy the documentation to another Data Base file.*

This is useful when you are not using the AppleWorks program in a RAM drive. The reason for putting Data Base template documentation on another database is simple: AppleWorks can change between Data Base files faster than between files of two different programs.

When a Data Base template requires considerable documentation, write the documentation on the Word Processor. Using the same procedures described in the tip on printing multicolumn text, send the text to a Data Base file. Remember that the text requires only one category. Widen the first and only category in multiple-record layout. If the application is named LIST, the documentation file should be named LIST.DOC.

USING THE APPLEWORKS MAILING PROGRAM

The inexpensive AppleWorks Mailing Program (AMP) from International Apple Core generates form letters. Although it has been marketed for that purpose, it has at least as much value for extended Data Base reporting.

In addition, AMP provides a model for writing Applesoft BASIC programs that are compatible with AppleWorks. The disk contains two versions of the program. The first version includes complete remark (REM) statements. The second, which you normally use, does not.

Tip: *Edit the AMP instruction files before you print them.*

The AppleWorks Mailing Program comes on a single disk in a plastic mailer. To get a copy of the instructions, you simply print the three AppleWorks Word Processor files on the disk. Use Apple-Z to review the formatting instructions and delete those that are inappropriate for your needs. For example, the CI settings are variously 4, 10, 12, and 15 (pointless if you have a daisy-wheel printer or prefer simplicity).

Tip: *AMP is easy to modify.*

The instructions provided with the program explain how to change one line in the program to adapt AMP for printer interface cards other than the Apple parallel card. Although the program was written in Applesoft BASIC, it runs fast enough for most mail-merge purposes. Because the disk includes a version of the program with complete remarks, you can make your own modifications. Anyone interested in using AppleWorks screen design conventions in Applesoft BASIC programs will want to study this listing.

Caution: *To use AMP, you must add another printer for printing to disk.*

AMP requires Word Processor files that have been printed to disk using your standard printer, normally assigned to slot 1. The process is similar to printing ASCII files to disk, except that AMP wants the file to include any AppleWorks character enhancements and other printer options you have used.

The only way you can get a printer to print to disk is to specify that this is how the printer will be accessed. Surprisingly, there is no way to change the printer access option, as you can with other options. Therefore, you must add another printer to AppleWorks.

If your standard printer is listed, add the same listed printer again, with one difference: on the menu for adding a printer, specify that the printer will be accessed by printing onto disk.

If your standard printer is a custom printer, you must make another copy of the AppleWorks Program disk, delete the custom printer, and then add a custom printer dedicated to printing to disk. On the menu for adding a printer, specify that the printer will be accessed by printing onto disk.

Tip: *AMP uses standard Data Base report formats.*

Some mail-merge programs require report formats with special characters (such as dollar signs) beginning each report category. AMP lets you use your existing report formats to print unformatted text (ASCII) files to disk.

Form letters for AMP must be written with data-merge indicators, such as [MERGE1], to identify places where AMP must enter information. The mailing label report format in Chapter 3 can be used to supply the form letter heading shown in Figure 5.16. Notice that the letter uses a first-name greeting. The asterisk in [MERGE3*] means that the line will be omitted if that category has no information. AMP sets up each letter individually, typically every six to ten seconds if you use a printer buffer. Otherwise it waits for the printer.

If you need the telephone number category in the letter, you can add that category at the bottom of the mailing labels report. Use Apple-L from within the report format. Any or all of the database categories can be added this way, and AMP will count them from left to right, top to bottom in the report format.

AMP's simple approach has another advantage: it can also use Spreadsheet data printed to an unformatted ASCII file. Each row is treated as a record, each column as a category. To create

```
File: Merge.Markers           REVIEW/ADD/CHANGE           Escape: Main Menu
=====|====|====|====|====|====|====|====|====|====|====|====|====|====|===

December 8, 1985

[MERGE1] [MERGE2]
[MERGE3*]
[MERGE4*]
[MERGE5] [MERGE6] [MERGE7]

Dear [MERGE1]:

     The text of the letter can also include merged information
from each Data Base record.  For example, if you want readers to
verify information in their respective records, you can list the
remaining categories in the following form:

Telephone: [MERGE 8]




-----------------------------------------------------------------------------
Type entry or use @ commands          Line 16  Column 47      @-? for Help
```

Figure 5.16: *Form letter*

special reports, you can move columns, arrange records, and define the worksheet block to be printed.

Tip: *Use AMP for extended Data Base reporting.*

There will be times when the reports you need will require more than the Data Base can provide. For example, you may want to write narrative reports with information from records inserted within sentences, or in tables between paragraphs.

Although AMP is called a mailing program, it can manage all 30 fields for this kind of extended Data Base reporting. The housing example used in Chapter 3 (Figure 3.20) might well use AMP to advantage. Suppose you want a standard narrative report on each of several properties. This report resembles a common form letter, except that the merges occur within the report text rather than in the heading. Each report is intended for someone interested in acquiring the property.

You could begin with a paragraph that provides a context for the specific information. The second paragraph might include the following:

The property at [MERGE1] [MERGE2] includes a [MERGE3]-family house. The recorded back taxes amount to [MERGE4], and the recorded lien on the property is [MERGE5].

Caution: *You must design applications around AMP's specific limitations.*

The limitations are well documented. AMP can handle from one to six merges per line, but it cannot make adjustments for lines that are shortened or extended by merged information. It will not print category names when they are specified in the report format. Sometimes you will have to plan carefully to allow for these limitations.

DATA BASE AND SPREADSHEET

It is sometimes difficult to know whether an application belongs in the Data Base or in the Spreadsheet. Large advanced applications often begin in the Data Base and then transfer data to the Spreadsheet for specialized calculations.

In general, you should use the program you know best. Some people prefer to use the Spreadsheet because they can move the cursor to any piece of information quickly. Others prefer the Data Base because of the single-record entry screen. Sometimes you simply understand one program better than the other and can make it do more.

Tip: *Develop your own rules of thumb about when to transfer information.*

Recall the Apple IIe system budget we developed in Chapter 4 (Figure 4.3). Suppose you want to list everything related to the system: current prices, suppliers, and so on. You would soon have a large block of information. Should that information be a database? In this case, my advice would be to keep it as a worksheet unless there happened to be some need for a labels-style report format. The Spreadsheet can provide enough functions for this purpose, including arranging (sorting) by rows and finding text entries.

Adding other information, such as supplier addresses, might tip the balance toward the Data Base. Or suppose you want to use a complicated record-selection rule. With the worksheet on the screen, you can make a Data Base file as follows:

1. Press Apple-P and then B to print a block of information.

2. Use the arrow keys to highlight the block and press Return.

3. Select the option to print to a DIF file and press Return.

4. Press 2 for the column option. Enter a brief path name and press Return.

5. When the file has been saved, return to the Main Menu.

6. Create a Data Base file from the DIF file. Enter the path name and press Return.

7. Enter a name for the Data Base file and press Return.

8. Name each of the numbered categories you intend to use.

Tip: *Use the Spreadsheet to analyze quantitative information from the Data Base.*

Report formats and record-selection rules permit transfer of data subsets from the Data Base to the Spreadsheet for such things as statistical analysis and applications requiring many calculations, which only the Spreadsheet can handle.

Tip: *Use the Spreadsheet and Data Base capacity limits to complement one another.*

If you need to manage a database with fewer than 999 records but more than 30 categories, the Spreadsheet is a logical choice. For example, suppose you have 100 records with 50 categories. Even though each record may have fewer than 1,024 characters, a single Data Base file cannot accommodate them.

If you need to manage a database with fewer than 999 records but more than 1,024 characters, the Spreadsheet is again a logical choice. For example, suppose you have 100 records with up to 1,500 characters each. Even though the file may have only 30 categories, a single Data Base file cannot accommodate them.

If you need to manage a database with more than 999 records, the Data Base is the logical choice. But what happens if you have more than 30 categories or 1,024 characters? There are three choices: parallel Data Base files, parallel Spreadsheet files, or both.

A description of the third option effectively describes the first two as well. Suppose you have a file of 1,200 records with 36 categories. Ten categories are descriptive text, such as name, address, and so on. The other 26 categories are values, many of which will be used in calculations. Follow these steps to set up parallel files:

1. Make a Data Base file from a template (such as the LIST template described in Chapter 3).

2. Give each record a unique identification number, preferably values from 1 to 1,200.

3. Enter data into the first ten information categories.

4. Make another parallel Data Base file and assign corresponding identification numbers to the records.

5. Enter data into the remaining 26 information categories.

6. From the second Data Base, print 600 records to one DIF file and 600 records to another.

7. Make two new Spreadsheet files from the DIF files.

Now there are two Data Base files and two Spreadsheet files. The categories most often used with record-selection rules should be in the first Data Base file. The categories most often calculated should be in the Spreadsheet files. The Data Base files are the master files. Any revised information goes into the master file, from which new DIF and Spreadsheet files are generated.

Parallel files can remain forever separated, linked only by shared identification numbers for respective records. Parallel files can also trade categories if necessary. For example, you can print one Data Base category to a column-order DIF file as follows:

1. Arrange all files by ascending identification numbers.

2. Create a tables-style report format for just the selected category.

3. Select the first 250 identification numbers and print to a DIF file.

4. Create a new Spreadsheet file from the DIF file.

5. Copy the 250 rows to empty rows (such as 700 through 950) in the destination Spreadsheet file.

6. Copy the blocks within the destination file, then delete rows 700 through 950.

7. Repeat the process until the category entries have been added to all the records in the Spreadsheet files.

After following this complicated process, you can understand the importance of designing applications to avoid unnecessary transfers.

Tip: *When you move data back and forth between the Data Base and Spreadsheet, use the column-order option.*

The DIF column-order option means that a Spreadsheet column will become a Data Base category. Column-order is the only option available in the Data Base. In the Spreadsheet you must be careful to specifically select column order, because row order is the default selection.

Caution: *In transfers from the Spreadsheet to the Data Base, the order of the origin and destination files must match.*

When you use DIF files to transfer data from the Spreadsheet to the Data Base, the Spreadsheet column order must match the Data Base original category order.

These DIF data transfers are never direct: going from the Spreadsheet you must make a new Data Base file from the DIF file, copy records to the clipboard, and then move the records from the clipboard to the destination file. In this kind of transfer it is best to first move columns on the origin worksheet to match the Data Base original category order.

When you use DIF files to transfer data from the Data Base to the Spreadsheet, the Data Base report format order need not match the Spreadsheet column order. Going from the Data Base you must make a new Spreadsheet file from the DIF file, copy records to the clipboard, and then move the records from the clipboard to the destination file. Before copying to the clipboard, you can move columns to match the column order of the destination worksheet.

Tip: *You can also use ASCII files to transfer data from the Spreadsheet to the Data Base.*

Using ASCII files has an advantage: it maintains the number of decimal places specified for value cells on the origin worksheet.

Transfer data from the Spreadsheet to the Data Base by printing a selected block of cells to an unformatted text (ASCII) file on disk. Create a new Data Base from the ASCII file, copy the records to the clipboard, and then move the records from the clipboard to the destination file. In this kind of transfer it is best first to move columns on the origin worksheet to match the Data Base original category order.

You cannot transfer data by ASCII file from the Data Base to the Spreadsheet, because the Spreadsheet cannot accept these files.

Caution: *Earlier versions of AppleWorks have trouble recognizing DIF files.*

When you attempt to create a Spreadsheet file from a DIF file, earlier versions of AppleWorks may respond incorrectly, repeatedly asking for the path name of the DIF file. If you first have the Data Base find the DIF file, the Spreadsheet program will respond correctly. Here's how to make the Data Base find the file without actually creating a Data Base:

1. Return to the Main Menu, and choose option 1 to add files to the Desktop.

2. Select the option to create a Data Base file from a DIF file.

3. Specify from 1 to 30 categories for the file.

4. Specify the path name of the DIF file.

5. When asked to enter a name for the Data Base file, escape to the Main Menu.

6. Begin the process again, this time to make a new Spreadsheet file from a DIF file.

If you repeatedly transfer data between the Data Base and Spreadsheet, you should use version 1.2 of AppleWorks.

Tip: *Data takes up a little less memory in the Data Base.*

There is a small advantage to using the Data Base over the Spreadsheet: the same data uses less memory space. For example, an 80K database in the Spreadsheet may require only 70K in the Data Base. For applications near the limits of your Apple system's memory, this may be a significant factor when you decide which program to use. The Data Base can also arrange more records—1,350 (and potentially more than 5,000) compared with a maximum of 999 for the Spreadsheet. In short, although database applications tend to be large, the Data Base uses memory very efficiently.

PRODOS AND DOS 3.3

AppleWorks teaches you about some of the things you can do with ASCII files, and the lesson continues beyond AppleWorks to other software. In transferring files, you will sometimes need to convert from DOS 3.3 format to ProDOS format. It takes just enough time to make you think twice about commuting along that route every day.

If you have an Apple IIe, you probably have the ProDOS User's Disk Utilities. If you have an Apple IIc, you have a disk called the ProDOS System Utilities. These are the disks you need for transferring files between ProDOS and DOS 3.3.

Tip: *Learn the differences between DOS 3.3 and ProDOS files.*

DOS 3.3 and ProDOS files differ in many ways, but one difference is particularly important: a disk formatted for ProDOS has a volume name preceded by a slash mark (/). The volume name is separated from any file name by another slash. The name can be brief, such as the /P used throughout this book.

ProDOS volume names can be no more than 15 characters long. The same rule applies to ProDOS file names. Volume names commonly precede file names, as in /P/Filename. Together they are called the path name.

Tip: *Think of a ProDOS volume as a disk.*

For most AppleWorks purposes, a ProDOS volume is the same as a standard 136K floppy disk. Although a ProDOS volume can have subdirectories, there is really no need to use them with a two-disk-drive system. An AppleWorks data disk seldom has more than about 20 AppleWorks files, so there is rarely any confusion. If you have a hard disk or a high-capacity floppy disk, however, subdirectories provide branching paths for finding your way through many files.

Caution: *The ProDOS utilities have limitations when converting ASCII files from ProDOS to DOS 3.3.*

The Convert program correctly converts text files up to about 30K. (Note that it shows mouse characters instead of file names on the Apple IIc and Enhanced Apple IIe.) The equivalent Apple IIc program for changing disk formats is even more limited—to about 11K. The bottom line is that the path from ProDOS to DOS 3.3 is far more difficult than the route the other way. A following tip about on-line information services includes information on a useful ProDOS text-file splitter that enables you to limit the size of your files so the Convert program can handle them.

TO AND FROM APPLEWORKS

In most cases, AppleWorks will meet all your needs. But occasionally you will need to find a program that does something

AppleWorks cannot do. Consider overall efficiency when deciding which program to use for a given application. In engineering or navigation, where trigonometrical functions are used extensively, you may be better off using SuperCalc 3a or advanced VisiCalc than the AppleWorks Spreadsheet. You can always transfer information back to AppleWorks later. In this section we will look at some representative applications.

File transfers between ProDOS programs can be efficient enough for consistent use. File transfers between DOS 3.3 and ProDOS programs are more likely to be once-and-for-all transfers to the latter.

Tip: *Many word processors create ASCII files that you can easily convert to the AppleWorks Word Processor.*

Many AppleWorks users have some DOS 3.3 files that they want to convert to ProDOS. Suppose, for example, you want to convert a Screenwriter II text file to an AppleWorks Word Processor file. Because it is an ASCII file, the conversion proceeds as follows:

1. Insert the ProDOS utilities disk in drive 1 and turn on your Apple.

2. Press C to select the file-conversion utility. On the Convert menu, note that the arrow path is going the way you want—from DOS 3.3 in drive 2 to ProDOS in drive 1.

3. Insert the DOS 3.3 disk in drive 2.

4. Insert a formatted ProDOS disk in drive 1 and press P to set the ProDOS prefix (the name of the disk).

5. Press S to select the "slot and number" option, then press Return three times. The disk (ProDOS volume) will enter its own name.

6. Press T to transfer the file from DOS 3.3 to ProDOS.

When the disk drive stops running, you have a ProDOS file.

Now you can load AppleWorks and go to the Main Menu. Then proceed as follows:

7. Begin a Word Processor file from an ASCII file.

8. Enter the path name for the ASCII file and press Return.

9. Enter a Word Processor file name and press Return.

When the disk drive stops running, you have a usable Apple-Works Word Processor file.

Tip: *If a database manager can generate ASCII files, use that route to the AppleWorks Data Base.*

General Manager is a respected DOS 3.3 database manager capable of managing more than 60,000 records per file on a hard disk. It can generate reports that serve as address files for Screenwriter II, and those reports can include every field (category) in the record. General Manager accepts up to 99 fields on a parent screen, but the AppleWorks Data Base handles only 30, so there are obvious transfer limitations.

Suppose you have selected entries in 29 categories in a General Manager database that you want to transfer to an AppleWorks Data Base. Generate an address file in General Manager. Convert that file to an ASCII file, and create a Data Base file from that ASCII file. Every record ends with a line containing only a slash (/) (used to signal Screenwriter II). If you have 29 categories, you must count the line with the slash as category 30. This keeps the data transfer working correctly. Once you have named the new Data Base file and entered the appropriate category names, the transfer is complete.

Caution: *If you use DIF files to transfer information to the Data Base, make certain that the file is in column order.*

The Data Base will accept row-order DIF files, but the results may not be what you had in mind. For example, categories will then become records and vice versa. When in doubt, load DIF files first into the Spreadsheet, which can then generate a DIF file in the same order or rotated 90 degrees.

Tip: *Use other word processors for writing form letters.*

Some other word processors include mail-merge capabilities that are more powerful than those of the AppleWorks Mailing Program. For example, Screenwriter II uses logical tests to insert text blocks based on specified conditions.

Suppose you want to write a general letter of thanks to all members of a library association, and you want to add a special paragraph to those who contributed $50 or more during the past year. Screenwriter II can add such a paragraph. The logical test is written in code and can be paraphrased as follows:

"If the value in category 9 is greater than or equal to $50, print the following text block, otherwise go to the next signal character (typically an exclamation mark at the beginning of a line)."

Screenwriter II can use ASCII files generated by the Data Base and converted to DOS 3.3. The last category must contain a specified record delimiter such as a slash mark (/). Here the limits of the Convert program are particularly frustrating, because ASCII files used to generate form letters are often longer than 30K.

Tip: *Use specialized ProDOS database managers to complement AppleWorks.*

Though AppleWorks has a good multipurpose database manager, the Bookends Extended program from Sensible Software is a good specialized database manager that can be used to complement the AppleWorks Word Processor. Bookends Extended has special capabilities for managing citations, including the ability to store and select two forms of journal titles (which are often abbreviated in published articles). It has special capabilities for bibliographical information. For example, it can format reports for footnotes or bibliographies in any one of several styles, inserting the correct punctuation for each. As you may recall, the citation database in Chapter 3 was punctuated for one form of bibliography only.

Suppose you want to transfer a complete set of footnotes from Bookends to the AppleWorks Word Processor for use in a research paper. Bookends uses the ProDOS operating system, so you simply print a text (ASCII) file to disk and create a new Word Processor file from that file. Note, however, that with an ASCII file you must add your own underlining in the Word Processor.

Tip: *Use specialized ProDOS spreadsheets to complement AppleWorks.*

SuperCalc 3a and the ProDOS version of advanced VisiCalc have many functions that the AppleWorks Spreadsheet lacks. These include date-calculation functions used in accounting, trigonometric functions for engineering, and the option to retrieve text as the result of a formula.

AppleWorks will translate VisiCalc files quickly, within the limitations documented in Chapter 4. SuperCalc 3a will translate AppleWorks Spreadsheet files, albeit slowly, within the limitations documented in the remarkably thorough SuperCalc manual. Both SuperCalc 3a and advanced VisiCalc accept and receive DIF files created by AppleWorks.

Tip: *You can transfer information from files of many other programs.*

Many other programs, including most spreadsheets, can print text files to disk. You can convert these ASCII files from DOS 3.3 to ProDOS, and then begin a Word Processor file from the ASCII file. Once you have the data in AppleWorks, you can think about how it must be edited for transfers to the Data Base or Spreadsheet. The carriage return is a surprisingly useful tool in such cases.

One classic transfer example involves the graph format in standard VisiCalc. In that program you can specify the display of a number as an equivalent number of asterisks. With formulas, you can equate any number of units with each asterisk. However, there is no way to transfer the graph format to the AppleWorks Spreadsheet, which lacks that function. The pound function (#) in VisiCalc will preserve only the value, not the asterisks.

VisiCalc can print a text file to disk, and that allows you to transfer that graph format to the Word Processor. Chapter 4 includes an example (Figure 4.26). Notice that this is a formatted text file.

Caution: *The Word Processor default margins can make transferred spreadsheet print files look scrambled.*

The Word Processor one-inch left and right margins, along with the default setting for 10 characters per inch, limit intact transfers to 60-character lines rather than 77-character lines. That may make some spreadsheet print files look scrambled. Once the information is in the Word Processor file, resetting the margins to 0 inches should make most print files readable.

Tip: *Use information utilities to supplement AppleWorks.*

CompuServe, Delphi, and The Source are commonly used information services. You can download ASCII text from each. The ASCII files saved from the Apple memory buffer to disk can be edited and used in the Word Processor. Several communications programs are now available in ProDOS versions. The best known of these is ASCII Express. If you have DOS 3.3 communications software, convert your files to the ProDOS format first.

The following example is typical of the information you can acquire from the Micronetworked Apple Users Group (MAUG) on CompuServe and Delphi. The modem system described is a Zoom Telephonics Modem IIe with DOS 3.3 Netmaster communications software.

Each on-line information service has its own procedures for connection. For example, the Modem IIe can automatically dial a previously loaded CompuServe network telephone number for the initial connection. After a brief procedure of entering an identification number and password, you can go directly to the MAUG and access their files. If you are not already a member, you must sign on and come back the next day to access the most useful information.

One example of useful information is the ProDOS Text File Splitter, an Applesoft BASIC public domain program by Larry Miller. It splits ProDOS text files into a specified number of parts approximately equal in size. This program has two important uses. First, if you want to convert an existing large ProDOS ASCII file to DOS 3.3, you can break it into files of less than 30K. Second, if you download a large file from an information service and it exceeds Desktop memory, you can break it into smaller files.

The Netmaster program has a 42K text trap that can automatically save to memory everything transmitted to the screen. When the trap is full, you can save it to disk with a simple manual procedure. Some programs, such as ASCII Express, will save to disk automatically. In either case, your Apple can acquire the ProDOS Text File Splitter while you are reading from the screen. It is sent to disk as a text file, and in the next section you will learn how to convert it quickly to a working BASIC program.

APPLESOFT BASIC PROGRAMS

Many AppleWorks users want to download programs from information services. Many want to write Applesoft BASIC programs or modify existing programs for specific purposes. You may even want to develop programs that add capabilities to AppleWorks by processing ASCII or DIF files. The Word Processor can be a big help here. The program example in this section generates natural logarithms. You will remember, of course, that neither the Data Base nor Spreadsheet have logarithmic functions.

Tip: *The Word Processor is a useful Applesoft BASIC editor.*

AppleWorks can help you write and edit programs in Applesoft BASIC. The Word Processor provides many advantages for developing programs, such as the find and replace commands.

When working in BASIC, use uppercase letters, even where you might not in AppleWorks. The Apple IIc and enhanced Apple IIe can interpret lowercase letters in Applesoft BASIC programs, but other Apple IIs cannot.

To work with the following example, begin a Word Processor file from scratch, depress the Caps Lock key, and begin entering the numbered lines of code listed below. This program will generate natural logarithms in the form of an ASCII file that can then be loaded into the Data Base.

```
10   REM THIS PROGRAM PRINTS A LIST
20   REM OF VALUES AND THEIR LOGS
30   REM TO A DESIGNATED TEXT FILE
40   D$ = CHR$ (4)
50   INPUT "FILE:";XX$
60   PRINT D$;"OPEN";XX$
70   PRINT D$;"WRITE";XX$
80   FOR X = 3 TO 4 STEP 0.1
90   PRINT X
100  PRINT LOG (X)
110  NEXT X
120  PRINT D$;"CLOSE";XX$
130  END
```

When you have typed in the program, follow these steps to convert the Word Processor file into a working Applesoft BASIC program:

1. Print from the beginning of the file to a text (ASCII) file on disk. Enter the path name /P/LN.

2. Leave AppleWorks and load ProDOS in drive 1. When the menu appears, press B for BASIC. Note that the data disk can remain in drive 2.

3. Catalog the disk by entering CAT,S6,D2 and check to see that LN is there.

4. Enter EXEC LN to convert the text file to a BASIC file. Here you will see a series of right brackets (]).

5. Enter LIST to see the program.

6. Type SAVE LN2 to save the file as a BASIC program under a different file name.

7. Enter RUN to make it run. The program first asks you to name the file of logarithms it will be creating.

8. Enter the name LOGS in response to this prompt.

What is the program doing? Look at line 80 first. This program finds natural logarithms for specified values of X, in this case from 3 to 4, in increments of 0.1. The program will print a range of values and their natural logs to a text file (LOGS). The list will be 22 lines long in a single column, beginning as follows:

```
3
1.09861229
3.1
1.13140211
```

Notice that the values and natural logs alternate in a single column. This is an important feature, because you will be using the information in the Data Base. Now follow these steps:

1. Reload AppleWorks and start making a new Data Base file from a text (ASCII) file.

2. Specify two categories for the Data Base file, because each record is composed of a value and its natural log.

3. Designate the file with the proper path name, here /P/LOGS.

4. Give the new Data Base file a name.

Notice that the values and their respective natural logarithms are now in parallel columns, as shown in Figure 5.17. As you will remember from other examples in this chapter, this data can be transferred from the Data Base to the Spreadsheet in a DIF file.

This tip has provided a simple demonstration of an important concept. You can use Applesoft BASIC programs to perform special processing beyond the capabilities of AppleWorks, and the results can then be transferred to AppleWorks for editing and reporting. The program calculations, here confined to lines 80 through 110, could have been far more complex. Instead of having LN2 print to an ASCII file, you could have programmed it to print to a DIF file. For more on BASIC routines for creating DIF files, see Douglas Hergert's *Mastering VisiCalc* (SYBEX, 1983).

There are additional things to know. Save at least one copy of the original Word Processor file, so that you can use it to make necessary program revisions later. You can also write the program with no line numbers for the remark (REM) lines. When you run EXEC to convert the ASCII file into a BASIC program, those lines will be excluded from the program, making it run faster.

```
File: DB.LOGS               REVIEW/ADD/CHANGE           Escape: Main Menu

Selection: All records


Category 01    Category 02
=================================================================================
3              1.09861229
3.1            1.13140211
3.2            1.16315081
3.3            1.19392247
3.4            1.22377543
3.5            1.25276297
3.6            1.28093385
3.7            1.30833282
3.8            1.33500107
3.9            1.36097655
4              1.38629436




---------------------------------------------------------------------------------
Type entry or use @ commands                                      @-? for Help
```

Figure 5.17: Values and logarithms in the Data Base

Tip: *You can convert an Applesoft BASIC program back into an ASCII file.*

Suppose you want to revise a program that came on a disk. Or suppose you forgot to save a Word Processor version of your last program. Following is a short subroutine that will convert an Applesoft BASIC program back into a text file.

Begin a Word Processor file from scratch, depress the Caps Lock key, and enter these lines:

```
63500   D$ = CHR$(4)
63506   INPUT "FILE:";XX$
63508   PRINT D$;"OPEN";XX$
63510   PRINT D$;"WRITE";XX$
63512   LIST 1,63499
63514   PRINT D$;"CLOSE";XX$
63516   END
```

The unusual numbering in this program allows you to append it to virtually any Applesoft BASIC program ever written. The program is reprinted from page 163 of *The ProDOS Handbook,* by Timothy and Karen Rice (SYBEX, 1985), where additional notes on the utility of this program are included. Note how it resembles the structure of the LN2 program. Where LN2 calculates, this program simply lists. In fact, you could have entered it by editing the Word Processor file from which LN2 was created.

You can use this subroutine to make the BASIC file LN2 into a text file once again, in this case simply to demonstrate how you can use AppleWorks to edit it. Follow these steps:

1. Print from the beginning of the Word Processor file to a text (ASCII) file on disk. Enter the path name /P/ REVERSE.

2. Leave AppleWorks and load ProDOS in drive 1. When the menu appears, press B for BASIC. Note that the data disk can remain in drive 2.

3. Catalog the disk by entering CAT,S6, and check to see that LN2 and REVERSE are there.

4. Enter LOAD LN2.

5. Enter EXEC REVERSE.

6. Enter LIST to see the two programs merged.

7. Enter RUN 63500.

8. When requested, enter a file name such as LNX, because you may still have the original LN text file on the disk.

Now all you have to do is reload AppleWorks, make a new Word Processor file from the ASCII file named LNX, and the cycle is complete.

SUMMARY

This chapter has examined many techniques for transferring information within AppleWorks, as well as to and from Apple-Works. Some of the techniques are simple, some necessarily complicated. This chapter concludes the discussion of AppleWorks information processing. In the next chapter you will find some additional printing techniques that can be used with each of the three AppleWorks programs.

If you are interested in additional possibilities for applications development and information transfer, Appendix A looks at the potential for AppleWorks over the next few years.

6
Installing Printers

*T*his chapter discusses the mechanics of installing printers, interface cards, and buffers. If you are having problems with your printer, read this chapter first. Printer problems include such curious things as an "80N" printed at the beginning of a Word Processor file, too many spaces between lines, and similarly frustrating anomalies. You can generally tell when a printing problem is a printer problem, because it occurs with the simplest text formatting.

Once you have configured your printer correctly, you can use the standard printing options described in the first five chapters of this book. This chapter also includes advanced printing options that require an understanding of your printer's specific control codes. You may or may not be able to use all the techniques described in this chapter. If you discover some options that are important to you and your printer does not have them, make a check list to use whenever you buy another printer.

Information on printing appears in Chapter 13 of the Apple-Works Reference Manual. Read that chapter first if you have a printer listed there. If your printer is not listed there, read Appendix B of the Reference Manual. Consult this chapter if your printer is not working as you had expected.

This chapter provides tips and techniques for installing printers in seven sections. It begins with the most general tips, then moves on to tips on using interface cards. The following section provides techniques for using printers included on the AppleWorks list of available printers. Following that is a section on custom printers, providing important information on installing printers that Apple-Works has not included on its list. You will also learn why some listed printers should also be added as custom printers as well. A section on control codes includes several advanced methods for substituting and "piggybacking" codes. (Note that control codes are sometimes called command codes in printer manuals.)

In the section on printing techniques, you should pay particular attention to the cautions about differences between tenths of an inch and other fractions, particularly if you regularly print onto forms. The last section contains reference information on using printer buffers, one of the most cost-effective investments you can make.

GENERAL PRINTER TIPS

The following tips provide the most basic information about using printers with AppleWorks. If you are looking for a printer, pay special attention to considerations in choosing a printer. If you already have a good printer, take out your manual and read up on the things you will need to know for this chapter.

Tip: *Consider the printing speed, print quality, and level of noise when you choose a printer.*

Objective information on printers is surprisingly difficult to find. Few periodicals have conducted independent comparative tests of decibel ratings, printing speed, and print quality. These measurements sometimes differ markedly from manufacturers' claims.

If you cannot find good, independent tests of printers you are considering, develop a benchmark printing test on a known printer. How long do printers A and B take to print the same Word Processor file? One printer may be faster moving through white space (as on invoices), while another may be faster printing characters. Design the test to reflect your most common printing needs.

Note that some dot-matrix printers are very fast, but only in draft fonts you may not find easy to read. Some fonts are easy to read but different from daisy-wheel print. If you really need true letter-quality print for letters and reports, there are some good, small daisy-wheel printers.

Listen to the printer run in an otherwise quiet place. Sit as near to it as you would in normal use. If the sound irritates you, consider choosing another printer. For example, a letter-quality printer running at less than 15 characters per second may sound enough like a human typist to be familiar and quite tolerable. That may be a more important consideration than marginally greater speed or a slightly lower decibel rating.

Caution: *Before you buy a printer, find out whether the tractors are unidirectional or bidirectional.*

This caution is particularly important for those who use superscripts and subscripts, which require paper movement in both directions on most printers. Almost any printer can do this in the friction-feed mode, but some cannot do it with their pin- and tractor-feed mechanisms. If you print long papers with footnotes, for example, you need a bidirectional tractor. Friction feed is never quite good enough, because the paper slowly drifts on the roller, just a little to the right or left with each page.

Tip: *Keep your printer manual nearby.*

Of all the manuals you own, your printer manual is the one you will use most often. Make photocopies of the pages that list control codes, and insert the copies in your AppleWorks notebook. Use a yellow marker to highlight important information, and add tabs to key pages. Consult the manual when you enter special printer codes in the Data Base and Spreadsheet.

Tip: *Printers are listed in the order you added them.*

When you first tell AppleWorks you want to print, the proposed printer is always the one at the top of the list. To have your printer there you must configure it first, even if that means removing the Apple Dot Matrix Printer and the Imagewriter that Apple has already added. It helps to have your standard printer on top, so you can use Return to step through the printing menu sequence.

INTERFACE CARDS

Earlier versions of AppleWorks made no provision for changing interface card control codes. Version 1.2 finally makes it easy to install non-Apple interfaces, many of which offer remarkable performance at reasonable prices. You can also find Apple-compatible parallel interface cards for less than $50.

Tip: *If your printer prints incorrectly, check the interface card configuration first.*

Even if you have a listed printer, your interface card may not respond to the default control codes entered for Apple interface cards. AppleWorks version 1.2 lets you change the control codes yourself, as shown in Figure 6.1. Control-I 80N is the default setting, but if you have installed a Grappler card, for example, Control-I 0N (zero N) is what you need.

AppleWorks versions 1.0 and 1.1 assume that you have an Apple interface card, so these versions do not provide any other configuration options. Many people with earlier versions of AppleWorks and Grappler cards find 80N printed at the beginning of every Word Processor file. If this is your problem, bring your original AppleWorks disks to an Apple dealer for a free disk

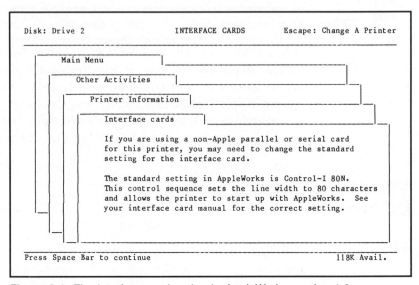

Figure 6.1: *The interface card option in AppleWorks version 1.2*

upgrade to version 1.2 and change the interface card control code. Then if you change interface cards at some point in the future, you can change the control codes easily.

Tip: *If you use AppleWorks version 1.1, Apple offers a free patch for non-Apple interface cards.*

Apple dealers provide technical support for Apple hardware and software. Through the dealer network, Apple offers a free program for version 1.1 called the AppleWorks Interface Card Configuration Utility. Another way to obtain this program is to capture it as a text file through CompuServe from the Micronetworked Apple Users Group (MAUG) mentioned in Chapter 5.

With this Configuration Utility, you can modify a copy of the AppleWorks Startup disk so that it supports the Grappler card. When you have the Startup disk of version 1.1 modified for the Grappler card, the first screen will say "V1.1G USA". Note, however, that almost everyone would be wiser simply to upgrade from an earlier version to version 1.2.

APPLEWORKS PRINTERS

AppleWorks allows you to install three printers, one of which can be a custom printer. A fourth "printer" is already installed for printing unformatted ASCII files to disk. (When AppleWorks prints to disk, it has to pretend that it's accessing a printer.) In this section we will cover the mechanics of installing the first three printers. We will install two of these printers to perform specialized functions.

Tip: *Install your standard printer and test print to it.*

Suppose you want to install a Qume Sprint 5 daisy-wheel printer as your standard printer. This printer is option 9 on the

Add a Printer menu shown in Figure 6.2. Install it as the first printer by removing any existing printers and then selecting option 2 on the Printer Information menu. Give the printer a name such as Qume.5 and specify that it will be accessed from slot 1. If you have an Apple or an Apple-compatible parallel interface card, there is no need to change the interface control code. If you have another type of card, use the control code suggested in the interface card instructions. With the Grappler interface card, for example, the code would be Control-I 0N (zero N). Figure 6.3 shows one printer installed.

Suppose you want to install an Abati LQ-20 daisy-wheel printer as your standard printer. Any printer not listed on the Add a Printer menu is considered a custom printer. A custom printer is option 12 on the Add a Printer menu's list of printers. Install it as you would the first printer by selecting option 2 on the Printer Information menu. Give it a name such as Abati.LQ. Configure the interface card if you have a non-Apple card.

Unless otherwise specified, the first printer on your list will be the designated printer for producing hard copies of the screen with the Apple-H command. In this example case, our other two printers will be printing to disk, and that disqualifies them from being designated as Apple-H printers.

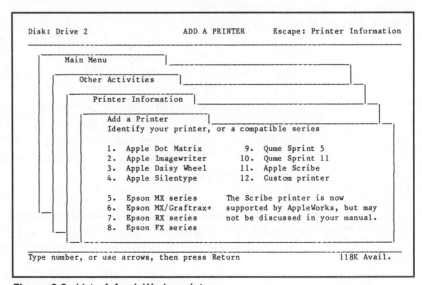

Figure 6.2: List of AppleWorks printers

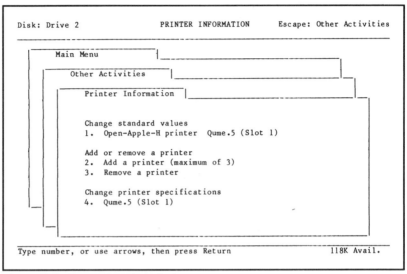

Figure 6.3: *One printer installed*

Tip: *Install your standard printer again to print to disk.*

The AppleWorks Mailing Program requires Word Processor files that have been printed to disk using your standard printer, normally assigned to slot 1. The process is similar to printing ASCII files to disk, except that the file includes any AppleWorks character enhancements and other printer options you have used.

The only way you can get a printer to print to disk is to specify that this is how the printer will be accessed. Surprisingly, there is no way to change the printer access option, as you can with other options. Therefore, you must add another printer to AppleWorks.

If your standard printer is listed, add the same listed printer again, with one difference: on the menu for adding a printer, specify that the printer will be accessed by printing onto disk.

If your standard printer is a custom printer, you must make another copy of the AppleWorks Program disk, delete the custom printer, and then add a custom printer dedicated to printing to disk. On the menu for adding a printer, specify that the printer will be accessed by printing onto disk.

Tip: *Install a dummy Silentype printer.*

Apple no longer sells the Silentype printer, but it is listed in AppleWorks as option 4 on the Add a Printer menu. It is a basic thermal printer, quieter than most. In this case, basic means that the Silentype default settings are ten characters per inch and six lines per inch, with no character enhancements available (not even underlining). In AppleWorks these settings make the Silentype a useful dummy for printing formatted text files to disk.

Install the Silentype as the third printer by selecting option 2 on the Printer Information menu. Name the printer Silentype and specify that it will print to disk. You can change the platen-width setting to 8 inches for the sake of conformity, but the Silentype will accept much wider platen widths no matter what the setting. Configure the interface card as you did for your standard printer. Figure 6.4 shows that we now have three installed printers.

Although the actual Silentype prints only ten characters per inch, the dummy will also print to disk at 12 and 17 characters per inch. If you have any character enhancements entered in Word Processor text, the Silentype will completely ignore both the enhancements and their markers.

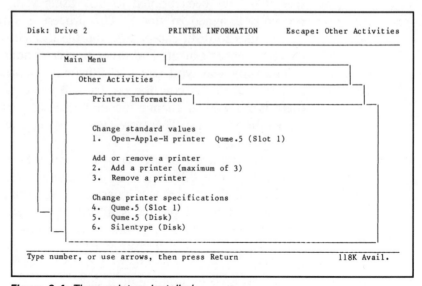

```
Disk: Drive 2              PRINTER INFORMATION      Escape: Other Activities
--------------------------------------------------------------------------
    Main Menu            |
        Other Activities     |
            Printer Information  |

                Change standard values
                1.  Open-Apple-H printer  Qume.5 (Slot 1)

                Add or remove a printer
                2.  Add a printer (maximum of 3)
                3.  Remove a printer

                Change printer specifications
                4.  Qume.5 (Slot 1)
                5.  Qume.5 (Disk)
                6.  Silentype (Disk)

--------------------------------------------------------------------------
Type number, or use arrows, then press Return               118K Avail.
```

Figure 6.4: Three printers installed

Tip: *The printer for unformatted text (ASCII) files has no name.*

One useful option offered on the print menu in each program represents a dummy printer that is just as important as the dummy Silentype. Think of it as a printer, even though it has no name, and remember the distinctions between formatted and unformatted text files noted in Chapter 5. In Figure 6.5 this "noname" printer is option 6.

Tip: *Although the Apple IIc uses a serial interface, it has a similar approach to installing printers.*

When you install a standard printer for the Apple IIc, Apple-Works offers a choice of two serial ports (rather than six slots). Serial connections transfer bits of data in single-file sequence, rather than in eight parallel paths. The AppleWorks serial interface configuration includes options to set the baud rate, data

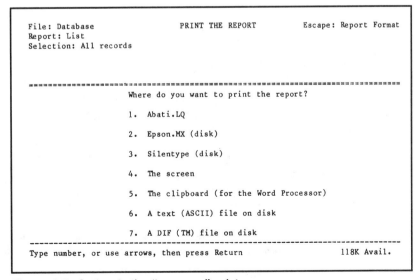

Figure 6.5: *Option 6: the "no name" printer*

format, and parity, all of which are explained in the AppleWorks Reference Manual.

Note that the Apple IIe can use a serial interface card and serial printers. Serial-to-parallel conversion devices allow the Apple IIc to use parallel printers. Many printers come in both parallel and serial versions, but few come with both connections on one version.

CUSTOM PRINTERS

Most people will eventually read Appendix B of the Apple-Works Reference Manual for two reasons. First, neither the widely used Okidata 92 dot matrix nor the widely emulated Diablo 630 daisy wheel are listed printers. Second, even if your printer is listed, there are significant advantages to entering a custom version of the same printer: a listed printer may have more capabilities that you can access from codes entered in the listing.

Tip: *Your printer may be compatible with a listed printer.*

Before you enter your printer as a custom printer, notice that the menu says "Identify your printer, or a compatible series." For example, because the Epson MX series has been so popular for so long, some other printers use Epson-compatible control codes. Check your printer manual to see if your printer uses the same codes as one of the other listed printers.

Tip: *Before you install your custom printer, find the list of control codes for it.*

The instructions for preparing a custom printer are easy enough to understand. The only difficulty is determining which codes to enter. A good printer manual will usually contain a table of

ASCII printer control codes written as keystroke sequences or combinations, such as Escape D or Control-H. Some manuals provide only the ASCII decimal values (such 29 or 31). Conversions from ASCII values to keystroke sequences are provided in Appendix B. Some of the conversions requiring the Control key are listed in Table 6.1. The ASCII values 1–26 are the letters in alphabetical order. (Note that in some printer manuals the Control key may be signified by CTRL or by a caret (^).)

Control-[is equivalent to simply pressing Escape. Thus, an ASCII decimal value listed as 27 56 is the same as the keystrokes Escape 8. Everything else is easy once you have the list of ASCII codes. We will refer to them throughout this chapter.

Tip: *A listed printer can also be a custom printer.*

Some printers have more options than AppleWorks can hold in the space allocated to one printer. For instance, some printers have two different fonts available at ten characters per inch or some other density. The Epson MX series (with optional Graftrax) provides an example. These printers are very reliable, and are often used in combination with a Grappler card. This remains a

---

Table 6.1: Selected Control-key ASCII conversions

ASCII Value	Keystroke Combination
0	Control-@
1	Control-A
26	Control-Z
27	Control-[
28	Control-\
29	Control-]
30	Control-^
31	Control-_

dependable system for draft printing and graphics, and almost all software includes a printer driver for this Epson.

An MX-80 can be entered as a listed printer under option 5, the Epson MX series. We can name it Epson.MX in this case. It can also be entered as a custom printer under a different name, such as Custom.MX.

When you enter the custom printer codes, type Escape E in the space for 10 characters per inch. The custom MX will then print entirely in emphasized mode, which is identical to the boldface option on the Printer Options menu. It is true that you can use Control-B to select emphasized mode for the listed printer, but the emphasized print continues only for the remainder of that paragraph. If you wanted to print in emphasized mode continuously, you would normally have to use Control-B at the beginning of each paragraph. By installing a custom MX on the same Program disk, you can solve that problem.

You can also enter "piggyback" codes (two or more independent codes merged in one entry) on the interface card control sequence, which means you can get the same effect without having to use the custom printer option. Version 1.2 of AppleWorks allows you to use up to three different interface cards—one for each printer. Hence you can add the listed Epson MX-80 twice and add Escape E to one interface card setting.

Tip: *The Okidata 92 really does work with AppleWorks.*

The Okidata 92 is widely used with the buffered Grappler + interface card. Together they make for an unusually fast and dependable system. The correspondence quality print on the Okidata 92 is remarkably attractive and readable. Unfortunately, many people believe that the Okidata 92 will not work with AppleWorks.

The Okidata 92 and 93 printer series, as well as the newer 192 and 193, all work perfectly with AppleWorks version 1.2. In fact, all the drafts of this book were written with AppleWorks and printed on an Okidata 92. The most commonly used font control codes for the Okidata printer series are given in Table 6.2.

Table 6.2: *Font control codes for the Okidata printer series*

Pitch	Keystroke Sequence
Draft quality print	
10 CI	Escape 0 Control-^
12 CI	Escape 0 Control-\
17 CI	Escape 0 Control-]
Near-letter-quality print	
10 CI	Escape 1 Control-^
12 CI	Escape 1 Control-\

Escape 1 turns on near-letter-quality (NLQ) print, and Escape 0 turns it off. Escape 0 must be included in draft-quality codes to clear any previous NLQ setting. There is no NLQ font for 17 characters per inch, but you must include Escape 0 to access 17 CI after using any NLQ font. (It actually prints at 17.1 CI.) Other important control codes are given in Table 6.3.

Table 6.3: *Print setting codes for the Okidata printer series*

Print Setting	Keystroke Sequence
Six lines per inch	Escape 6
Eight lines per inch	Escape 8
Boldface on	Escape T
Boldface off	Escape I
Subscript on	Escape L
Subscript off	Escape M
Superscript on	Escape J
Superscript off	Escape K
Underlining on	Escape C
Underlining off	Escape D

Note that this printer uses start and stop underlining commands—option 2 on the Underlining configuration menu.

Caution: *You may need two or more Program disks to use all the options on your custom printer.*

The Okidata 92 has a problem similar to that of the Epson MX with 10 CI print. Entering Escape 1 for 10 characters per inch produces near-letter-quality print. Because you can list only one custom printer per Program disk, as shown in Figure 6.6, you will need to configure a second disk to access 10 CI in draft quality.

In practice, you may want to reserve 10 CI for fast printing of drafts and 12 CI for near-letter-quality printing. That makes it possible to work with just one Program disk. (Note that the printer configuration is loaded into memory when you first load AppleWorks, so you cannot just put another Program disk in the drive to change fonts.)

There is a technique for accessing both draft quality and near-letter quality from one 10 CI setting. Enter 10 CI as Control-^ and 12 CI as Escape 1 Control-\. The 10 CI will then print in draft quality after you use 17 CI, and in NLQ mode after you use 12 CI.

Caution: *Some of the installed codes for listed Epson printers are incorrect.*

In earlier versions of AppleWorks, the Epson MX series with Graphtrax+ has the most problems. Once started, the underlining will not stop until the end of a paragraph. If you want to underline, you must enter a custom version of the same printer using codes from the Epson manual.

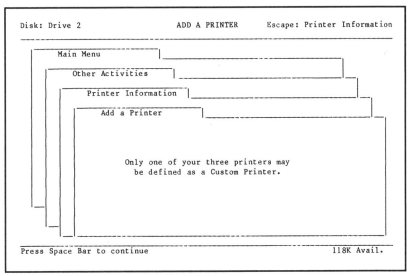

```
Disk: Drive 2                    ADD A PRINTER      Escape: Printer Information
--------------------------------------------------------------------------------
         | Main Menu                    |
              | Other Activities        |
                   | Printer Information    |
                      | Add a Printer         |


                      Only one of your three printers may
                         be defined as a Custom Printer.




--------------------------------------------------------------------------------
Press Space Bar to continue                              118K Avail.
```

Figure 6.6: Only one custom printer permitted

In earlier versions and version 1.2, the 16.5 CI font appears to have been entered as 17 characters per inch, with complications described in the following tip.

Tip: *If your printer has a fractional character-per-inch font, enter that setting rounded down.*

For example, if you want to configure an Epson custom printer for 16.5 characters per inch (Escape F Control-O), enter 16 rather than 17 on both the Add a Printer menu and the Printer Options menu in each program. The 16 CI setting will always leave you with enough platen width (a maximum of 128 characters of 132 possible with an 8-inch platen width), but 17 CI can cause a short extra line when the characters go beyond the platen width (136 characters attempted when only 132 are possible). When you enter 16, you can still include all 132 characters by setting an 8.3-inch platen width. AppleWorks will be fooled, but the printer will work correctly.

Tip: *Many good letter-quality printers emulate Diablo 630 commands.*

The Juki 6100 is one of several inexpensive daisy-wheel printers that emulate Diablo 630 printer codes. The inexpensive Silver-Reed 400 also emulates Diablo 630 codes. The print enhancement codes for the Diablo 630 are given in Table 6.4.

On printers emulating the Diablo 630, Escape D and Escape U are used in one order for superscripts and in the opposite order for subscripts. Escape U causes the paper to feed up a half line, so the character ends up striking below the normal print line. Esc D then feeds the paper back down a half line to the normal printing position.

Other printers emulate the Diablo 630 in part. For example, the Abati LQ-20 uses Qume daisy wheels and ribbon cartridges, but its codes are similar to those of the Diablo 630: Escape Q and Escape & turn boldface on and off. Escape D and Escape U turn superscript on and off. Escape _ and Escape R start and stop underlining.

Table 6.4: *Print enhancement codes for the Diablo 630*

Print Enhancement	Keystroke Sequence
Boldface on	Escape O
Boldface off	Escape &
Subscript on	Escape U
Subscript off	Escape D
Superscript on	Escape D
Superscript off	Escape U
Underlining on	Escape E
Underlining off	Escape R

Tip: *There are many more custom printer tips.*

As you have seen, many printers, including listed printers, can use the custom printer option to considerable advantage. You will undoubtedly find many variations and extensions of the techniques described in this chapter. Members of the Micronetworked Apple Users Group have even documented locations within AppleWorks for listed printer settings that can be changed to permit new listed printers.

For more on custom printer tips, read David Simerly's *Practical AppleWorks Uses* (SYBEX, 1985). It contains complete instructions for creating a Macintosh custom printer in AppleWorks to transfer text to a Macintosh word processor. In fact, he used that connection extensively to illustrate the book.

CONTROL CODES

This section provides additional techniques for using printer control codes, as well as tips for using boldfacing and underlining codes in ways you may never have considered. If your printer is not discussed in this section, take out your list of control codes for reference while you read the tips below.

Tip: *Use control codes as soft switches whenever you can.*

Some of the settings you may want to change on your printer are controlled by dip switches. Because these switches are so small, you may have trouble switching just one without disturbing the others unless you use a very small screwdriver. Sometimes these switches are hidden away inside the printer. You can often avoid using them by using control codes instead.

For example, the Apple DMP has dip switches to select character sets for different languages—French, German, Italian, Spanish, and Swedish. Suppose you want to write a letter in French at 10 CI. Suppose you also want the zero printed with a slash through it, so that no one will mistake it for a capital O. You can do all this at once by entering Escape N Escape D61 in the printer configuration option for 10 characters per inch, as shown in Figure 6.7.

When you finish the letter, change the entry back to the default Escape N for 10 CI. This technique saves the time and trouble of opening up the DMP to access its dip switches.

Tip: *Use "piggyback" codes for specific purposes.*

The Apple DMP example given in the previous tip uses what is sometimes called a "piggyback" code: two or more independent codes merged in one entry. AppleWorks can accept up to 38 characters in a single merged code (13 in the Data Base and Spreadsheet special codes option). Empty spaces, Escape, and Control count as one character each in printer control code entries, so the example in Figure 6.7 used only six character spaces.

Tip: *You can exchange control codes.*

Suppose you will eventually print the final draft of a long report at 12 CI on a letter-quality printer. Your letter-quality printer runs at 14 characters per second, while your dot-matrix printer runs at 90 characters per second. You want to proofread the whole report and see the lines as they will break when you later print the final draft. You can print the report at 17 CI on the dot-matrix printer with the exact 12 CI line breaks of the letter-quality printer by entering the wrong control codes.

For simulating 12 characters-per-inch layout with 17 CI dot-matrix print, select the 12 CI option in printer configuration and

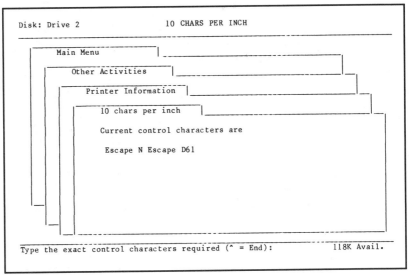

```
Disk: Drive 2                    10 CHARS PER INCH
_____

     | Main Menu            | _____
        | Other Activities    | _____
           | Printer Information | _____
              | 10 chars per inch  | _____

                 Current control characters are

                   Escape N Escape D61




_____
Type the exact control characters required (^ = End):    118K Avail.
```

Figure 6.7: *Using merged (or "piggyback") codes*

insert the code for 17 CI. The printout also leaves you plenty of white space for editing marks and comments.

Tip: *You can change boldfacing or underlining control codes to print superscripts.*

Suppose that you use underlining and superscripts (for footnotes) frequently, but you don't use boldfacing. When specifying the printer configuration, enter the control code for superscript begin under "boldface begin". Enter the code for superscript end under "boldface end". This allows you to use Control-B to turn superscript on and off in the Word Processor, without having to enter the Printer Options menu.

If other people use your Apple and AppleWorks, of course, you'll have to tell them what you did. Better yet, keep your modified Program disk to yourself. And remember, when you trick AppleWorks, it can trick you in return if you forget about the modification.

Tip: *You can change boldfacing or underlining control codes to print more than one character size per line.*

Suppose you want to use an 8.5 CI font in part of a title line. In printer configuration, enter the control code for 8.5 characters per inch under "boldface begin". Enter the code for the normal font under "boldface end". This allows you to use Control-B to turn 8.5 CI on and off quickly. Because the CI menu option works only for whole lines, this is the only way to mix character sizes on the same line. Furthermore, AppleWorks will not count these characters accurately, so use a carriage return at the end of the line.

Tip: *You can change boldfacing and underlining control codes to call up alternate character sets.*

Alternate character sets include italics, scientific symbols, and foreign character sets. Use the same technique described in the previous tip, this time to access an alternate character set. In each case the screen will show the standard keyboard input, but the printer will print the substitute you designated for that character.

Remember that Control-B and Control-L remain in effect only to the end of a paragraph. (In AppleWorks, a paragraph ends when a line ends in a carriage return.) Italics, scientific symbols, and foreign character sets used for limited purposes can be accessed with this technique. For longer text applications, use the "piggyback" method previously described.

PRINTING TECHNIQUES

The mechanics of printing can be tedious. You have to spend time making certain that the paper fits just right, not too high or too far left. It takes a while to work accurately with sixths, tenths, and twelfths of an inch if you have already spent years using eighths and sixteenths. When you make everything fit, however, you waste considerably less paper and time.

Tip: *Learn the dimensions of the print head, platen, and roller on your printer.*

The platen width is the distance the print head travels across the printer roller. Most printers have a platen width of 8 inches, although standard paper is 8½ inches wide. Paper is usually aligned so that the left-most character just barely fits on the paper when the left margin is set at 0 inches.

For layout purposes, the most important things to know about a printer are where the platen begins on the roller and where the characters are printed in relation to the top of the print head.

Printers that use a fixed pin-feed system with an 8-inch platen may set quarter-inch margins on each side as a matter of course. You have to consider this in any additional margins you specify. For example, if you want an inch margin on the left, you can use a 0.7 or 0.8 setting and get very close to what you want.

Tip: *Maximum platen-width settings vary considerably within AppleWorks.*

The maximum platen width you can specify on the Add a Printer menu is 16.0 inches; Figure 6.8 shows that it can indeed be entered. In the Word Processor, however, the maximum platen width you can specify on the Printer Options menu is 13.2 inches, while the Data Base and Spreadsheet Printer Option limits are 25.5 inches. These settings override any settings on the Add a Printer menu. The Data Base and Spreadsheet platen limits make it easy to print formatted text files to disk for special purposes, even though few printers used with the Apple have platen widths wider than 13.2 inches.

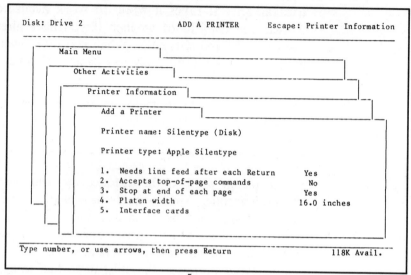

Figure 6.8: *Maximum platen width in option 4*

Caution: *The top-of-page command can produce unwanted results.*

If your printer feeds too much paper between blank cards or labels, return to the Main Menu and then go to the printer information section of the Other Activities menu. You probably need a "no" response to option 2: "Accepts top-of-page commands". In general, if a page length differs from the standard 11 inches, turn off the top-of-page command.

The Data Base and Spreadsheet printer options allow you to enter special codes to control page length, which means that your printer can continue to accept top-of-page commands. Note, however, that the control range on your printer may be limited.

Caution: *Sixths and tenths of an inch rarely match up.*

Most printing is done at six lines per inch (6 LI), in which a top margin of 0.5 inches equals 3 lines. Tenths and sixths are otherwise poorly matched. In Data Base report formats, use multiples of 0.5 for top and bottom margins, and an empty report line or two for the leftover sixths.

Table 6.5 shows how the number of lines decreases as you change from a bottom margin of 1 inch to a bottom margin of 2 inches on standard 11-inch paper. A top margin of 0 is assumed in each case. Notice that in some cases two different settings can provide the same number of lines per page.

Table 6.5: *Lines printed per page with various bottom margin settings*

Bottom Margin in Inches	Number of Lines per Page 6 LI	8 LI
1.0	60	80
1.1	59	79
1.2	58	78
1.3	58	77
1.4	57	76
1.5	57	76
1.6	56	75
1.7	55	74
1.8	55	73
1.9	54	72
2.0	54	72

Caution: *Twelfths and tenths of an inch rarely match up.*

Most printing is done at ten characters per inch (10 CI), in which one tenth of an inch is equal to one character. Most printers offer additional choices for 12, 15, or other numbers of characters per inch. Let's take a closer look at the relationships between tenths of an inch and character spaces as the print pitch increases.

Table 6.6 shows how the number of characters per line decreases in various print pitches as you increase the right margin from 0 to 1 inch on a standard 8-inch platen width paper. A left margin of 1 inch is assumed in each case. Notice that you cannot print some line lengths, such as 77 characters in 12 CI and 92 characters in 15 CI.

Table 6.6: Characters printed per line with various right margin settings

Right Margin in Inches	Characters per Line		
	10 CI	**12 CI**	**15 CI**
0.0	70	84	105
0.1	69	82	103
0.2	68	81	102
0.3	67	80	100
0.4	66	79	99
0.5	65	78	97
0.6	64	76	96
0.7	63	75	94
0.8	62	74	93
0.9	61	73	91
1.0	60	72	90

Tip: *You can create your own tables for margins and characters per line.*

Because there are many different character pitches available on different printers, this tip offers a method for creating your own tables. Follow the steps listed below:

1. In a new Word Processor document, type in 60 characters of the continuing series 123456789.123456789. within the default margins.

2. Copy the line to the clipboard, then from the clipboard twice, to the next two lines.

3. Remove the carriage return markers from the first two lines.

4. Copy the three-line section to the clipboard, then from the clipboard ten times, leaving a blank line between each section.

5. Press Apple-1 and select the number of characters per inch that you intend to use for the test.

6. Before each section, set a new right margin that is a tenth of an inch larger than the previous setting, as shown in Figure 6.9.

7. Print the test pattern to paper and count the characters per line for each margin width. Because the lines are numbered, the counting is easy.

Remember that some printers have pitches measured in fractional numbers of characters per inch. That is why the Data Base and Spreadsheet Printer Options menus show estimated (est) characters per line. AppleWorks neither accepts nor calculates fractional CI settings. All three AppleWorks programs correctly calculate the line lengths for all whole-number CI settings between 4 CI and 24 CI.

```
File: Margin.Copy              REVIEW/ADD/CHANGE          Escape: Main Menu
=====|====|====|====|====|====|====|====|====|====|====|====|====|====|====|===
--------Chars per Inch: 15 chars
--------Left Margin:  1.0 inches
--------Right Margin:  0.0 inches
123456789.123456789.123456789.123456789.123456789.123456789.1234567
89.123456789.123456789.123456789.123456789.123456789.123456789.1234
56789.123456789.123456789.

--------Right Margin:  0.1 inches
123456789.123456789.123456789.123456789.123456789.123456789.1234567
89.123456789.123456789.123456789.123456789.123456789.123456789.1234
56789.123456789.123456789.

--------Right Margin:  0.2 inches
123456789.123456789.123456789.123456789.123456789.123456789.1234567
89.123456789.123456789.123456789.123456789.123456789.123456789.1234
56789.123456789.123456789.

--------Right Margin:  0.3 inches
123456789.123456789.123456789.123456789.123456789.123456789.1234567
89.123456789.123456789.123456789.123456789.123456789.123456789.1234
---------------------------------------------------------------------
Type entry or use @ commands          Line 1  Column  1      @-? for Help
```

Figure 6.9: Copy for testing print lines at various margin widths

Caution: *The Word Processor screen uses 77-character lines.*

The screen shows 80 character columns per line, but even with no margins, the words will wrap at column 78. The maximum line length on the screen is 77 characters. You should know all this when you set wide margins.

Because the margins are set in tenths of inches rather than character spaces, only the 10 CI setting matches the screen to the printer. If the printer option settings allow more than 77 characters, the printer will not print the text exactly as you see it on the screen. Given the screen's effective 77-character width, margin settings of 0.3 on the left and 0 on the right will print the text as it appears on the screen. The appropriate margins for other print pitches are problematic: see the previous tips on margin widths and characters per line.

Tip: *You may be able to produce any line length by tricking AppleWorks with hard switches.*

As Table 6.5 shows, you cannot normally print 77 characters per line at 12 CI. However, there is sometimes a way around this limitation. Many printers use both hard and soft switches. Although soft switches generally override hard switches, most printers can respond to either alone. For example, the Abati LQ-20 has dip-switch controls for 10, 12, and 15 characters per inch. If the Printer Options menu and the printer dip switches are set for 12 CI, but no CI codes have been entered for printer configuration, AppleWorks calculates in 10 CI.

The reason for this is simple: AppleWorks defaults to 10 CI calculations in the absence of all the information it needs. Therefore, when the Abati dip switches are set for 12 CI, you can simply change the platen width setting in the Printer Options menu to a setting of 9.7 inches. With the default left and right margins in effect, the printer will then print a 77-character line at 12 characters per inch.

There are other uses for this technique. In this book, for example, all the screen copies were printed at 12 CI by using hard switches with no CI control codes installed in AppleWorks.

Tip: *Print a ruler to measure characters per inch.*

Many data processing suppliers offer rulers that measure characters at 10, 12, or 15 characters per inch. If you need to measure forms infrequently, print your own from a template. Figure 6.10 shows two ruler templates: one for 10 CI with a caret every five characters and one for 12CI with a caret every six characters. The two rulers are the same length on the screen, but the 12 CI version will be shorter when printed.

You can print any ruler of any length in the number of characters for which it will be used. Make long rulers in the Spreadsheet. When you use the ruler, align the first vertical bar points with the mid-point of the first letter. In this sense it is slightly different from a common wooden ruler.

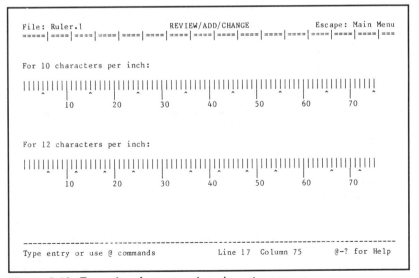

Figure 6.10: Two rulers for measuring character spaces

| **Caution:** | *Many daisy print wheels include non-ASCII characters.* |

Non-ASCII characters are typically substituted for ASCII decimal numbers 92, 94, 96, and 123–126. Two of these characters are particularly important for AppleWorks: print wheels may substitute the copyright symbol in place of the caret, and the paragraph symbol in place of the vertical bar.

This means that you will have no vertical bar when printing hard copies of the screens and no caret when printing Spreadsheet formulas. Some mail-order suppliers offer daisy print wheels with the correct ASCII sequence of characters: these wheels are generally labeled ASCII 96.

Prestige Elite is one of the few fonts available in both word processor and ASCII 96 sequence. With timely wheel changes you can then have all the characters of both. Figure 6.11 compares the ASCII characters to the substitute characters. The copy was made by taking the printer off line to change daisy wheels after the ASCII 96 characters were printed.

	92	94	96	123	124	125	126
ASCII 96	\	^	`	{	|	}	~
Prestige Elite	®	©	°	§	¶	†	™

Figure 6.11: Characters typically substituted in the ASCII sequence

PRINT BUFFERS

The efficiency of AppleWorks makes printing seem inefficient, but print buffers can minimize the time spent waiting to get back to AppleWorks. Most printers come with small internal buffers (2K or less). Printers commonly used with the Apple IIe print from 12 to 100 characters per second. By using larger buffers

(8K–64K), you can regain use of the Apple within seconds after using the print command. For example, AppleWorks can send a 12K file to a buffer in about 14 seconds, and about 1K per second for anything beyond that size.

Tip: *Expand the buffer in your printer if you can.*

Some printers can hold more memory chips. For example, the standard 2K buffer within the Juki 6100 can be expanded to 8K. That is still not quite enough for most reports, but you need not send an entire file at once. Remember also that a Spreadsheet printout uses less memory than the worksheet from which it is derived.

There is an important advantage to having a buffer in the printer: you can clear the buffer by turning off the printer, without affecting the program running in AppleWorks. For example, suppose you print four pages of single-spaced text. It goes to the buffer in the printer in several seconds, about the time it takes to realize that your margins are wrong. If the Word Processor has returned to the text and the cursor is flashing, you can simply turn off the printer, empty the buffer instantly, reset the margins, and start over again.

Tip: *A buffered interface card requires more thought than a buffered printer.*

Consider the buffered Grappler + card for the Apple IIe. It comes with 16K memory, expandable to 32K or 64K. It was designed so that you can use Control-Open-Apple-Reset to boot another program without disturbing the buffer. To clear the buffer you must depress Control-Reset for two seconds, which takes you out of the AppleWorks program. If you want to continue with AppleWorks, you must reboot with the Startup disk. You must clear any buffer in the printer as well, even if it is a small one.

To minimize the inconvenience of starting over whenever you make a formatting mistake, place a pause marker early in a document. If anything is wrong, you can press Escape from the print menu to get back to the program without committing everything to the buffered Grappler. On the other hand, if the document is printing correctly, just press the Space bar to keep loading.

Tip: *If you have a buffered Grappler+ card, install more 64K dynamic RAM chips.*

You can add 4164 DRAM chips to the buffered Grappler+ card just as you would add RAM chips to an 80-character extended memory card. The 4164 DRAM chips cost about two dollars each, and the Grappler manual explains how to install them. Adding two chips doubles the original 16K buffer, and may be one of the best productivity investments available for an Apple IIe system. The 32K should be adequate for about 90 percent of your printing. Adding four chips beyond that increases the capacity to 64K.

SUMMARY

In this chapter we have reviewed solutions to the most difficult printer installation problems. We have discussed some techniques for tricking AppleWorks into providing more options. At this point you can return to Chapters 2 through 5 to try out these options. Make notes on how each technique works, and keep the information in your AppleWorks notebook.

The all-important ASCII table appears in Appendix B. Keep it near at hand, along with your printer manual. You may even want to write your own one-page manual for the Silentype.

Appendix A, which follows this chapter, includes a discussion of the prospects for AppleWorks during the coming years, including developments in printer interfacing. Appendix B offers some insights on using the AppleWorks keyboard. Appendix C provides an overview of general reference information, followed by an annotated AppleWorks bibliography in the last appendix.

Appendix **A**
An AppleWorks Prospectus

*I*n a world of marketing hyperbole, it is easy to get carried away with new products. Conversely, it is easy to overlook something worthwhile that has not been heavily promoted. In the process of evaluating new hardware and software, it is important to remember what makes AppleWorks such a valuable program.

The strength of AppleWorks is its ability to start quickly and perform common tasks efficiently. Thanks to software firms such as Norwich Data Systems, AppleWorks can now run on older Apple II models. AppleWorks can also share files with the Apple III and III E-Z Pieces. Any future changes in AppleWorks should respect these important contributions.

And AppleWorks will be changing. During the months this book was written, the cost of 256K RAM chips decreased by 50 percent. The tip in Chapter 1 about installing 64K chips on an extended-memory card remains important, but more as a concept than a specific suggestion. Because some things change faster than books can be written and revised, this appendix discusses some of the things that might happen to affect AppleWorks during the coming years.

APPLEWORKS: AN APPLE II FEATURE

Perhaps the most logical possibility in the future of Apple-Works is that Apple will decide to offer it with the Apple IIc and Enhanced IIe in one "bundle," just as Apple includes the Pro-DOS operating system. That would make the integrated package a standard feature of the Apple II system, and other software firms would almost certainly design more software to use Apple-Works file formats.

Even if Apple were never to bundle AppleWorks, however, the option remains so logical that the possibility alone may well discourage the development of other integrated packages for the Apple II series.

Apple has probably underestimated the appeal of AppleWorks as a construction package and therefore underestimated its utility as well. In my opinion, AppleWorks deserves equality with Pro-DOS as a common feature of the Apple II series.

THE MACINTOSH CONNECTION

Apple has attempted to minimize the apparent differences between the Apple II and Macintosh series, generally by making the former work more like the latter. For example, the Apple IIc and Enhanced Apple IIe offer mouse characters that can be used to build mouse-controlled, pull-down menus, thereby simulating some advantages of the bit-mapped screen used in the Macintosh.

We can probably expect to see a pull-down menu version of AppleWorks. Pull-down menus can be mouse- or cursor-controlled, and many Apple II users will wisely choose the latter: a mouse requires additional surface area better allocated to oatmeal cookies, and it is time consuming to constantly shift between the mouse and the keyboard.

If both the Apple II and Macintosh series eventually use double-sided 3½-inch disks, we can probably expect to see a utility program that will translate AppleWorks files to a Macintosh version of AppleWorks and vice versa. This would offer a significant complement to both the Apple II and Macintosh series.

All this means relatively little if you plan to stay with your existing system. And that would be a wise choice, because the Apple II with 136K disk drives and AppleWorks version 1.2 will remain highly productive for a long time to come.

CORRECTING UNDOCUMENTED PROBLEMS

The first priority of any marketing-oriented firm should be getting the basics right, because it saves grief for everyone. Apple should correct the problems of the Convert program included in the ProDOS utilities and provide Apple IIc users with a copy.

Within AppleWorks, some problems are more significant than others. Because the package is targeted for beginning users, making the record-selection rules work correctly probably qualifies as the highest priority. And the Spreadsheet formula capacities for worksheet rows should be fully explained in the documentation.

The underlying Standard Apple Numerics Environment (SANE) module, which handles calculations in AppleWorks, deserves a special comment. It provides remarkable accuracy, beyond the needs of most Spreadsheet users, but it seems to be the source of the rounding problems described in Chapter 4.

Apple should also make their list of known problems available to AppleWorks users through dealers and Apple users groups. This book has amply demonstrated that there are many ways around problems. The lack of information about a problem is far more damaging than the problem itself.

DESIGN CHANGES

AppleWorks was designed to provide adequate Desktop memory within a 128K Apple II system and fast operation using a 6502 or 65C02 microcompressor. Hundreds of thousands of Apple II systems will remain within these boundaries. Accepting this fact, how should the design of AppleWorks be changed?

There are obvious areas where additional information in the AppleWorks Reference Manual would be more useful than changing the program. Here are some examples:

1. The rules for paragraph integrity are acceptable, given that they minimize the amount of program code required, but the rules need to be explained with common examples.

2. The Spreadsheet requires block formatting to control the format of unfilled cells. This is a good design choice, but the AppleWorks Reference Manual should explain why it is necessary.

3. The printer option for special codes in the Data Base and Spreadsheet serve practical purposes that need to be explained with examples.

There are several areas where AppleWorks needs some minor design changes. Here are four examples:

1. Boldfacing should not be turned off at the end of each paragraph. You should be able to boldface text selectively, regardless of carriage return markers.

2. The default position for the first tab stop should be the fifth character, not the sixth, because most people prefer paragraph indents on the fifth character.

3. While a Data Base file remains on the Desktop, the cursor should always return to the record from which the file was saved, because you will most often want to return to entering data in that record.

4. All Spreadsheet values should include a buffer space on the right, no matter what their formats. This would make worksheets easier to read.

Finally, in defense of AppleWorks, there are some good design choices that should be retained. Here are two examples:

1. When you view the Desktop Index, the Escape key rightly brings you back to the Main Menu, not back to the file shown behind the Index, which is handled by the Return key.

2. The AppleWorks menu system is so easy to use that pull-down menus can only be justified if they require less program code.

Additional Functions

As AppleWorks gains capabilities, the program segments will require more memory and a faster microprocessor to maintain essentially the same operating speed for common tasks. We may therefore see a standard AppleWorks and an enhanced Apple-Works. The suggestions below are for an enhanced AppleWorks that can still run on 128K systems. They may well prompt some friendly disagreements.

Apple's file format documentation for AppleWorks reserves specific locations for two additional features: a mail-merge capability for using Data Base reports with Word Processor files, and an @IRR function for internal rate of return in the Spreadsheet. The AppleWorks Mailing Program minimizes the need for a built-in mail-merge capability, and Chapter 4 includes a simple model for internal rate of return. Memory can be better allocated for other purposes.

The Word Processor needs at least a limited capability for true macro writing, and the clipboard capacity should be increased to at least 500 lines of text. (Some users would undoubtedly like to be able to change characters per inch within text lines, but this would contribute little: boldfacing and underlining serve that purpose far more effectively.)

The Data Base cannot scroll across all categories in multiple-record layout; adding this capability would be a significant improvement. In addition, transfers with DIF files would be easier if the Data Base could distinguish between labels and values, as the Spreadsheet does.

The Spreadsheet would benefit most from a graph format that represents values with asterisks (*). After that, I would like to see the capability to return the contents of label cells as the result of formulas, as in advanced VisiCalc. Blank label cells and the asterisk could produce a broad range of useful graphics within worksheets.

Patch Programs

AppleWorks can be modified easily at the byte level with one of several good byte modification programs, among them Pro-Byter from Beagle Brothers. The problem is in learning what is where on the Startup and Program disks. Don Lancaster's *Apple-Works Disassembly Script* (Synergetics, 1985) should provide most, if not all, of that information for version 1.2. (As of this writing, Lancaster's project is nearly complete.)

Knowing where each part of the program resides means that you can produce programs that offer menus of available patches to change listed printers, error messages, default margin widths, and so on. Applied Engineering and Checkmate Technology have effectively created patch programs for use with their respective extended-memory cards.

RELATED SOFTWARE

AppleWorks can be greatly strengthened by related software, much as Lotus 1-2-3 has been strengthened. AppleWorks is not copy protected, nor should related software be copy protected—that compromises too much, including essential trust. There is a certain comfort in working with people who could easily make copies of copyrighted software but don't.

There are many items on the shopping list of needed software to supplement AppleWorks, and I will mention but a few. The first is an unprotected spelling checker that combines the speed and accuracy of Sensible Speller with an efficient design similar to that used by Beagle Brothers. The spelling checker should come with a comparative review of paperback dictionaries, if not the preferred dictionary itself. Sensible Software fills an important niche in the world of Apple by producing quality software for limited professional markets, and in this case they have something that could be abridged and packaged for a broader market.

AppleWorks needs a related innovative mapping and graphics program that provides for efficient visual display of quantitative data. Read the graphics section of Chapter 4 on this subject, and note that Edward Tufte (see Appendix D) is one of several important sources of information in this emerging field.

Several programs for the IBM market add a cluster of small programs—a memo writer, a calculator, and so on—for use with integrated software and other programs. Once loaded into RAM, each of these small programs can be accessed quickly whenever needed, then returned to the background in favor of the main program. These background programs can be useful in long work sessions. As they begin to appear for AppleWorks, consider whether they offer benefits to you.

RELATED HARDWARE

During the next two years, AppleWorks users will probably benefit most from two hardware items already available. During the autumn of 1984, Applied Engineering developed a memory card and software patches that made AppleWorks a serious program for professional applications development on the Apple IIe. They also developed a memory extension for the Apple IIc (which you can now take apart). Both products have been continually improved, and other firms now offer similar products. During the months this book was written, Apple announced its own extended-memory card, and it may well become *a* design standard, but probably not *the* design standard.

Innovations in extended-memory cards have encouraged larger applications and longer sessions on the Apple II. This brings new importance to the nonglare monitor screen. AppleWorks users often work in too much light and glare. Amber monitors are slightly easier to read when light levels are above the preferred level of 30 footcandles, but a nonglare screen is still more important than color choice. As noted in Chapter 1, the Apple II uses relatively few dots to create letters on the screen, so you need every other available advantage in differentiating between letters. Characters on the screen should not persist (or "ghost") during scrolling.

The next significant Apple II innovation will probably be the replacement of the 65C02 microprocessor with the 65816 16-bit microprocessor. This will allow faster operation and direct access to more memory. If Apple offers a reasonably priced replacement motherboard for the Apple IIe, I suspect that many people will upgrade.

RELATED BASIC PROGRAMMING

As of this writing, no one has yet released a compiler for the ProDOS version of Applesoft BASIC. A good compiler makes BASIC a feasible programming language for larger programs.

The AppleWorks Mailing Program would benefit considerably from compiling.

Extra K, from Beagle Brothers, is a particularly useful software package with two important functions. Applesoft BASIC programs can normally occupy and access only 48K of memory, even when the Apple II has 128K. Among other things, Extra K allows BASIC to use variables in the auxiliary (or extended) memory, thus permitting larger programs that can offer more extensive support to AppleWorks. Extra-K also includes a fast copying program that copies disks in less than 35 seconds on a two-disk-drive system.

The standard texts on writing BASIC programs to create and read DIF files have been included in the annotated bibliography in Appendix D.

APPLEWORKS SUPPORT SERVICES

Apple relies heavily on its dealer network for technical support of its hardware and software, including AppleWorks. Other hardware manufacturers and software publishers are developing technical support centers for their products, and AppleWorks support needs to be revised in this direction as well.

Many integrated software packages include in their user's manual a telephone number for a technical support center, where you can ask questions about such things as undocumented problems or confusing instructions. The user typically makes a long-distance call, provides the software registration number for identification, asks the question, and receives an accurate answer.

This kind of technical support has significant benefits for the software firm. Because one technical support center handles all the questions, staff members hear many questions again and again. They learn to field common questions efficiently, and they can then provide important insights for upgrading instructional materials. Additional clarification or expansion in a reference manual can often greatly reduce the frequency of a given question (and hence the workload of the center).

A technical support center also learns about undocumented problems from the small percentage of users who find such problems during advanced applications development. Staff members can run tests to identify the causes and limits of these problems. They get very good at what they do, and their experience can be used to improve subsequent releases of the software package.

Given potential productivity advantages, technical support centers will increasingly integrate product testing, development of technical support databases, development of user's manuals, and publication of advanced materials. In coming years it may be virtually impossible to survive in the hardware and software markets without centralized technical support.

The advanced materials mentioned above include newsletters, periodicals, and books. *Lotus,* a monthly magazine, is one good example of a technical support periodical. Although it is written for specific integrated software packages, it is surprisingly useful for users of almost any integrated software that includes a spreadsheet. Some of the articles in *Lotus* focus on applications development in specific professions, which leads us to the subject of professional support.

Professional Support

Specific professions, such as agricultural management, library science, and health care, tend to have specialized hardware, software, and information needs. A users group for a specific profession can provide needed specialized information about hardware and software, as well as information about applications development and current events in the field.

If such a users group does not exist, an interested hardware or software firm may start one. Its newsletter could be little more than an extension of direct-mail advertising, or it could be a serious publication reflecting long-term commitment to the profession. The best example of the latter is the Apple Library Users Group quarterly newsletter. Apple's own librarian, Monica Ertel, has made this one of the most useful publications currently available in information science.

Apple Users Groups

Most Apple users groups cover specific geographic areas. In some groups AppleWorks users list their phone numbers and offer to answer questions. Some newsletters publish articles or a continuing column on AppleWorks. Apple should provide these users groups with the information necessary to simplify technical support, including a database of undocumented problems and an improved Convert program for Apple II owners to copy.

One users group, the A.P.P.L.E. cooperative in Washington state, publishes a monthly magazine with an international circulation. Another, the Micronetworked Apple Users Group, appears on the CompuServe and Delphi information services. Together, they fill an important niche for AppleWorks information.

Appendix **B**

The AppleWorks Keyboard

ppleWorks uses the keyboard differently for each of several purposes: text entry, number entry, editing, and control code entry. This appendix explains how to work more efficiently in each case, as well as how to make your own keyboard templates.

TEXT ENTRY

The interaction between the user and the keyboard is the slowest interface in AppleWorks. If you know touch typing, you can significantly speed up your work. If you don't know touch typing, your thoughts will always run ahead of your fingers. Moreover, touch typing lets you think about your writing rather than about where the next key might be. If you want to learn touch typing, Jeremy Grossman's *Quick Typing* (John Wiley and Sons, 1980) is a good paperback self-teaching guide that includes additional information useful for typing on a word processor.

Touch typing is basically the ability to use all ten fingers on the correct keys without looking at the keyboard. To do this you need to know at least the following: the four fingers of the right hand touch keys J K L and the semicolon, reach up to U I O P and also 7 8 9 0 on the higher rows, and reach down to M , . / on the bottom row. The four fingers of the left hand touch keys A S D F, reach up to Q W E R and 1 2 3 4, and reach down to Z X C V. The index fingers reach to the middle keys, and the right thumb controls the Space bar. The little fingers cover the keys to the right and left of the alphanumeric keys—most importantly the Return and Shift keys.

The D and K keys on the Apple each have a little bump on them so your middle fingers know when they are home. (The → key is also embossed.) Note that the right Shift key is used with the left-hand keys (such as A and S), while the left Shift key is used with the right-hand keys (such as L and P).

Practice using each finger until the muscles seem to remember on their own. The little fingers have the most difficult work. Remember that this keyboard layout was a 19th-century scheme to keep people from jamming mechanical linkages while typing. There are faster keyboard designs: the Apple IIc converts to the Dvorak layout, on which the most commonly used keys are the most easily accessible.

NUMBER ENTRY

If you enter numbers often, as accountants do, you may want to use the equivalent of touch typing for number entry. On many personal computers, the number keys appear both on the top row of the keyboard and on a numeric keypad to the right of the keyboard. If you learn the keypad by touch, you can type numbers quickly with your index, middle, and ring fingers.

You can purchase a separate numeric keypad for the Apple II series. Left-handed users will appreciate the fact that this keypad can be used on either side of the keyboard. Most numeric keypads cluster the number keys in four rows: 7 8 9 at the top, then 4 5 6, then 1 2 3, and finally 0 and the decimal point at the bottom. Most keypads include basic arithmetic function keys. Some keypads also include unexpected keys: for example, > may be included because it quickly moves a VisiCalc cursor to a specified cell coordinate.

EDITING

Editing is typically a process of correcting spelling, changing punctuation, and moving text. Sometimes you will need to add whole sentences or paragraphs, but editing is generally quite different from text entry.

During editing you will spend most of your time on the bottom rows of the keyboard, using the Apple and arrow keys. The zoom, copy, move, and file-naming commands are all on those rows.

The Apple-E command, for changing between the insert and overstrike cursors, is one of the most frequently used commands in editing. Because the letter E is directly above the Open-Apple key, it is almost always easier to use Solid-Apple-E during editing. Learn to change back and forth between the insert and overstrike cursors quickly, even when replacing just a few characters.

ASCII VALUES

Entering control codes for printers requires no special typing skills, but you must know which keystrokes to enter for ASCII values. Keep a table of ASCII values near at hand for reference. You will most likely need to convert ASCII decimal values found in your printer manual into keystrokes. Table B.1 provides all the information you will need. (You may want to add a tab to this page to make it easier to find.) Pay special attention to the first 31 ASCII values, and remember that when you add printers to AppleWorks, pressing Control-[is the same as pressing Escape.

KEYBOARD TEMPLATES

Keyboard templates offer a simple but effective way to remember the things you need to know to work most efficiently with the keyboard. You can design your own templates, print them on paper or card stock, make several backup copies, highlight specific information, and pencil in comments as needed. You can make more templates for specific applications or use self-adhesive Post-It notes for reminders.

There are basically two kinds of templates. The first is for people who are learning AppleWorks or using it only occasionally. The template sections shown in Figures B.1 and B.2 work together as a template for beginners. The template is designed for getting around in the Word Processor and for using existing Spreadsheet and Data Base applications. The abbreviations WP, SS, or DB are used whenever a command is limited to one or two programs.

The letter keys for AppleWorks commands were wisely allocated for mnemonic purposes (they are easy to remember). However, some people need time to adapt to using AppleWorks

---

Table B.1: *ASCII character codes*

ASCII	Hex	CHR	Control Code	ASCII	Hex	CHR	Screen
0	00	NUL	Control-@	32	20	space	
1	01	SOH	Control-A	33	21	!	!
2	02	STX	Control-B	34	22	"	"
3	03	ETX	Control-C	35	23	#	#
4	04	EOT	Control-D	36	24	$	$
5	05	ENQ	Control-E	37	25	%	%
6	06	ACK	Control-F	38	26	&	&
7	07	BEL	Control-G (Bell)	39	27	'	'
8	08	BS	Control-H (←)	40	28	(	(
9	09	HT	Control-I (Tab)	41	29	)	)
10	0A	LF	Control-J (↓)	42	2A	*	*
11	0B	VT	Control-K (↑)	43	2B	+	+
12	0C	NP	Control-L	44	2C	,	,
13	0D	CR	Control-M (Return)	45	2D	-	-
14	0E	SO	Control-N	46	2E	.	.
15	0F	SI	Control-O	47	2F	/	/
16	10	DLE	Control-P	48	30	0	0
17	11	DC1	Control-Q	49	31	1	1
18	12	DC2	Control-R	50	32	2	2
19	13	DC3	Control-S	51	33	3	3
20	14	DC4	Control-T	52	34	4	4
21	15	NAK	Control-U (→)	53	35	5	5
22	16	SYN	Control-V	54	36	6	6
23	17	ETB	Control-W	55	37	7	7
24	18	CAN	Control-X	56	38	8	8
25	19	EM	Control-Y	57	39	9	9
26	1A	SUB	Control-Z	58	3A	:	:
27	1B	ESC	Control-[	59	3B	;	;
28	1C	FS	Control-\	60	3C	<	<
29	1D	GS	Control-]	61	3D	=	=
30	1E	RS	Control-^	62	3E	>	>
31	1F	US	Control-—	63	3F	?	?

Table B.1: *ASCII character codes (continued)*

ASCII	Hex	CHR	Screen		ASCII	Hex	CHR	Screen
64	40	@	@		96	60	`	`
65	41	A	A		97	61	a	a
66	42	B	B		98	62	b	b
67	43	C	C		99	63	c	c
68	44	D	D		100	64	d	d
69	45	E	E		101	65	e	e
70	46	F	F		102	66	f	f
71	47	G	G		103	67	g	g
72	48	H	H		104	68	h	h
73	49	I	I		105	69	i	i
74	4A	J	J		106	6A	j	j
75	4B	K	K		107	6B	k	k
76	4C	L	L		108	6C	l	l
77	4D	M	M		109	6D	m	m
78	4E	N	N		110	6E	n	n
79	4F	O	O		111	6F	o	o
80	50	P	P		112	70	p	p
81	51	Q	Q		113	71	q	q
82	52	R	R		114	72	r	r
83	53	S	S		115	73	s	s
84	54	T	T		116	74	t	t
85	55	U	U		117	75	u	u
86	56	V	V		118	76	v	v
87	57	W	W		119	77	w	w
88	58	X	X		120	78	x	x
89	59	Y	Y		121	79	y	y
90	5A	Z	Z		122	7A	z	z
91	5B	[	[		123	7B	{	{
92	5C	\	\		124	7C	|	|
93	5D	]	]		125	7D	}	}
94	5E	^	^		126	7E	~	~
95	5F	_	_		127	7F	DEL	

commands, particularly if they have used other programs. For example, VisiCalc users may have difficulty remembering Apple-L for layout (rather than /F for format). Unlike the AppleWorks reference card and help files, the sample template sections in Figures B.1 and B.2 redirect you to the AppleWorks terminology where appropriate. You can photocopy these template sections, paste them up side by side, and photocopy them again onto card stock. Make some copies for friends.

When you make your own templates, consider their layout carefully. With the Apple IIc it is best to use freestanding templates. Print or copy needed information sideways on $8\frac{1}{2} \times 11$-inch

---

ARRANGE (means sort)
Apple-A arranges SS rows,
    DB records

BLANK
Apple-B blanks SS cells

CALCULATE
Apple-K calculates WP page breaks,
    recalculates SS
Apple-V, R, F, M set SS manual recalc

CHANGE (see QUICK CHANGE, EDIT,
    LAYOUT, NAME, REPLACE, WIDTH)

COPY (see also MOVE)
Apple-C, W copy within files
Apple-C, T copy to clipboard
Apple-P to menu for printing SS, DB;
    to clipboard for use in WP
Apple-C, F copy from clipboard

CURSOR MOVES
Apple-→ moves one word right in WP;
    one screen right in SS
Apple-↓ moves one screen down
Apple-1 moves cursor to first line
Apple-9 moves cursor to last line
Apple-2. . .8 moves cursor to first
    line of each eighth-section

DEFAULT VALUES
Apple-V sets SS, DB default value

DELETE
Control-Y deletes to end of WP line,
    SS edit line, or DB category
Apple-D deletes selected segments
Delete erases character to left

EDIT
Apple-E switches between insert and
    overstrike cursors
Apple-U edits SS cell

ESCAPE
Escape to menu, file, or status listed
    in upper right of screen

FIND
Apple-F finds word or text block in WP,
    SS cell coordinate,
    DB record

FORMAT (see LAYOUT)

HELP
Apple-? lists available commands

INSERT
Apple-I inserts SS row or column,
    DB record

LAYOUT (means format)
Apple-L changes SS cell layout,
    DB record layout
Apple-O for Printer Options menu

Figure B.1: *AppleWorks template, sections A–L*

white card stock, using up to about 6 inches. Then fold back the rest of the card to serve as a base. (Note that the top slots of the Apple IIc should never be covered because they vent heat.)

Templates for the Apple IIe can fit just above the keyboard. Print or copy needed information sideways on $8^{1}/_{2} \times 11$-inch white card stock, using up to about 4 inches. Cut the card to make a template that is $4^{1}/_{2} \times 11$ inches. Fold back a quarter-inch

---

MARGINS
Apple-O for options menu

MOVE (see also COPY)
Apple-M, W move WP text, DB records,
    SS rows, columns within files
Apple-M, T move to clipboard
Apple-M, F move from clipboard

NAME
Apple-N new name for file in use

PRINT
Apple-P to printing menus
    Note: Allows printing to text
    file, clipboard (SS, DB),
    DIF file (SS, DB),
    screen (DB)
Apple-H prints hard copy of screen

QUICK CHANGE (means change files)
Apple-Q quick change to another file
    on the Desktop

QUIT
Escape to main menu, then option 6
    Note: use option 3 to save
    Desktop files instead

RENAME (see NAME)

REPLACE
Apple-R replaces WP text,
    DB record-selection rules

REPORT
Apple-P for DB report menus
    Note: Apple-P goes to report menu
    before print menu
Apple-J justifies DB report category
Apple-G adds or deletes DB group totals

SAVE
Apple-S saves file to data disk

SORT (see ARRANGE)

TAB
Apple-T sets tabs in WP
Tab moves to next setting in WP,
    next SS cell,
    or next DB category

VALUES
Apple-V sets SS, DB default values

WIDTH
Apple-L, C, Return, C, Apple-→ widen
    selected SS column(s)
Apple-L, Apple-→ widen DB category

WINDOWS
Apple-W creates SS windows
Apple-J jumps to other SS window

ZOOM
Apple-Z to WP layout mode and back,
    to SS formulas and back,
    to DB single record and back

Figure B.2: AppleWorks template, sections M–Z

at the bottom of the card (below the last line of information), and fit it into the space just above the top row of keys. You will need to trim one-eighth inch off each end of the insert tab. (You may also want to round off the top corners of the template to the radius of a nickel or quarter.)

If you need to include more information than these guidelines allow, print it first on a larger sheet. Later you can copy it onto $8^1/_2 \times 11$-inch card stock. Many quick-print shops can make reduced photocopies to about 77% of original size, and sometimes to any specified reduction.

More specialized templates are used primarily by people who design applications. For example, Figures B.3 through B.5 provide information that could appear on such a template—in this case for use on the Spreadsheet. Figure B.3 includes less frequently used commands that even experienced users can forget. For example, after several days away from AppleWorks, you may need to check the template before resetting manual recalculation in the Spreadsheet.

ARRANGE (means sort)
Apple-A arranges selected rows
    Note: A–Z option for labels

CALCULATE
Apple-V, R, F, M set manual calculation

COPY
Apple-C, W copy rows, columns,
    and "blocks" within file
Apple-C, T copy to clipboard
Apple-P to menu for printing to
    clipboard for use in WP
Apple-C, F copy from clipboard
    Note: You can copy complete
    rows only. You can copy from
    the clipboard repeatedly.

LAYOUT (means format)
Apple-L changes cell layout
Apple-O changes print format options

PRINT
Apple-P to printing menus
    Note: options include printing
    to printer, ASCII file, DIF
    file, clipboard

TITLES
Apple-T fixes row or column titles
    from cell below or to right

VALUES
Apple-V sets global default values
    for column width, formats, cell
    protection, recalculation

WIDTH
Apple-L, C, Return, C, Apple-→ widen
    selected column(s)

WINDOWS
Apple-W creates windows
Apple-J jumps to other window

Figure B.3: Selected Spreadsheet commands

Figure B.4 provides a list of all the Spreadsheet column letters with corresponding numbers for each column. The list can be simplified to show only columns E through O, then every fifth column thereafter.

A	1	AG	33	BM	65	CS	97
B	2	AH	34	BN	66	CT	98
C	3	AI	35	BO	67	CU	99
D	4	AJ	36	BP	68	CV	100
E	5	AK	37	BQ	69	CW	101
F	6	AL	38	BR	70	CX	102
G	7	AM	39	BS	71	CY	103
H	8	AN	40	BT	72	CZ	104
I	9	AO	41	BU	73	DA	105
J	10	AP	42	BV	74	DB	106
K	11	AQ	43	BW	75	DC	107
L	12	AR	44	BX	76	DD	108
M	13	AS	45	BY	77	DE	109
N	14	AT	46	BZ	78	DF	110
O	15	AU	47	CA	79	DG	111
P	16	AV	48	CB	80	DH	112
Q	17	AW	49	CC	81	DI	113
R	18	AX	50	CD	82	DJ	114
S	19	AY	51	CE	83	DK	115
T	20	AZ	52	CF	84	DL	116
U	21	BA	53	CG	85	DM	117
V	22	BB	54	CH	86	DN	118
W	23	BC	55	CI	87	DO	119
X	24	BD	56	CJ	88	DP	120
Y	25	BE	57	CK	89	DQ	121
Z	26	BF	58	CL	90	DR	122
AA	27	BG	59	CM	91	DS	123
AB	28	BH	60	CN	92	DT	124
AC	29	BI	61	CO	93	DU	125
AD	30	BJ	62	CP	94	DV	126
AE	31	BK	63	CQ	95	DW	127
AF	32	BL	64	CR	96		

Figure B.4: *Spreadsheet column letters and corresponding numbers*

You may also want to print important formulas on your template. Figure B.5 shows an example of how this can be done. Here the brief comments are the most useful part, because you will often copy the actual formulas from a PARTS file like the one described in Chapters 4 and 5.

No matter how experienced you are with AppleWorks, you will always be learning something new that you have not quite mastered. This is the kind of information that belongs on a keyboard template. Save some space to pencil in additional information during the life of the template. And when the template is no longer needed, set it aside and make another for your present needs.

```
=====B====C====D====E=====
1    .5    .22   .52   2
2    .12   10    20    40
3    3.99
```

FORMULAS (data above)	RESULTS	COMMENTS
+B2+C2/D2*E2	20.24	Left-to-right order of operations
+E1^.5	1.414214	Same as square root of 2
@IF(B2<=1,C2+D2,0)	30	.12 is less than 1
@INT(B1*B3*100+.5)/100	2.00	Rounding formula for accounting
@SUM(E1. . .E3)	42	Includes E2
@COUNT(E1. . .E3)	2	Empty E3 does not count
@AVG(E1. . .E3)	21	Sum divided by count
@MAX(E1. . .E3)	40	Finds maximum value in series
@MIN(E1. . .E3)	2	Empty E3 not considered
@NPV(B2,C2. . .E2)	53.34	C2 is year 1 (or period 1)
@CHOOSE(E1,20,10,40)	10	E1=2, so second value is chosen
@LOOKUP(B1,C1. . .E1)	10	.5 is less than .52, hence the value beneath .22 is selected

Figure B.5: *Sample formulas with comments*

Appendix **C**
On-Line Information Sources

*T*his appendix reviews general concepts about obtaining information for processing in AppleWorks. Some people think that access to on-line information services will someday be the prime reason for owning an Apple. At this time, however, only a small fraction of AppleWorks users subscribe to information services. In the process of looking at other information sources, you will begin to understand why. The material in this appendix will not cover everything you need to know, but it will point you in the right direction.

On-line information services typically cost $20 or more to join, with most of that cost going for a users' manual. In addition, whenever you access information from a service, you are charged for the time you are connected. These connect costs are typically between $6 and $20 per hour, with the lowest rates on nights and weekends.

AppleWorks has no communications program. Before you buy a modem, a communications program, and a subscription to an information service, find out what the service provides and then look at your own bookshelf and in a public (or college) library. Do you have at least a paperback dictionary, grammar book, almanac, one-volume paperback encyclopedia, and the most commonly used reference book in your own field? Unless you have all of the above, get those books first.

Then check the information in your local library against your list of what the information service provides. The printed word still serves us well for most information. For example, although information services offer encyclopedias, on-line access offers no distinct advantage over print (except perhaps for students who want to produce term papers with minimal effort). The chances are very good that your bookshelf and nearby library will be far more useful than an on-line information service, but there are important exceptions.

Some information changes too quickly to print and distribute effectively. One classic example is the Official Airlines Guide (OAG), available on CompuServe and other information services. In a deregulated airline industry, fares, routes, and schedules change frequently. The electronic edition of OAG keeps track of these changes with daily fare updates and weekly schedule updates. Furthermore, it provides information that may not be available to a given travel service. In short, this is exactly the kind of information that belongs on an information service.

An on-line information service may also have useful programs that can be downloaded as text files, and these programs may be available nowhere else. In fact, the Micronetworked Apple Users Group (MAUG) may be the most important reason for Apple-Works users to consider subscribing to CompuServe or Delphi.

On-line information services are often most valuable when you need specialized information. In these situations you may need to search the literature in a particular field or download specialized data.

The information found on specialized databases is similar to Official Airlines Guide information: it changes too quickly to print and distribute effectively. The information may be a specialized citation index in environmental science, or it may be continuously updated climate data.

When you know what information you need, the important question is where to acquire the data at the least cost. Specialized on-line databases are generally more expensive than broader-based information services. However, information costs vary considerably from source to source, even for the same information. When the information belongs to the federal government, it is sometimes available at little or no cost to the user. Note also that some databases are easier to search than others and therefore require less connect time.

The best introductions to this subject are Matthew Lesko's article "Low-Cost On-Line Databases," in the October 1984 issue of *Byte,* and his monthly column for *inCider,* the Apple II journal. Lesko has also written the most useful books available on information sources in the federal government and on-line databases. Both his books and the journals are commonly available in libraries.

Appendix **D**
An AppleWorks Bibliography

*I*nformation on AppleWorks comes from many sources: the on-line Micronetworked Apple Users Group, books, articles, users-group newsletters, and advertisements. The following annotated bibliography, although not comprehensive, suggests the range and quality of sources for intermediate and advanced users. It includes references that are not specifically AppleWorks related but can be quite valuable to AppleWorks users.

Hardware and software manuals can sometimes be unexpectedly useful AppleWorks sources. The Checkmate Technology MultiRam manual is a good example: in addition to installation instructions, it includes AppleWorks performance tests and information on practical uses of the enlarged Desktop. Users' manuals for scientific calculators can also be invaluable.

For those who want to write BASIC programs for use with AppleWorks, Tom Weishaar's *Open-Apple* newsletter provides good utility information. The August 1985 issue included an extended article on AppleWorks that inspired additional tips on the Silentype printer.

ANNOTATED BIBLIOGRAPHY

Alexander, Penny. "Automating the Miniledger." *Business Computing*. II, 5 (May 1984), pp. 68–72.
> Good example of a periodical column (from a periodical that is no longer published). Each template respects the limits of VisiCalc. Other particularly useful topics include project scheduling (September 1984) and invoicing (November 1984).

Arganbright, Deane. *Mathematical Applications of Electronic Spreadsheets*. New York: McGraw-Hill, 1985.
> Carefully designed templates in mathematics and statistics, with useful insights on circular references and iteration.

Beil, Donald. *The DIF File*. Reston, VA: Reston Publishing, 1983.
> Thorough and easily understood reference; a landmark book.

Cerati, Rodolfo. "Spreadsheet in BASIC." *Byte.* IX, 6 (June 1984), pp. 154–56, 457–62.
Thought-provoking discussion of a single-purpose program that looks exactly like a spreadsheet.

Checkmate Technology. *MultiRam C Users Manual.* Tempe, AZ: Checkmate Technology, 1985.
A remarkable manual that includes many performance tests and tips on AppleWorks.

Dooley, Thomas, and David Spiller. *Financial Planning in Transit.* Washington: US Dept. of Transportation, 1983.
Good example of spreadsheet information from an unexpected source. The concepts can be generalized.

Englander, Jim. "Making a Utilities Diskette for Spreadsheet Creation." *Spreadsheet.* I, 19 (June 1983), pp. 1–2.
Article that inspired the PARTS file, in a monthly newsletter that incorporated *Software Arts Technical News,* the VisiCalc newsletter.

Flast, Robert. *54 VisiCalc Models.* New York: Osborne/McGraw-Hill, 1983.
Sound reference for finance and statistics, with formula listings for everything, including labels.

Frazier, Howard. "Customers on File." *inCider.* II, 10 (October 1984), pp. 56–65.
Good Quick File II article that applies to the AppleWorks Data Base as well.

Grupe, Fritz. "Tips for Better Worksheet Documentation." *Lotus.* I, 4 (August 1985), pp. 68–70.
One of many articles in *Lotus* that has broad utility for spreadsheet users.

Hergert, Douglas. *Mastering VisiCalc.* Berkeley: SYBEX, 1983.
Useful information on BASIC programs for handling DIF files.

Jacques, Jeffrey. "THE Spreadsheet Sheet: Data Analysis." *CALL-A.P.P.L.E.* VI, 12 (December 1983), pp. 21–25.
First of a continuing series on statistics. See Chapter 4 for a table describing the complete series.

Kersey, Bert, and Jack Cassidy. *Pro-Byter.* San Diego: Beagle Brothers, 1985.
> All software manuals should be this interesting, informative, and fun.

Koons, J.B. "SANE Programming on the Apple." *CALL-A.P.P.L.E.* VIII, 7 (July 1985), pp. 19–20.
> Good review of the Standard Apple Numerics Environment discussed in Appendix A.

Lancaster, Don. *AppleWorks Disassembly Script.* Thatcher, AZ: Synergetics, 1985.
> This will undoubtedly be the classic on AppleWorks at the byte level.

Mason, Archie. "AppleWorks," *inCider,* II, 7 (July 1984), pp. 81–83.
> The most competent early review I have seen, particularly good on the Spreadsheet.

Oliva, Ralph et al. *The Great International Math on Keys Book.* Lubbock: Texas Instruments, 1976.
> Classic collection of useful formulas, written for a scientific calculator. TI manuals continue to be invaluable for spreadsheet users.

Ross, Paul. "Letter Quality Printing with AppleWorks and Epson FX-80." *Washington Apple Pi.* VII, 4 (April 1985), pp. 30–31.
> Good example of printer installation information found in Apple users group newsletters.

Rubin, Charles. *AppleWorks.* Bellevue, WA: Microsoft Press, 1985.
> Well-written, intermediate-level book, with considerable detail on information transfer.

Simerly, David K. *Practical AppleWorks Uses.* Berkeley: SYBEX, 1985.
> An insightful book with useful applications. Although written for intermediate-level users, it includes the most advanced information available on connections with the Macintosh.

Tufte, Edward R. *The Visual Display of Quantitative Information*. Cheshire, CT: Graphics Press, 1983.

A landmark book, finely crafted and with many illustrations.

Weishaar, Tom. "Big Boy Data Managers." *Open-Apple*. I, 2 (March 1985), pp. 23–24.

Good, efficient writing about the AppleWorks Data Base and database management in general.

INDEX

@AVG, 191, 358
@CHOOSE, xvii, 242, 358
@COUNT, xvii, 191, 227–228, 237
@ERROR, 210, 243
@IF, 196, 207, 210, 219–226, 228, 245, 358
@INT, 233–234, 358
@LOOKUP, 202, 221, 230–232, 358
@MAX, 191, 240, 358
@MIN, 191, 358
@NA, 227
@NPV, 196, 228–232, 242, 245, 358
@SQRT, 192, 194–196
@SUM, 189–191, 196, 209–210, 358

Accounts, posting, 219–222
Apple keys, xx, 351
Apple II and III series, xiv, 337
Apple IIc, xiv, 30–31, 313–314
Apple IIe, xiv, 25–27, 33, 182–183
AppleWorks (program)
　copying master disks, 37
　data disk location, 20–21
　hardware needed, xiv
　installing printers, 307–321
　earlier versions, xiv, xxiv–xxv, 75–119, 289, 308–309
　technical support for, 344–346
　terms used in, xxi, 185, 255
AppleWorks Mailing Program, 49, 280–284
Arrow keys, xx, 18, 53
Arranging
　Data Base records, 125–128
　Spreadsheet rows, 186, 250–251
ASCII Express (program), 296
ASCII text files
　creating, 20, 259, 263–265
　downloading with modem, 296–297
　formatted, 258, 262, 277, 295–296
　splitting, 297
　unformatted, 258, 262, 270, 288–289, 292–295, 299, 301
ASCII values
　conversion table, 315, 352–353
　in arranging, 17, 125, 249–251

BASIC programs, 297–302, 343–344
Baud rate, 313
Bibliographies, 169–174, 294–295, 365–367
Binary files, 246
Boldface, 78, 139, 323–324, 340
Bookends Extended (program), 294–295
Budgets, 157–158, 184–185

Calculating
　Spreadsheet formulas, 187–189
　Word Processor pages, 71–75
Calculator, scientific, 44, 90–91, 367
Cards for Apple IIe slots
　clock, 33, 160–161
　80-column, 25–33
　microprocessors, 27, 182, 339, 343
　modem, 296–297
　MultiRam memory, 26, 365–366
　printer interface, 307–309, 332–334
　RAMWORKS memory, 26–33
Caret symbol, 192, 315, 317, 332
Carriage return. See Return key
Categories, in Data Base
　calculated, 135–136, 154–155, 157–158, 166–169
　deleting, 130, 149
　inserting, 151
　naming, 100, 149, 156
　original order, 146–148, 162–165
Cautions
　Data Base, 110, 114, 116, 119, 125–126, 129–131, 139, 153, 159, 173
　Desktop, 8, 13, 15, 19–21, 34, 35
　installing printers, 307, 318, 326–327, 330, 332
　Spreadsheet, 188, 191–192, 194, 197, 200, 204, 213, 217–218, 226, 228, 233, 238, 240, 242–243, 246, 249
　transferring information, 261, 275, 278, 281, 284, 288–289, 291, 293, 296
　Word Processor, 66–70, 72–76, 78, 84, 89
Cells
　formatting, 213, 215, 339
　protecting, 210
Centering text, 65
Changing
　file names, 18, 182
　files, 8
Characters
　alternate sets, 324
　counting, 88–89, 331
　deleting, 54
　lowercase letters, 4–5, 181–182
　per inch, 319, 324, 331
　per line, 199, 319, 326–327, 330
　uppercase letters, 4–5, 100
Clipboard
　copying to and from, 22–25, 56, 258, 341
　moving to and from, 22–25, 56, 113, 258
　printing to, 258–259
Clock, 33, 160–161
Columns
　letters and numbers, 155, 357
　width, 159–160, 203–205, 208–209, 245, 354, 356

Computer Specific

Apple II—Macintosh

THE PRO-DOS HANDBOOK
by Timothy Rice/Karen Rice
225 pp., illustr., Ref. 0-230
All Pro-DOS users, from beginning to advanced, will find this book packed with vital information. The book covers the basics, and then addresses itself to the Apple II user who needs to interface with Pro-DOS when programming in BASIC. Learn how Pro-DOS uses memory, and how it handles text files, binary files, graphics, and sound. Includes a chapter on machine language programming.

THE MACINTOSH™ TOOLBOX
by Huxham, Burnard, and Takatsuka
300 pp., illustr., Ref. 0-249
This tutorial on the advanced features of the Macintosh toolbox is an ideal companion to The Macintosh BASIC Handbook.

THE MACINTOSH™ BASIC HANDBOOK
by Thomas Blackadar/Jonathan Kamin
800 pp., illustr., Ref. 0-257
This desk-side reference book for the Macintosh programmer covers the BASIC statements and toolbox commands, organized like a dictionary.

PROGRAMMING THE MACINTOSH™ IN ASSEMBLY LANGUAGE
by Steve Williams
400 pp., illustr., Ref. 0-263
Information, examples, and guidelines for programming the 68000 microprocessor are given, including details of its entire instruction set.

THE EASY GUIDE TO YOUR APPLE II®
by Joseph Kascmer
147 pp., illustr., Ref. 0-122
A friendly introduction to the Apple II, II plus, and the IIe.

BASIC EXERCISES FOR THE APPLE®
by J.P. Lamoitier
250 pp., 90 illustr., Ref. 0-084
Teaches Applesoft BASIC through actual practice, using graduated exercises drawn from everyday applications.

THE APPLE II® BASIC HANDBOOK
by Douglas Hergert
250 pp., illustr., Ref. 0-115
A complete listing with descriptions and instructive examples of each of the Apple II BASIC keywords and functions. A handy reference guide, organized like a dictionary.

APPLE II® BASIC PROGRAMS IN MINUTES
by Stanley R. Trost
150 pp., illustr., Ref. 0-121
A collection of ready-to-run programs for financial calculations, investment analysis, record keeping, and many more home and office applications. These programs can be entered on your Apple II plus or IIe in minutes!

YOUR FIRST APPLE II® PROGRAM
by Rodnay Zaks
182 pp., illustr., Ref. 0-136
This fully illustrated, easy-to-use introduction to Applesoft BASIC programming will have the reader programming in a matter of hours.

THE APPLE® CONNECTION
by James W. Coffron
264 pp., 120 illustr., Ref. 0-085
Teaches elementary interfacing and BASIC programming of the Apple for connection to external devices and household appliances.

THE APPLE IIc™: A PRACTICAL GUIDE
by Thomas Blackadar
175 pp., illustr., Ref. 0-241
Learn all you need to know about the Apple IIc! This jargon-free companion gives you a guided tour of Apple's new machine.

Selections from The SYBEX Library

THE BEST OF EDUCATIONAL SOFTWARE FOR APPLE II® COMPUTERS
by Gary G. Bitter, Ph.D. and Kay Gore
300 pp., Ref. 0-206
Here is a handy guide for parents and an invaluable reference for educators who must make decisions about software purchases.

YOUR SECOND APPLE II® PROGRAM
by Gary Lippman
250 pp., illustr., Ref. 0-208
The many colorful illustrations in this book make it a delight for children and fun for adults who are mastering programming on any of the Apple II line of computers, including the new IIc.

THE MACINTOSH™: A PRACTICAL GUIDE
by Joseph Caggiano
280 pp., illustr., Ref. 0-216
This easy-to-read guide takes you all the way from set-up to more advanced activities such as using Macwrite, Macpaint, and Multiplan.

MACINTOSH™ FOR COLLEGE STUDENTS
by Bryan Pfaffenberger
250 pp., illustr., Ref. 0-227
Find out how to give yourself an edge in the race to get papers in on time and prepare for exams. This book covers everything you need to know about how to use the Macintosh for college study.